Egypt and Syria in the Early Mamluk Period

Providing a modern English translation of a key selection of Ibn Faḍl Allāh al-ʿUmarī's *Masālik al-abṣār*, this book offers a rich description of Egypt and Syria under the Mamluks in the first half of the fourteenth-century A.D. It provides a fascinating snapshot of the physical and administrative geography of this crucial region as well as insights into its society and the organization and functioning of the Mamluk state.

D.S. Richards is an Emeritus Fellow of St Cross College, University of Oxford.

Egypt and Syria in the Early Mamluk Period

An extract from Ibn Faḍl Allāh al-ʿUmarī's *Masālik Al-Abṣār Fī Mamālik Al-Amṣār*

Translated by D.S. Richards

Routledge
Taylor & Francis Group
LONDON AND NEW YORK

First published 2017
by Routledge
2 Park Square, Milton Park, Abingdon, Oxon OX14 4RN

and by Routledge
711 Third Avenue, New York, NY 10017

Routledge is an imprint of the Taylor & Francis Group, an informa business

British Library Cataloguing in Publication Data
A catalogue record for this book is available from the British Library

Library of Congress Cataloging in Publication Data
Names: Ibn Faḍl Allāh Al-'Umarī, Aḥmad ibn Yaḥyā, 1301–1349, author. | Richards, D. S. (Donald Sidney), 1935- translator.
Title: Egypt and Syria in the Early Mamluk Period : an extract from Ibn Faḍl Allāh Al-'Umarī's Masālik Al-Abṣār Fī Mamālik Al-Amṣār / translated by D. S. Richards.
Description: New York ; London : Routledge, 2017. | Includes bibliographical references and index.
Identifiers: LCCN 2016037486 (print) | LCCN 2016039947 (ebook) | ISBN 9781138208599 (alk. paper) | ISBN 9781315458816
Subjects: LCSH: Ibn Faḍl Allāh Al-'Umarī, Aḥmad ibn Yaḥyā, 1301–1349. | Egypt—History—1250-1517. | Mamelukes—History. | Egypt—Description and travel. | Syria—Description and travel.
Classification: LCC DT96.4 .I25413 2017 (print) | LCC DT96.4 (ebook) | DDC 956.91/02—dc23
LC record available at https://lccn.loc.gov/2016037486

ISBN: 978-1-138-20859-9 (hbk)
ISBN: 978-1-315-45881-6 (ebk)

Typeset in Times New Roman
by Swales & Willis Ltd, Exeter, Devon, UK

Contents

Preface vi

Introduction 1

The Faḍl Allāh family 1
The family tree 2
Shihāb al-Dīn (Ibn Faḍl Allāh) al-ʿUmarī 3
The Masālik al-abṣār 6
The chapter on Egypt and Syria 10

The translation 13

Notes 91
References 114
Index 120

Preface

Several decades ago I began to work on an edition of a chapter of Ibn Faḍl Allāh al-ʿUmarī's encyclopaedic work, *Masālik al-abṣār fī mamālik al-amṣār*, that is the section in which he describes his own part of the world, Egypt and Syria. My work was fairly well advanced when two other editions appeared in quick succession. The first was that of Ayman Fuad Sayyid, published in 1985 by the Institut Français d'Archéologie Orientale in Cairo; this edition also includes a re-edition of the much shorter chapter which deals with the Yemen. The other was prepared by Dorothea Krawulsky and was published by al-Markaz al-islāmī li-l'buḥūth (the Islamic Research Centre) in Beirut in the following year, 1986.

In those circumstances I put my own unfinished edition aside. However, I had at the same time prepared a translation, partly as a check on my own understanding of what is not always a transparent text (and the critical reader with a knowledge of Arabic must judge how successfully the translation interprets the text), and partly with the thought that the work possesses an inherent interest and deserves to be better known and to be made more widely accessible. This translation has now been revised in the light of the editions prepared by the other two scholars.

This part of Ibn Faḍl Allāh al-ʿUmarī's great work was written during what one may consider to have been the zenith of the Mamluk Sultanate, the third and final reign of the Sultan al-Nāṣir Muḥammad ibn Qalāwūn (died 741/1341). It presents a proud and confident picture of the core lands of the Sultanate. Without a doubt Ibn Faḍl Allāh's description of Egypt and Syria served as a source, not always fully acknowledged, for several later writers, who attempted systematic presentations of the nature and organisation of the Mamluk state. Its central importance will justify this offering of an English version.

Introduction

The Faḍl Allāh family

Our author, Shihāb al-Dīn Aḥmad ibn Yaḥyā ibn Faḍl Allāh, was born into a family that had already attained the highest ranks in the sphere in which both he himself and several other members of the family were to continue to shine, namely the *inshā'* or chancery branch of the Mamluk administration. It appears that the family, which claimed descent from the Caliph ʿUmar I (hence the al-ʿUmarī in their full name), may at some time have had connections with Kerak. However, they came to prominence in Damascus, and although various members of the family went to the centre to serve in Cairo, they retained an important presence in Damascus.

The first generation, the three sons of Faḍl Allāh, of whom himself little seems to have been recorded, were all senior officials. The least important was Badr al-Dīn Muḥammad, whose career appears to have been confined to Damascus. In 699/1299–1300 he was one of the local officials appointed to serve the deputy of the Ilkhān Ghazān after the latter's departure from Syria. How this is to be reconciled with the information that he was taken off into captivity and only returned from Ghazān's territory in 704/1304–5[1] is not clear. Sharaf al-Dīn ʿAbd al-Wahhāb was the first to come to a position of eminence. By 661/1262–3 he headed the Chancery Bureau in Damascus and was in due course called to Cairo in 692/1293 by Sultan Khalīl. He continued to serve there (declining to accompany the Sultan al-Nāṣir Muḥammad to Kerak in 708/1308–9[2]) until his dismissal in 711/1311–2 and his return to his former position in Damascus, where he replaced the youngest of the three brothers, Muḥyī al-Dīn, and remained until his death in 717/1317. Muḥyī al-Dīn had first entered the service of the Chancery in Damascus under his brother in 661/1262–3. By 708/1308–9 we find him appointed in his turn to be head of the Bureau in Damascus until replaced by his returning brother, as has been said. The top position in Cairo was given him in 729/1328–9, and this he continued to hold until his death in 738/1338, although there had been a break in 732–3/1331–3 when he had been sent back to Damascus and replaced by a grandson of al-Shihāb Maḥmūd, not because he was out of favour but owing to his hardness of hearing.

Of the next generation the three sons of Muḥyī al-Dīn alone need concern us here. The line continuing from Sharaf al-Dīn seems to have concentrated more on the military career and produced an emir[3] of forty at Damascus. One of Muḥyī al-Dīn's sons, another Badr al-Dīn Muḥammad, was the head of Chancery in Damascus from 744/1343 till his death in 746/1345. Another son, Shihāb al-Dīn Aḥmad, our present author, had accompanied his father to Egypt and from the date of his father's reinstatement as *Kātib al-Sirr* (Privy Secretary), as the head of the Chancery Bureau was called, in 733/1332–3, we find him fulfilling the functions of the office as his father's deputy. Just before his father's death (738/1338), Shihāb al-Dīn was replaced by his younger brother, ʿAlāʾ al-Dīn, as the acting head of the Bureau, and subsequently the latter was confirmed in the full position, which he held for upwards of thirty years and served eleven sultans with great prestige and authority.

The family tree

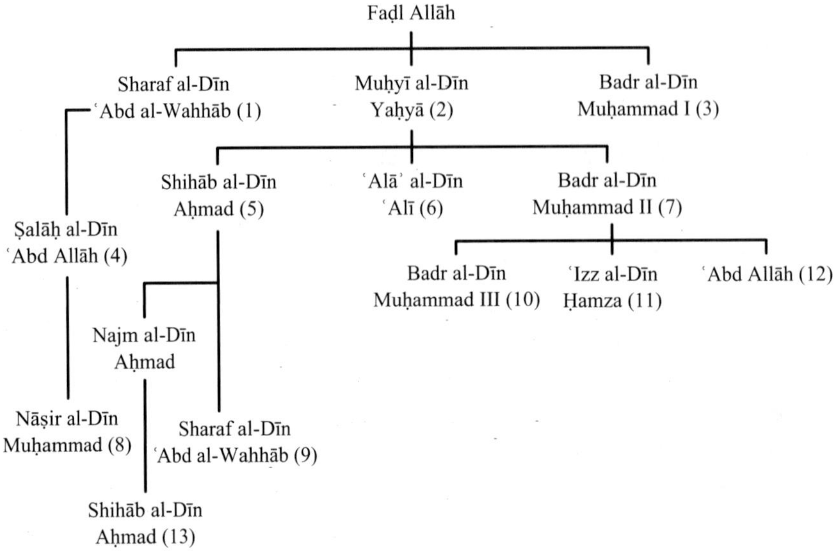

Notes

1 Ibn al-Suqāʿī, no. 305; *Sulūk*, ii, p. 179: b. Ḥijja 623/Nov. 1226, d. 3 Ram. 717/8 Nov. 1317.
2 Ibn Ḥajar al-Asqalānī, v, pp. 199ff: b. Shawwāl 645/Jan.–Feb. 1248, d. 9 Ram. 738/1 Apr. 1338.
3 al-Ṣafadī, iv, p. 328; Ibn Ḥajar al-Asqalānī, iv, p. 254: b. 634/1236–7. d. Jum. I 706/Nov. –Dec. 1306.
4 Ibn al-Suqāʿī, no. 305: d. Raj. 719/Aug. –Sept. 1319.
5 al-Ṣafadī, viii, pp. 252–70; Ibn Ḥajar al-Asqalānī, i, p. 352; Ibn Kathīr, xiv, p. 229; Ibn Qāḍī Shuhba, ii, p. 570: b. 3 Shawwāl 700/11 June 1301, d. 9 Ḥijja 749/28 Feb. 1349.
6 Ibn Ḥajar al-Asqalānī, iii, p. 212; *Sulūk*, ii, p. 166: b. 712/1312–3, d. 9 Ram. 769/28 Apr. 1368.
7 al-Ṣafadī, v, p. 211; Ibn Ḥajar al-Asqalānī, v, p. 53: b. 710/1310–11, d. 26 Raj. 746/22 Nov. 1345.
8 Ibn Ḥajar al-Asqalānī, iv, p. 95; *Sulūk*, iii, p. 88: b. 704/1304–5, d. Qaʿda 764/Aug.–Sept. 1363.
9 Ibn Ḥajar al-Asqalānī, iii, p. 38: d. Shawwāl 754/Oct. –Nov. 1353.
10 Ibn Ḥajar al-Asqalānī, iv, p. 215; *Sulūk*, iii, p. 821; Ibn Furāt, ix, p. 391: d. 20 Shawwāl 796/18 Aug. 1394.
11 Ibn Furāt, ix, p. 419: d. early Muḥ. 797/early Nov. 1394.
12 "the last of the family", *Sulūk*, iv, p. 472: d. 821/1418–19.
13 Ibn Qāḍī Shuhba, i, p. 94: d. Rabīʿ II 784/June–July 1382.

Our author had at least two sons, of one of whom it is recorded that he served as a secretary at court, that is as a *muwaqqiʿ al-dast*. A grandson was Privy Secretary at Tripoli and briefly in Damascus. However, the pre-eminence of the family stayed with the sons of ʿAlāʾ al-Dīn. Badr al-Dīn Muḥammad III was appointed to succeed his father a few days before the latter's death in 769/1368, and he held office, with two interruptions, until his own death in 796/1394. His brother, ʿIzz al-Dīn Ḥamza, "one of the court secretaries", acted as a deputy for him, and of him it is said that "he was the last of the Faḍl Allāh family of any eminence". The last surviving son of ʿAlāʾ al-Dīn, a certain ʿAbd Allāh, died in 821/1418–9 "obscure and very poor". For a century the family had been a dominating one amongst the ranks of the *kuttāb al-inshāʾ*, the Chancery secretaries.[4]

Shihāb al-Dīn Aḥmad (Ibn Faḍl Allāh) al-ʿUmarī

His career

Al-ʿUmarī (the name we shall use for our author from now on) was born on 3 Shawwāl 700/11 June 1301 in Damascus, where his father was making his career in the chancery administration. The fullest and most authoritative biographical notice, and a very laudatory and respectful one, is provided by his younger contemporary, al-Ṣafadī, who was on terms of friendship with him. As is customary in such sources, we are given an account of al-ʿUmarī's teachers, who included Ibn Taimiyya in the field of law (*fiqh*) and Shihāb al-Dīn Maḥmūd, a celebrated government official, in the literary field, poetry and rhetoric. According to Ṣafadī, al-ʿUmarī united four qualities rarely found together: the ability to grasp matters quickly and commit them to memory, an excellent long-term memory, acuteness of mind and literary flair, both in prose and poetry. To illustrate the breadth of his intellectual range, Ṣafadī records that he was the acknowledged authority on history, especially that of the Mongols of Jenghiz Khan's lineage and of the Turkish rulers of India, that he was a licensed jurisconsult (*muftī*) of the Shāfiʿī school of law, that he was an authority on astrolabes and astronomy generally, and that his standing in geography was generally recognised.

His administrative career was mostly carried out as the deputy of his father. However, from 733/1332–4, as has been said, he held effective authority in the Chancery, while his father, now old and indisposed, was nominally in charge. Detailed information about the way he fulfilled his duties cannot, of course, be hoped for. On the basis of what is available, however, one might hazard that he, like one or two others of his family, was outspoken and jealous of the powers and prerogatives of the bureau he was responsible for, and eager to maintain its standards and proper forms. His character is said by a contemporary to have been "hot-tempered and forceful".[5] This same source records that al-ʿUmarī clashed with the Dawādār, an official of the military sphere who functioned alongside the civilian bureaucracy. The title means "pen-box holder". This incident ended with the Dawādār's being outmanoeuvred and his dismissal and banishment secured (11 Ramaḍān, 733/26 May 1333).

Sometime before the death of his father, which occured on Wednesday, 9 Ramaḍān 738/1 April 1338, the attitudes ascribed to him above brought him trouble and the need to withdraw quietly from the scene, while his father smoothed over what was regarded at the time as being a situation with probable fatal consequences for al-ʿUmarī. He had spoken out far from discreetly against Sultan al-Nāṣir Muḥammad's ratification of Tankiz's appointment of a Coptic convert to Islam as *Kātib al-Sirr* in Damascus. Not only was Tankiz, the Vicegerent of Damascus, a great favourite of the Sultan at that time who denied him nothing, but also the Sultan could not tolerate any questioning of his decisions. He increased the titles and salary of the "Copt" and al-ʿUmarī resigned in blunt terms. It was at this point that his father intervened to save both al-ʿUmarī and the family position. His other son, ʿAlāʾ al-Dīn ʿAlī, although young, was brought in to fill the office. To explain the hostility of al-ʿUmarī to Tankiz's nominee, it may be that we imagine al-ʿUmarī to have some proprietry feeling about the post in Damascus. Apart from that, a straight prejudice against Copts, converted or not, may be too simple an answer in the light of our author's remarks (see Section 34, p. 33), in which he adopts an essentially unbigoted stance in connection with the common criticisms of the Copts in the administration, and points out that much of what is said is exaggeration based on ignorance and unfamiliarity. The clue to his reaction lies perhaps in his remark, as it is attributed to him, when protesting to the sultan, "This is a Copt who does not know this discipline", meaning, of course, the professional skills and practice of the Chancery, as opposed to those of the financial bureaux where frequently the Copts were recognised to be indispensable. In other words, we may infer that he was objecting on professional grounds.

After his father's death, although he himself was out of employment, it seems that he exerted some influence on his brother, ʿAlāʾ al-Dīn, which caused the sultan some annoyance. That, plus the fact that al-ʿUmarī imprudently brought himself to the sultan's notice by petitioning to be allowed to depart to Damascus, led to his being arrested on 24 Shaʿbān 739/7 March 1339, and given into the hands of the then Dawādār. The threat of torture was enough to persuade him to put his signature to a requisition order for 10,000 dinars. By selling property and other effects in Damascus he raised 140,000 dirhems and on receipt of that the authorities were satisfied. However, he stayed in prison in the Citadel for a little over seven months until he was released on 13 Rabīʿ II 740/18 October 1339. Despite the money taken from him, he remained a man of property and wealth. According to Ibn Kathīr he built a splendid residence for himself at the foot of Mount Qasyūn.

His memory helped here, because it is said that he was the only person to whom the sultan could turn for information about a certain secretary who had been imprisoned for forging the sultan's signature and was now petitioning to be released. With this case satisfactorily explained, both the secretary and al-ʿUmarī were restored to favour and released. Al-ʿUmarī had, when this man was first convicted, saved him his hand which the sultan had ordered to be cut off. In the following year (741/1340–1), having been appointed head of Chancery in

Damascus, he was instrumental in saving the hand of his predecessor, Yaḥyā al-Qaisarānī, which the sultan had ordered the Ḥājib Barsbughā to cut off.

In Ṣafar 743/July 1342 he was replaced in Damascus by his brother, Badr al-Dīn II, and in the following year was summoned to Cairo because of "the multitude of complaints against him". With the support of his brother, ʿAlāʾ al-Dīn, who was still head of Chancery in Cairo, he avoided further extortion and was returned to Damascus without office but provided with a sufficient pension. He died in Damascus on 9 Dhūʾl-Ḥijja 749/28 February 1349, not long after his wife, a cousin of his, with whom he had set out intending to perform the Pilgrimage to Mecca. He was also hoping to avoid an outbreak of the plague but en route his wife had died and had been buried at Jerusalem. He himself died in the family house within the Paradises' Gate at Damascus and was buried in the tomb he had built at the foot of Qasyūn.

His works

During his relatively short, busy bureaucratic career al-ʿUmarī found the time and the energy to write a sizeable amount. The biographical notices dedicated to him describe him as a consummate man of letters. An authoritative entry is to be found in the biographical dictionary of al-Ṣafadī,[6] who had personal contact with al-ʿUmarī. It was his all-round ability that was admired and, as is often the case, his facility that was striking. Ṣafadī wrote:

> He was one of the perfect men of letters I have known. With the word "perfect" I have in mind those who follow literature both in theory and practice, in prose and poetry and with a knowledge of the careers of contemporaries and the various earlier generations and of outstanding calligraphers and doyens of the secretarial arts. . . . His many letters, both official and private to his intimate friends, flowed from his pen spontaneously, as I witnessed, producing staggering results. I have never seen anyone of comparable ability.

Leaving aside his *magnum opus*, the *Masālik al-abṣār*, which will be dealt with separately below, his output was considerable. He was a poet and a fair amount of his poetry is quoted by al-Ṣafadī, although it is classed as only "moderate" by one source. There are also a number of titles of a belles-lettres character which are attributed to al-ʿUmarī:

- i At Leiden there survives in manuscript a collection (with the title of *al-Shatawiyyāt*) of letters (*rasāʾil*), including some of the replies, on the theme of a particularly bad winter at Damascus in 744/1343.[7]
- ii A work entitled *al-Nubdha al-kāfiya fi maʿrifat al-kitāba waʾl-qāfiya* (*The Sufficient Modicum on Composition and Rhyme*).[8]
- iii *al-Durar al-farāʾid* is a shortened version of a collection of biographies of notables in various fields from the Islamic West. The original was written

by al-Fatḥ ibn Khāqān (died 535/1140–1). This is most likely to have been a preparatory exercise for incorporation in his *Masālik al-abṣār*. A manuscript is preserved in the Taimuriyya Library at Cairo, dated 720/1320.

iv In praise of the Prophet Muḥammad he wrote a volume of poems, entitled *Ṣubābat al-mushtāq* (*The Lover's Longing*). Ṣafadī gives an extract from one of them.[9]

v Probably following the much-imitated pattern set by al-Thaʿālabī in his *Yatīmat al-dahr*, al-ʿUmarī wrote biographies of his contemporaries with selections of their poetry in a work called *Dhahabiyyat al-ʿaṣr*.

vi A selection of al-ʿUmarī's official prose is referred to by al-Qalqashandī in his handbook for government secretaries, the *Ṣubḥ al-aʿshā*. It was called *al-Jawāhir al-multaqaṭa* (*The Gleaned Gems*).[10]

Other titles are given by various sources but as there is little or no indication of the contents, except for the near certainty that there was a large element of anthologising, it is not profitable to list them all.

His pride in the ancestry that his family claimed, that is, a direct line back to ʿUmar ibn al-Khaṭṭāb, the second of the so-called Rightly-guided Caliphs (the *Rāshidīn*), was probably the motive for his writing the *Fawāḍil al-samar fī faḍāʾil Āl ʿUmar*, or *Residues of Conversation*[11] *concerning the Excellencies of the Lineage of ʿUmar*, said to be in four volumes. No copy of this is known to survive.

It may be assumed that it was as a product of his professional expertise and interest that he wrote the handbook on current Mamluk diplomatic to which he gave the title *al-Taʿrīf biʾl-muṣṭalaḥ al-sharīf*. One might translate this as *Instruction in Royal Chancery Practice*. It is a solidly practical book which gives styles of address, model documents for different purposes, material on what one might call administrative and political geography,[12] some other material on the official postal services, and finally stock descriptive phrases on a variety of topics, suitable to adorn official documents with the flowery language deemed indispensable. This work was published initially at Cairo in 1312/1894–5, and has been re-edited by Muḥammad Ḥusain Shams al-Dīn (*Dār al-Kutub al-ʿIlmiyya*, Beirut, 1988).

The Masālik al-abṣār

Whether this work should properly be described as an encyclopaedia or not, it is in the general sense encyclopaedic by virtue of its great size and scope. The full title is *Masālik al-abṣār fī mamālik al-amṣār*, which is difficult to translate, as are so many of the rhyming titles so beloved by Muslim mediaeval authors, but could be rendered as *The Ways of Discernment into the Realms of the Capital Cities*. The presence in the title of the two key words *masālik* and *mamālik* ("routes" or "ways" and "realms" or "kingdoms") inevitably suggests a connection with the tradition of geographical writing, mainly of the tenth century A.D., which was basically interested in defining the "space" and the itineraries of the

Dār al-Islām, the Islamic world, and in establishing the realities of political order within the theoretical unity of the Caliphate. In particular one may refer to the well-known works which bear the title *Kitāb al-masālik wa'l-mamālik* by Ibn Khurdādhbih (died 300/911), al-Istakhrī (dates uncertain) and Ibn Ḥawqal (died after 362/973). Following their lead, al-ʿUmarī's work has a large geographical content but that is far from being the whole story.

Fuat Sezgin has led a project to publish a facsimile edition of the whole of the *Masālik al-abṣār*, employing a variety of available manuscripts, mostly from collections in Istanbul.[13] This facsimile edition comprises twenty-seven "books" (*sifr*), issued in twenty-two volumes. Al-Ṣafadī stated that the *Masālik al-abṣār* consisted of "ten large volumes".[14] These schemes of division refer, of course, to the physical production of any given set of volumes. See how in the Aya Sofya manuscript no. 3422 a note (*faṣl*) records that this and other volumes had been made a *waqf* (an inalienable donation) by Jamāl al-Dīn Maḥmūd, the *ustādār*[15] of the Mamluk Sultan al-Ẓāhir Barqūq, for his madrasa[16] in Cairo. It adds that the whole donation consisted of twenty-two volumes out of an original twenty-three, because of the loss of the eleventh volume of this particular set. Such a physical division is quite distinct from any internal plan of organisation established by the author.[17]

In this case, al-ʿUmarī set out his plan for the work in the introduction. The work is divided into two main parts (*qism*), the first dealing with "an account of the earth and what it contains by land and sea", and the second covering "the inhabitants of the earth, the various peoples". The first part commences in a very organised, regularly sub-divided manner, an extreme example of which is found in al-Qalqashandī's *Ṣubḥ al-a'shā*. The formal sub-divisions are not so evident in the second part but the very nature of the material imposes its own order with, as it were, built-in rubrics.

Part One (*al-qism al-awwāl*) is organised in two over-arching divisions (the Arabic term is *naw*ʿ, literally "a type"). The first division concerns "the routes" (*masālik*) and the second "the realms" (*mamālik*) of Islam, and each is further broken down into chapters (*abwāb*) and excursuses (*fuṣūl*). The "routes" division deals initially with physical geography, but most of its first chapter has a distinctly literary, indeed lexicographical, character, as it lists and explains obscure terms for various sorts of land, soil, dust, sand and so on. The world's mountains, rivers and lakes are then listed, and this is followed by significant Muslim and non-Muslim monuments or sites throughout the world, with many pages on monasteries and wine taverns famous in the literary tradition. One has the decided impression that much of this is produced only for the anecdotes and the verses that are associated with various places. The atmosphere of the anthology is palpable.

The second chapter brings us back to geography with an account of the seven climes and the cities, islands and so on. which each contains. Here we meet with the separate "summary discourse" (*kalām jumlī*) on the important Christian polities with information derived from a Genoese informant. The remaining chapters of this division touch on length of day in each clime, the seas and the *Qibla* (the direction of prayer).

The second major division of Part One contains fifteen chapters on different areas of the Islamic world. The chapter dealing with Egypt and Syria, of which a translation is to follow, is number six of this group. It is entitled "Concerning the realm of Egypt, Syria and the Hijāz", but the amount of text on the Hijaz is minimal, as will be seen. This is, no doubt, because Mecca with the Kaaba and Medina with the Prophet's Mosque are dealt with in the earlier section on the famous monuments of the world.

Part Two, headed "Concerning the inhabitants of the earth etc.", begins with summary biographical notices on leading cultural figures of Islam, keeping those from the East and West of the Islamic world separate from one another. The following categories are dealt with successively: Koran scholars, Hadith scholars, lawyers (*fuqahā'*), lexicographers, grammarians, rhetoricians, Sufis, sages (*ḥukamā'*), doctors, musicians, viziers, government secretaries, preachers and poets (in this case, including pre-Islamic figures). All this takes up no less than fifteen "books", far more than the four "books" for the whole of Part One. Then there are three further "books", two dealing with animals, birds, insects, fish and plants and one dealing with the inanimate creation.

The remaining five "books", which form the second main division of Part Two, consist of a treatment of religions (in one book only) and then a resumé of non-Islamic and Islamic history. From all this one may gather the enormous scope of this work and also appreciate that the geographical content, however widely that is interpreted, is far from being dominant. Indeed, it is not easy to categorise this work satisfactorily. It exemplifies the appetite of scholarship in the Mamluk period for vast compendia of knowledge.[18] The wish to have knowledge corralled and systematised, and even, in many cases, reduced, all for the sake of comprehensiveness and ease of reference, nevertheless resulted in works of a size that militated against the logistics of the manuscript age. In that light the *Masālik al-abṣār* is as much an encyclopaedia as it is anything else. It is a large-scale assemblage of much of the knowledge that the *kātib*, the secretary-literateur (that crucial figure of Arabic secular literature) would require, other than the strictly professional material, like that which our author had provided in the *Ta'rīf*.

Clearly a work of this size would have been written over a considerable period and there can be no certainty that it was compiled in the order in which it now is. In fact, it is clear that the work was never fully completed. The chapter on the Bedouin Arabs is abandoned with a rubric left dangling in the air, and the final year of the historical section is 744/1344. Its termination at that point is surely entirely random. One gains an idea of the span of time over which al-'Umarī was writing from the fact that the chapter on Andalus was being compiled in 738/1337–8,[19] while elsewhere the author records his visit to Hebron in Dhū'l-Ḥijja 745/April 1345,[20] and notes that he received certain information on the Bedouin of North Africa in Ṣafar 749/May 1348, only nine or ten months before his death.[21]

The following parts of the work have been edited, translated or commented on:
From Division 1 of Part One

i The author's introduction and Chapter 1: *Masālik al-abṣār*, i, ed. Aḥmad Zakī Pasha, Cairo (1924).
ii Part of Section 6 of Chapter 1: A.L. Mayer, "A Medieval Description of the Haram of Jerusalem", *Quarterly of the Department of Antiquities of Palestine*, i (1932), pp. 44ff, 74 ff.
iii Part of Section 6 (on monasteries) of Chapter 1: Ḥabīb al-Zaiyāt, *Naqd al-diyārāt fī'l-juz' al-awwāl min Masālik al-abṣār*, Cairo (1928).
iv Section 2 of Chapter 2: M. Amari, "Al ʿUmarī, Condizioni degli Stati cristiani dell' Occidente secondo una relazione di Domenichino Doria da Genova, Testo arabo con versione italiana e note", in *Atti della Reale Accademia dei Lincei, 1882–3, serie III, Memoire della classe di scienze morali, storiche e filologiche*, xi, Rome (1883), pp. 67–103.

From Division 2 of Part One

v Chapter 1: *Al-ʿOmarī's Bericht über Indien in seinem Werke Masālik al-abṣār etc.*, ed. & trans. O Spies, Sammlung orientalischer Arbeiten 14, Leipzig (1943).
vi Chapter 2: E. Quatremère, "Notice de l'ouvrage qui a pour titre: Mesalek alabsar etc.," *Notices et Extraits des Manuscrits de la Bibliothèque du Roi etc.*, xiii (1838), pp. 151–384; Klaus Lech, *Das mongolische Weltreich. Al-ʿUmarī's Darstellung der mongolischen Reiche in seinem Werk* Masālik al-abṣār *etc.*, Wiesbaden (1968).
vii Chapter 5: *al-ʿUmarī's Bericht uber Anatolien in seinem Werke* Masālik al-Abṣār, ed. F Taeschner, Leipzig (1929).
viii Chapter 6: *Masālik al-Abṣār etc., Dawlat al-mamālīk al-Ūlā,* ed. Dorothea Krawulsky, Beirut (1986); *Masālik al-Abṣār etc., mamālik Miṣr wa'l-Shām wa'l-Ḥijāz wa'l-Yaman*, ed. Ayman Fu'ād Sayyid, IFAO, Cairo (1985); M. Gaudefroy-Demombynes, *La Syrie à l'Époque des Mamelouks,* Paris (1923).
ix Chapter 7: *Masālik al-abṣār etc., al-qism al-khāṣṣ bi-mamlakat al-Yaman*, ed. Ayman Fu'ād Sayyid, Cairo (1974).
x Chapters 12, 13, 14: *Waṣf Ifrīqiya wa-Andalus etc*, ed. Ḥasan Ḥusnī ʿAbd al-Wahhāb, Tunis (1341/1922); M. Gaudefroy Demombynes, *L'Afrique moins l'Egypte*, Paris (1927); M. Gaudefroy Demombynes, "Quelques passages du Masalik el Absar rélatifs à Maroc" in *Mémorial Henri Basset. Nouvelles études nordafricaines et orientales*, i, Paris (1929), pp. 269–80.
xi Chapter 15: *Masālik al-abṣār etc.*, Book 15, *Qabā'il al-'Arab*, ed. Dorothea Krawulsky, *al-Markaz al-ʿIlmī li'l-Buḥūth*, Beirut (1985).

From Division 1 of Part Two

xii Part of Section 2: G.S. Colin, "Quelques poètes arabes d'Occident au XIVe siècle," *Hesperis*, xii, (1931), pp. 241–7.

From Division 2 of Part Two

xiii Eva Rodhe Lundquist, *Saladin and the Crusaders. Selected annals from* Masālik al-abṣār *etc.*, Studia Orientalia Lundensia 5, Lund (1992).

The chapter on Egypt and Syria

This description of the Mamluk state marks a proud and confident point in its history after the Crusader states had been finally suppressed and the even more dangerous threat from the Mongols of the Ilkhanid state had been met and overcome. The Mamluk state was not seriously challenged from any quarter and it stood as perhaps the most powerful and prestigious Islamic power, the centre of learning and the traditions of the caliphate. It is, however, noteworthy that al-ʿUmarī makes nothing of the continued presence in Cairo of an Abbasid caliph, a shadowy figure, although one not entirely without prestige abroad. The Mamluk state in all its aspects is given the highest praise and there is little or nothing that strikes a critical note in the author's description, unless one remarks on the rather extraordinary passage (Section 51) in which the author expresses sympathy for the Egyptian peasants and the burdens they bear. Early in the whole chapter (Section 4) he makes a special plea not to be thought of as biased. Indeed, he has, as he claims, rather abbreviated the paean of praise that he could be singing.

The author insists that he is writing about "one realm" and for a while the subject matter moves freely between Egypt and Syria with a sense of improvisation until one arrives at the account of the central power structures and routines. A division is then established with the treatment of the centre and then a more systematic description of Damascus. The treatment of successive Syrian towns and districts follows on. It is a little odd that the whole begins with a random air, that is, with an account of Egypt's emerald mines, hardly central to the matter at large, although interesting in itself. It can be seen, along with the section on the balsam plant, to be a reflection of the long-established *faḍāʾil* genre, the celebration of a place's "excellencies" and titles to fame. The description of the various aspects of the state, its natural resources and economy, the royal estate of the sultan, the army and its administration, the norms of dress of its various cadres etc., although valuable and suggestive, is far from being as exhaustively informative as a modern reader might wish. An impulse towards the purely poetic, however charming, often asserts itself. The element of "abbreviation" in the account, originally intended to refer to an economy in commendation, could well be given a much wider significance. In this case abbreviation could be understood to characterise the nature of the treatment of the material in general. The treatment of most places in Syria, for example, is disappointingly antiquarian, indeed, legendary, in tone.

It could be thought surprising that the mamluk system, which was so fundamental to the Mamluk state, was not given any more extensive exposition. The author in one brief passage (Section 18 below) remarked on the mixed origins of the regime's troops and states that "the majority are purchased mamluks". In Islam there was a lengthy tradition for states to seek military manpower from beyond the areas of Muslim political control by importing slaves (by which one should understand a favoured status of technical servitude without the negative connotations that the word has for Europeans), overseeing their conversion to Islam and subsequently manumitting them. These mamluks (the word means "owned") were for the most part Turks from the Asian steppe lands or Circassians from the Caucasus. The Turks especially were renowned for their mounted archery in the nomadic style. For centuries such troops provided the main force of Muslim armies and the elite members of society. From the thirteenth century the supporters of regimes became themselves the rulers and then continued to replace themselves by further purchases. This system reached its highest stage of development under the Mamluks when the whole of the state and society was defined by that term. One may accept that for al-ʿUmarī the mamluk system was a given phenomenon which required no explanation.

One date for the composition of this work is given within the text itself (see p. 8), namely the year 738/1337–8, the year in which al-ʿUmarī was writing the chapter on Andalus. The Sultan al-Nāṣir Muḥammad was still on the throne, as is fully obvious from the laudatory phrases used of him as the ruling sovereign. It appears that al-ʿUmarī had intended to dedicate the work to the sultan, but the latter died in 741/1341 by which time al-ʿUmarī had lost his active role in state administration. Despite his greater leisure for scholarly pursuits, the whole enterprise was never completely finished, as we have seen. Within this chapter itself there are perhaps signs of lack of revision. Material on both the emerald mines and the balsam product is repeated and a quotation from Abū Bakr al-Khwārizmī is used twice in different forms (see Sections 66 and 68).

In this chapter there are few acknowledged written sources. Al-ʿUmarī's own taste, no doubt, led him to quote the prose of al-Qāḍī al-Fāḍil, the celebrated stylist and official of Saladin (see Sections 11, 13, 51, 66, 73, 74 and 82). Short passages are taken from the geographical writings of al-Bakrī and Ibn Saʿīd (Sections 61 and 62), while the longest quotations are attributed to al-Tīfāshī[22] (Sections 39, 54, 56 and 63–5), through whom the writings of al-Idrīsī, Ibn ʿAsākir and others are indirectly cited. Amongst historians material is taken from al-Balādhurī and al-Ṭabarī, although most of the passages (Sections 72 and 83) cannot be traced in their extant works.

Oral sources are many and varied. Quite probably al-ʿUmarī used the method he outlines in his author's introduction, that is, to question each of his informants on different occasions to see whether their information remained consistent. He clearly sought out individuals with a direct or a specialist knowledge. For example, for information about conditions in Cyrenaica he questioned an officer, a former *muqṭaʿ*[23] in that area, and also a Bedouin sheikh and two *qāḍī*s with local connections (Section 62). For a point of comparison with conditions in the

Ilkhanid region he questioned the well-known merchant and diplomatic envoy, Majd al-Din al-Sallamī (Section 51), and for a section on the Ismāʿīlīs of Syria his informant was a leading member of the sect from those parts, Mubārak ibn ʿAlwān (Section 49). An obvious example of employing expert witnesses is the reliance on the two persons who knew the Egyptian emerald mines at first hand (see Section 2).

As one might expect, granted al-ʿUmarī's training and profession, his prose style is greatly influenced by the taste and practice of *inshā*ʾ, the official epistolographical manner. There are the typical balanced rhyming phrases, and his prose borrows much in way of vocabulary and imagery from poetry, and indeed citations of verses not infrequently punctuate the text. Very striking are passages of a sensitive awareness of nature and the beauty of certain scenes, such as the view from the Citadel or moonlight on the Nile, and the description of the Ghuta of Damascus.

The authority of al-ʿUmarī's account of the Mamluk state system was recognised by later writings, who quarried it for their own works. The extent of this use made by later writers will be evident from the many parallel passages to which reference will be made in the notes to the various sections of the translation that follows. The three writers who made significant use of the *Masālik al-abṣār* are al-Qalqashandī (d. 821/1418) for his *Ṣubḥ al-aʿshā*, al-Maqrīzī (d. 845/1442) for his topographical and historical work, normally known as *al-Khiṭaṭ*, and al-Suyūṭī (d. 911/1505) in his *Ḥusn al-muḥādara*.

Of the two editions, the one prepared by Krawulsky (*Masālik* (Beirut)) and that prepared by Ayman Fuad Sayyid (*Masālik* (Cairo)), the former may be considered as the base text for this translation, although I have not maintained an identical arrangement of the paragraphs and I have also adopted a few different readings, which will be indicated in the footnotes. In addition three manuscripts of the *Masālik al-abṣār* have been consulted in connection with this translation, namely:

- i Ms. Istanbul, Aya Sofya, no. 3416, part iii = A
- ii Ms. Istanbul, Top Kapi, Ahmet III, no. 2797, part ii = T
- iii Ms. Paris, Bibliothèque Nationale, no. 583 arabe = P

The figures within angular brackets in the text of the translation refer to the pagination of Krawulsky's edition.

The translation

<77> Concerning the realm of Egypt, Syria and the Hijaz

[1][24]

These countries form one realm. Most of Egypt is situated at the beginning of the third [clime], and most of Syria at its end. Aleppo, part of Syria, is in the fourth. It is a large realm of great wealth, whose seat of government is the Citadel of the Mount [in Cairo], and secondarily Damascus. It is one of the most glorious kingdoms on earth because it possesses certain revered sites, the Holy Land and places of worship that were founded in goodly piety. Within it are the three mosques "which are the goal of all pilgrims",[25] the tombs of the Prophets (the blessings of God be upon them), al-Ṭūr,[26] and the Nile and the Euphrates, the two rivers that flow from Paradise.[27]

[2][28]

<78> In this realm there is an emerald mine,[29] unrivalled anywhere in the world. The fact that Egypt is in sole possession of this mine and that distant foreign rulers seek its products from her is in itself a sufficient cause for pride. The following account of the mine I had from the notary[30] ʿAbd al-Raḥīm, the Clerk of the Mine:

> Travelling at the normal moderate speed it takes eight days to get there from Qūs. The Beja[31] camp around about it or in the vicinity to undertake the digging and guarding of it. The mine is in the mountains east of the Nile, to the north of a large peak called Qurshanda, the highest and noblest in the mountains there. The stretch of country in which it is situated has no permanent settlement, nor is there one around about or anywhere near. The nearest water is half a day's journey away or more, and is water collected from the rain, known as the Pool of Aʿyun. It is abundant when there is much rain and scarce when there is little.[32]
>
> The mine is at the heart of a lengthy cavern in white rock from which the emeralds are extracted. This white rock is of three kinds. The first is called *talq kāfūrī*,[33] the second is called *ṭalq fiḍḍa*[34] and the third is called <79> *ḥarawī* stone [?]. The rock is broken to reveal the emeralds, which are, as it

> were, veins within it. The best sort – and the emeralds are of three types – are the so-called *dhubābī* [fly-green].[35] These are the most splendid, but they are rare, no, rarer than rare; they are hardly ever found.

The notary, ʿAbd al-Raḥīm, reported that during all the time he was employed there he saw not a single one, nor was one mined in all that period, and he had to collect throughout the year all that was found by any worker there.

He continued:

> There is no fixed limit to the number of workers. It fluctuates according to the interest, or lack of it, in exploiting the mine. When an emerald is mined, it is thrown into linseed oil, then placed in cotton and the cotton is wrapped up in strips of linen, or something similar. Security in the mine is very strict. The workers are searched each day when they leave; even places which it is not proper to mention are searched.

This is what he has told me.

Another person, who knows all about this mine, told me that the workers in the mine, notwithstanding the strict security, have many devious ways of stealing emeralds.[36] For example, a man may steal such emeralds as he can, put them in a little purse, which he has with him, prepared for the purpose, tie it up and suspend it by a silk thread, tied securely to it, between his back molars. The top of the thread is tied firmly, and when the thread is suspended he works the knot between the two molars towards his cheek. The purse remains attached, and when he leaves the mine and reaches a safe place, he retrieves it and takes the contents.

[3]

<80> Balsam, that well-known substance, is found in Egypt. The rulers of Christendom most eagerly solicit it, for Christians generally have a particular belief concerning it, thinking that no Christian is fully made a Christian until some oil of balsam is put in the water of the font at his baptism.[37]

[4]

The various sources of income and revenue of this state, its regiments and troops, the communities that have taken refuge in it and the multifarious peoples that have come to live here, the goodly rule and long tradition of leadership for which its Sultans are known – all this is common knowledge and not concealed in obscurity from any person of perception. In previous passages of this work and in some others still to come my words find their justification. Let no-one believe or suppose that bias lies behind my words, because I am a native of these lands, subject to the authority of their rulers, and nurtured like my forefathers in the grace and favour of the Sultans. God forbid that I should speak anything but the truth or record what is not correct, especially concerning what will be repeated by generation after generation. Indeed, for this reason, I have rather abbreviated what I have to say.

[5][38]

The currency used is dirhems, which are two thirds silver and one third copper. The dirhem is 18 carob seeds, one of which equals 3 *qamḥa* (wheat grain). A *mithqāl* is 24 <81> carobs. One of these dirhems is worth 48 *fulūs*. The "army dinar"[39] is a nominal unit worth 13⅓ dirhems ordinarily, and the nominal equivalent of 40 "black" dirhems, one of which is a third of one of the dirhems mentioned above. In Egypt [generally] "black" dirhems exist only as nominal units of account, not as actual coins, but they are found in Alexandria, each worth half a [normal] dirhem.

There are various measures of volume used. In Cairo the ardebb is 6 *waiba*s, the *waiba* is 4 "quarters", the "quarter" is 4 *qadaḥ*s and each *qadaḥ* is 232 dirhems. Such is the ardebb in Cairo. In the countryside the volume of the ardebb differs from this. At its greatest it reaches 8 *waiba*s. The normal, commonly used measure is the ardebb mentioned above. [Of weights] the rotl is 12 okes and the oke is 12 dirhems; thus the rotl equals 144 dirhems.[40]

In Damascus the same currency is used, except that the standard weight differs, so that every hundred Syrian *mithqāl*s are the equivalent of only 98¾ Egyptian. The same is true of the dirhems. The rotl is 12 okes and each oke 50 dirhems, so that a rotl equals 600 dirhems.[41]

The *ghirāra* is used for produce and equals 12 "measures" (*kail*), each "measure" being 6 *mudd*s. A *mudd* is a little short of the Egyptian "quarter", and thus the relationship between the *ghirāra* and that of the ardebb is that <82> each *ghirāra* plus 1½ *mudd* equals 3 Egyptian ardebbs precisely. In the Damascus countryside the rotl and the *ghirāra* sometimes are bigger than the Damascus city variety. Because of the size of the extra amount in some places the discrepancy can be quite large. However, the Damascus measures and the Damascus rotl provide the accepted standard.

In Aleppo, Hama and Homs the rotls are larger than those of Damascus, while the *ghirāra* is unknown. The normal measure is the *makkūk*. Although the ratio between the two measures is variable, normally the *ghirāra* is from two *makkūk*s to two and a half, but all this is an approximation.

[6][42]

Egypt's agricultural land depends on the Nile when it rises and inundates whole areas, with the exception of a small amount of no great significance, which is rain-fed, such as the outlying districts of Buhaira, or which is irrigated from permanent flows, such as the Fayyum Oasis, watered from the Manha Canal of Joseph,[43] which branches off from the Nile and which, as is well known, never dries up.

Most of the good things of Egypt are imported. Indeed, one local even exaggerated and said, "The four elements are imports; water, that is to say the Nile, is imported from the south, soil is imported, being carried down by the water (otherwise Egypt would be pure sand that could grow no crop), the source of fire, in other words flint-stone, is only found there when it has been imported, and no air blows there except from one of the two seas, either [the breeze from] the Mediterranean or the one that issues from the Red Sea." This was excessive prejudice [against the country].

<83> Egypt has many grains and pulses – wheat, barley, beans, chick-peas, lentils, peas, lūbiyā-beans, millet and rice – and many flowers, such as penny-royal, myrtle, rose, nenuphar (Egyptian lotus), eglantine, the ben-oil tree, *fāmarḥanna* (?), wallflower and jasmine. There one finds the citron, orange, lemon, sorrel, bitter oranges, many bananas, and much sugar cane, dates, grapes, figs, pomegranates, mulberries, white mulberries, peaches, almonds, sycomore figs, Christ's thorn, plums, cherries and apples. Of quinces and pears there are few, and olives too are imported, except for an insignificant few from the Fayyum. There are only a very few nuts. Pistachios and hazel nuts do not grow there at all. There are yellow melons of various sorts and watermelons, also cucumbers[44] of different sorts, colocasia, turnips, carrots, cauliflowers, radish and multifarious vegetables.

[7][45]

The varieties of animal in Egypt include horses, camels, mules, donkeys, cows, water buffalo, sheep and goats. Those that have an excellent reputation are the donkeys for their liveliness and the cows and sheep for their size. Geese, hens and pigeons are found, and, among wild animals, gazelles, ostriches and hares. The varieties of birds, which are numerous, include cranes and geese.

[8][46]

Most of the time the average prices are as follows. An ardebb of wheat costs 15 dirhems, <84> and of barley 10 dirhems. All other cereal prices are proportionate to these. Rice, however, may cost more. The minimum cost of meat is half a dirhem a rotl, but it is generally higher. Chicken prices vary according to quality. A good bird may be bought for 2 dirhems, some cost 3 or even more; yet others cost only a dirhem. In Egypt oven-like "factories" are built, in which eggs are skilfully treated. When fired, the natural warmth provided by the brooding hen for her eggs is imitated, and so the chicks are hatched out in these factories. Most of their chickens [are provided in this way].[47]

The milk and cheese products are highly regarded, and honey is available in moderate amounts, neither abundant nor scarce. Sugar is very plentiful. The usual price is 1½ dirhems a rotl, and sometimes higher. An excellent refined sugar is produced, which may cost 2½ dirhems a rotl. Sugar in all its various sorts is exported by Egypt to many lands, where the previously famous sugar of Ahwaz is now forgotten.

[9][48]

Egypt possesses incomparable flax, which is exported all over the world, both as raw material and as linen textiles. <85> I was shown by the Khwājā (Master) Jamāl al-Dīn Yūsuf al-Māḥūrī[49] lengths of very fine white linen (*sharb*) of the *mumarrash* variety[50] (just like wasps wings they were!), which he had ordered[51] in Alexandria to present to the Sultan Abū Saʿīd.[52] I do not believe that any material in the world could match this. He also said that when he ordered them, each length, quite plain, cost him 700 dirhems, and the band, also plain, cost the same. So altogether each length cost 1,400 *waraq* dirhems, that is, 700 *nuqra* dirhems.[53] This material is made solely of linen, and of any silk that may be worked in the decorative band, though most of that is linen, for the background [lit. the white] is never made of silk, but the wording itself, which forms the decoration of the band, may be. He added that a dirhem weight of this linen fetches more than its weight in silver, and that what goes into the decorative band fetches many more times its weight. It is in this *sharb* product, rather than any other of the different sorts and varieties of material that are made there, that Alexandria excels.[54]

[10]

To return to our general account of Egypt, only a few buildings are of stone; most are constructed of mud brick, split palm trunks, palm branches and pine timber, which is imported from Asia Minor (*Bilād al-Rūm*) by sea and is known locally as *naqiyy*.[55] Within Egypt are found madrasas, Sufi convents, hospices, *zāwiya*s,[56] large mausolea, <86> fine and noble constructions and incomparable buildings, paved with marble, embellished with variously painted beams, dazzlingly picked out in gold and lapis lazuli, and clad in marble on some of their walls. There are as many different buildings as there are different people to build them.

[11][57]

The capital of Egypt comprises three great cities:[58] Fustat, built by ʿAmr ibn al-ʿAṣ,[59] which the Egyptians commonly call Old Cairo (*Miṣr al-ʿAtīqa*), Cairo (*al-Qāhira al-Muʿizziyya*), built by the general Jawhar[60] for his master, the Caliph al-Muʿizz ibn al-Qāʿim ibn al-Mahdī,[61] and the Citadel of the Mount,[62] built by Qarāqūsh for al-Malik al-Nāṣir Ṣalāḥ al-Dīn [Saladin] Abūʾl-Muẓaffar Yūsuf ibn Aiyūb (may God Almighty have mercy upon him), and first inhabited by his brother, al-ʿĀdil. These three were linked by a wall built by Qarāqūsh,[63] but now the wall is breached in several places.

This wall is the one about which al-Fāḍil[64] wrote as follows in a letter to Saladin:

> May God preserve my Lord alive till his belt encircles the two cities and his screen stretches around them both, for they are both like a spouse whose wrist

<87> should not be left without a bracelet, nor her waist left free without a golden girdle. Now are men's minds at rest for the wall protects them from any grasping hand or the unchecked advance of sinful ambition.

The city, which has grown great, contains the Manṣūrī Hospital, which cannot be matched anywhere for the vastness of its construction, the great amount of its endowed income, the amplitude of its budget, and the variety of its doctors, oculists and surgeons. It is on a noble scale, handsomely equipped, profuse in the benefits it offers, and was endowed by the Sultan al-Malik al-Manṣūr Qalāwūn (may God have mercy upon him).[65]

There too are fine gardens, delightful promenades and houses overlooking both the main river and the channels which extend from it when they fill at the time of high Nile. The Qarāfa cemetery[66] serves the population as its great burial place. The city has some impressive constructions, and charming pleasure-grounds. It is indeed one of the most beautiful cities in the world at spring time owing to the pools <88> that extend throughout it from the branches of the Nile, and the plants that border them when they have put forth their shoots and their flowers have burst into bloom.

[12][67]

Within Egypt are ancient monuments that indicate the wisdom of their builder, such as the pyramids, of which the two Great Pyramids at Giza are the most renowned, and the temples of Akhmim. The rest of the famous temples and theatres and arenas (*malāʿib*) at Ashmunain, Antinoupolis, Qift and Heliopolis, the Pharos of Alexandria,[68] the Green Temple[69] at Joseph's Camp (peace be upon him), have all been touched by time's disfiguring hand and most are in a ruined state. The Great Pyramids and the temples at Akhmim have begun to decay because they have been quarried for their stone and their glory has been altered.

Near the Great Pyramids is the large idol, called by the populace Abū'l-Hawl [the Sphinx], of which no more than about the top half is visible. Much has been said about the pyramids and temples. What is most likely to be true is that the pyramids are shrines to certain stars. As regards the temples, I was told by the learned Shams al-Dīn Abū ʿAbd Allāh Muḥammad ibn Shuqair of Damascus that he had seen <89> and most minutely examined them, and found them to contain all the dispositions of the firmament, and that, in his view, no one learned man or ruler had produced them, but that they were the consecutive work of one people after another until the completion of a whole cycle, namely 36,000 years, since such works could not be done without observations, which could not be completed in less than that time. Such is the information he gave me about the temples.[70]

[13]

The Qadi Muḥyī al-Dīn ibn al-Zakī[71] wrote a letter to the Qadi al-Fāḍil in which he referred to Egypt and called her a whore. Upset by this, al-Fāḍil in his reply wrote:

I had the temerity to ponder on a word which he applied to Egypt and with which he alluded to her. He disgraced her with the character he gave her and cut from [men's] hearts the ties [that bound them to her]. I believe he punished her for Pharaoh's sin, when the latter said, "I am your supreme lord", and "Is not the kingdom of Egypt mine?"[72] Just the same did al-Rashīd when he appointed al-Khaṣīb.[73] If he has come to this, then he has punished her for a sin <90> she did not commit and destroyed her for something not of her making. At all events, if it depended on me, I would be with him against her. If he were to despatch an arrow against her, my hand would undertake to direct it. He took me from my land by his magic[74] and has made his humble servant[75] regret the years of his life spent in Egypt. But he, in his indolence, does not now lift his gaze towards her. Her Nile is to him merely something less than Barada's[76] course and its running stream. If he looks at her red dinar, he says, "It is red for shame"; and if he looks on her black alluvial mud, he says, "From the blackness of its work"; if he beholds her two [great] pyramids, he says, "Her breasts droop"; and if he sees her two encompassing sandy wastes, he says, "Her temples have turned gray". Then I read again, and found that the word, which my lord had applied to her, namely whore, rejects the association. How may he impugn her decency with such slander and assail her honour with this description, when he came to her from his Syria at the time when Unbelief had seized his Islam by the throat.[77] She aided and succoured him, she quieted and removed all dread. He returned to his past responsibilities. Men said, "This is no mortal, this is naught but an angel."[78] If Damascus is a freedwoman of Egypt, then there is no boast for her in her mistress' being a whore. I have drawn a veil over this word. We shall imagine it never found its way into his letter or his salon.

[14][79]

In Syria most agricultural land is rain-fed and produces all the cereals and pulses mentioned for Egypt. Some parts, though they are few, are irrigated from rivers. One finds <91> all sorts of trees and varieties of fruits, such as figs, grapes, pomegranates, quinces, apples, pears, plums, cherries, mulberries, both white and black, apricots, medlars and peaches, which locally are called *durrāqin*. Of most of these fruits the most excellent are found in Damascus in their various sorts and numerous different varieties. Some of these fruits come in the autumn and continue until spring, such as quinces, apples, pomegranates and grapes. There too grow walnuts, almonds, pistachios and filberts, and lemons, citrons, oranges, bitter oranges and bananas. Sugar cane from the lowlands is brought in from about two or more days' journey away. Yellow melons and watermelons of different sorts are grown, and also cucumber (in two varieties), bottle-gourds, turnips, carrots, cauliflower, asparagus, aubergine, Jew's mallow, blite, purslane and other varieties of edible vegetables.

[15][80]

Damascus' special river is the Barada, but there are other streams and rivers extending over the vicinity.[81] Geese, hens, pigeons and many species of birds are found there. Chickens are only hatched naturally, not as is done in Egypt. It has been told that a certain person came from Egypt in the summer time and constructed a battery chicken factory in the suburb of al-ʿUqaiba[82], where they were successfully hatched, but when the autumn came, the system failed. He lost his money, gave it all up and returned to Egypt.

Meat prices are cheaper than those of Egypt. Chicken is about the same, but goose is more expensive. The honey is moderate, and sugar is produced there, some of it refined, but at a higher price than in Egypt and not in large quantities.

<92> Many species of flowers grow, including myrtle, roses, violets, nenuphars, delphiniums, narcissi, wallflowers, jasmine, balm, marjoram, wild thyme and eglantine. The roses and violets are supreme; indeed the roses and the rose water extracted from them have quite eclipsed the renowned products of Jūr and Nisibis.[83] Syrian rose water is exported to most lands. Olives too are abundant in Syria and widely exported. The country possesses many things for which it is especially known.

[16][84]

Most buildings in Syria are of stone. Houses there are of smaller dimensions than those in Egypt, but more highly decorated, for, although marble is rarer there, it is of finer varieties. The inhabitants of Damascus devote great care to their buildings, and in their gardens they have some in which Damascus excels and which are handsomely laid out. Although Aleppo may be more magnificently built because of the care taken over the masonry work, Damascus is more attractive and more beautiful owing to the way in which water permeates the city and holds sway over all its parts.

In all of Syria charitable institutions are numerous, including madrasas, Sufi convents, hospices, *zāwiya*s for men and women, hospitals, and charitable trusts and alms of various sorts, but especially in Damascus, for in this respect her scope is unrivalled and her lofty position unassailable. The Great Mosque sets her apart from all other cities and in its beauty surpasses all buildings.[85]

[17]

<93> In this realm, Egypt and Syria together, are beautiful objects and elegant artifacts sufficient to make it celebrated, and it possesses a variety of craftsmen for the production of weapons, fabrics, embroideries, dyed stuffs, inlaid metalwork and more besides, of which it is more or less the sole producer, and of spears too, than which none better are made anywhere in the world.

[18][86]

The armies of the realm are partly resident at the Sultan's court and partly distributed around its provinces and throughout its lands. Some of them are nomads, such as the Arab tribesmen and the Turcomans. The regular troops are mixed in origin, being Turks, Circassians, *Rūmīs*,[87] Kurds and Turcomans. The majority are purchased mamluks. They are ranked as follows. The greatest are those who hold an emirate of a hundred troopers together with a command of a thousand, from which category come the most important vicegerents. At times this figure may be increased for some by ten or twenty troopers. Next are the *ṭabl-khānah*[88] emirs, the majority of whom have an emirate of forty, although there may be those for whom that figure is increased to seventy. The *ṭabl-khānah* rank is not held with less than forty.

Then follow the emirs of ten, consisting of those who hold an emirate of ten, and sometimes including individuals who have twenty troopers, but who are still only counted as emirs of ten. Next come the troopers of the *Ḥalqa*,[89] whose diplomas[90] are issued from the Sultan, just as the diplomas of emirs are, while, on the other hand, the troops of emirs receive their diplomas from their emirs. For every forty of these *Ḥalqa* troops there is an officer (*muqaddam*), one of their number, who has no authority over them except on active military service, when they muster with him and he is responsible for their dispositions.

<94> In Egypt the *iqṭā*ʿ[91] of some senior emirs of a hundred, close to the Sultan, may amount to 200,000 army dinars,[92] and sometimes even more. For other emirs of this rank the figure progressively diminishes to around about 80,000 dinars. The *ṭabl-khānah* emirates amount to 30,000 dinars with fluctuations above and below, with a minimum of 23,000 dinars. The emirs of ten have an upper limit of 7,000 dinars. Some *iqṭā*ʿs of *Ḥalqa* troopers reach 1,500 dinars, this amount and those that come near it being the *iqṭā*ʿs of the senior members of the *Ḥalqa*, the officers appointed over them. Then come lesser amounts down to 250 dinars. For the troops of emirs, the value of their *iqṭā*ʿ is at the discretion of the emir.[93]

*Iqṭā*ʿs in Syria[94] do not come near these figures, but are worth two thirds of them, leaving aside what we have said about favoured senior emirs of a hundred, for this is unusual and without normal validity, and I am not aware of anything in Syria that comes anywhere near such a sum, except for what the Vicegerent of Damascus receives.

All the emirs' troops are reviewed through the Sultan's Army Bureau, and each man's name and personal description are recorded. No change can then be made by an emir, should he wish to make one, unless he registers his substitution and presents the substitute for inspection.[95]

[19][96]

The emirs receive annual gifts of clothing[97] from the Sultan. Those at court benefit abundantly from this, <95> and also receive horses that are bestowed on them annually. The emirs of a hundred receive them saddled and bridled, but the rest without accoutrements, this being one way the inner circle (*khāṣṣa*) is distinguished from the common run. All emirs at court, emirs of a hundred, *ṭabl-khānah* and those of ten, draw daily fixed allowances of meat and all its seasonings, and bread, barley and oil. Some also draw candles, sugar and clothing material annually.[98] The same applies to all mamluks of the Sultan, and to any troopers who hold an office.

Any adolescent son of an emir receives a grant of dinars, meat, bread and fodder till such time as he is eligible for an *iqṭāʿ* in the ranks of the *Ḥalqa*. Some may subsequently be transferred to an emirate of ten or to a *ṭabl-khānah* if they are fortunate and have good luck.

When the present Sultan rides to the Hippodrome (*maidān*) to play polo, he distributes gold belts to the commanders of a thousand. This takes place always on Saturdays in the hottest season for about two months of the year. At each session he gives them out to two at a time by rota; so for some their turn comes again after three or four years.

All emirs in Egypt in the inner service of the Sultan receive sugar and sweetmeats from him during Ramaḍān, and animals for sacrifice at the time of the Feast of Sacrifice on a scale appropriate to their rank, and also, for their horses' spring feed, clover, which during that period is in lieu of their allowance of fodder.

The practice of the ruler of Egypt is that his distribution of horses to his emirs should take place on two occasions. The first is when he visits his stud farms in spring at the completion of the spring feeding, at which time he gives the emirs of a hundred a horse with saddle and bridle and gold-embroidered caparison, <96> and the *ṭabl-khānah* emirs a horse unequipped. The second is when he plays polo in the Hippodrome, at which time he gives all of them horses saddled and bridled (minus caparisons) with light silver decoration. The emirs of ten do not benefit from this at all, except for what the Sultan may single them out to receive as a special act of grace. The especially favoured "inner" emirs, both of a hundred and *ṭabl-khānah*, may receive many extras on top of this, so much so that some may acquire a hundred horses in a year.[99]

There are other occasions on which he distributes horses to his mamluks, and he sometimes presents them to certain of the officers of the *Ḥalqa*. A general rule of the Sultan is that any mamluk of his who has a horse die, if he produces some of its flesh and a sworn statement to the loss, is given by him a replacement mount.[100]

Not one of the Syrian emirs participates in this beyond the single coat they are given to wear when winter comes, unless an individual happens to come to the notice of the Sultan on business and so becomes the recipient of his favour.[101]

Those special emirs who are close to the Sultan receive his bounty in various forms, for example, as estates or magnificent buildings, on some of which perhaps more than 100,000 dinars may have been spent, or clothing material of various fabrics, or, when they set out on their travels for hunting expeditions or such like, supplies of fodder and provisions.[102]

It is the custom of the present Sultan to go hunting several times a year. When he does so, he bestows on the senior emirs of a hundred (I do not mean the Sultan's favourites, but those senior in status and age), to each one, a thousand *mithqāl*s of gold, a horse[103] from the royal stable, saddled and bridled, and a gold-embroidered caparison.

Customarily, when he passes by the *iqṭāʿ*[104] of a great emir on his hunting trips, he is presented with a quantity of sheep, geese, chickens, sugar cane and barley, depending on the height of such a one's aspirations. <97> Having accepted this, he bestows a full robe of honour on the emir, and sometimes will order certain of them a sum of money.[105]

[20][106]

The following are the outward signs of sovereignty in this realm. When the Sultan formally enters any city he pays a visit to,[107] or on the Feast Day,[108] or on the days when he processes to the Hippodrome to play polo, he rides with the housing,[109] which has gold brocade on yellow satin and is draped over the horse's back from below his ears to his rump. Before him ride two of the corps of pages (*al-ūshāqiya*), mounted on two gray stallions with housings similar to the one the Sultan rides with, just as though they are ready for him to ride. The pages wear yellow surcoats, made of silk with decorative bands of gold brocade, and on their heads they have brocaded skull-caps. The saddle covering[110] is borne before him, which is made of leather embroidered with gold, and is carried before him by a groom on foot in the centre of the procession. A rider precedes the Sultan playing on a hautboy, not with the intention of giving pleasure by its music, but rather to strike whoever hears it with awe. Behind him come the reserve mounts (*janāʾib*),[111] while over his head are the royal banners, yellow and embroidered in gold with his name and titles.

On the two feast days and when entering the city, in addition to the above, the parasol is raised over <98> his head. Known as the *jitr*, this is of brocaded yellow satin, and on the top it has a cupola and bird of silver overlaid with gold. On those occasions one of the senior emirs of a hundred carries it, riding on horseback beside the Sultan. All the office holders and the arms-bearers come behind and to either side of him, and before him walk the Axe-bearers,[112] a contingent of Kurds who hold *iqṭāʿ*s and the rank of emir, bearing their naked axes in their hands.

[21]

It is the custom for emirs that, wherever one of them goes, he rides out with a reserve mount following him.[113] The greatest emirs frequently ride out with two. This is observed both in the capital and in other cities, and likewise in the country. Each one has a troop comprising most of his mamluks, who are proceeded by a chest (for the drums and instruments) carried on a single camel, which another rider on a camel leads along, and also by his treasure, carried on two camels.[114] Some have more than that. Before the chest go a number of reserve mounts, led by mamluks riding horses or dromedaries, and a group of Arab riders on dromedaries. Before these there are the dromedaries, with their saddles set athwart (?) for the drums etc., in one file of four [animals]. The procession of the dromedaries and [the animals carrying] the treasure is in two files. Some emirs may have more. Whether the number of his reserve mounts is greater or smaller depends on the individual emir and his personal circumstances. The reserve mounts, depending on his decision, may be saddled and bridled or simply have a leading rein[115] and nothing else.

[22][116]

<99> The members of the military class of the realm vie one with another in their splendid clothes and embellished saddles and splendid equipment. They dress as follows: Tatar coats with *takalāwāt*[117] over them, then the "Islamic coat" (*qabā' islāmi*) over that, round which is tied the belt and the sword. Furthermore, emirs, officers [of the Ḥalqa] and senior troopers wear short-sleeved coats on top, shorter than the under-coat, but with no great difference in the length of sleeve or of the garment overall, and also small *kalauta*-caps, generally of red Malatyan wool, with small turbans wrapped round them. They have spurs on their boots and a scarf is attached to the belt over the pouch[118] on the right side. Such is the fashion of the military of the realm. <100> Most of their belts are of silver, but some make them of gold, and sometimes they are made with jade.[119] They are not studded with jewels except when they form part of the apparel presented by the Sultan[120] to the senior emirs of a hundred. Most of them wear clothes with decorative *ṭirāz*-bands but only a person with an *iqṭā'* in the *Ḥalqa* may wear such or plate his spurs with gold. Those who receive a monthly pay may not follow this fashion.

To sum up, their dress is elegant and their equipment outstanding and expensive. Their clothes are variously made of *kamkhā*-silk, Chinese silk, Kanja-cotton, velvet, Alexandrian (linen), *sharb*-linen, a silk and linen mixture or wools.

[23][121]

Account of the manner in which the Sultan holds sessions to hear complaints

It is the practice of this present Sultan to hold a session on Monday mornings when he is in residence in the Citadel, except during the month of Ramaḍān, for no such session is held then. When held, the sessions take place in a vaulted hall outside his palace and near the entrance to it. It is a spacious hall, supported on columns, with a lofty ceiling, before which <101> is a broad square. This hall is called the Palace of Justice,[122] and it is also the place in which the common levée is held and where the envoys of foreign rulers are generally received.

The seat is set alongside the pulpit which is the throne of sovereignty. To his right sit the Chief Judges of the four schools of law, then the Steward of the Treasury, then the Inspector of the Ḥisba,[123] and to his left sit the Privy Secretary, and, in front of him, the Inspector of the Army and all the clerks, forming a complete circle. If there is at the time a vizier from the Men of the Pen, he sits between the Sultan and the Secretary, but, if the vizier is one of the Men of the Sword, he stands at a distance with the rest of the office holders. Likewise, if there should be a vicegerent at the time, he stands with the office holders. Behind the Sultan stand two rows, both to right and left, made up of arms-bearers, *jamdāriya*[124] and *khāṣṣikīya*.[125] At a distance of about 15 cubits on his right and left hand sit the senior emirs of a hundred, those of advanced years, who are the Emirs of the Council; next and below them come the senior emirs and the office holders, who stand, as also do the rest of the emirs behind the Emirs of the Council. Behind this ring which encompasses the Sultan stand the chamberlains[126] and the dawādārs to present the people's petitions and usher in the suppliants. The petitions are read out to the Sultan, and if, on any matter, he requires <102> to consult the judges, he does so, and if any matter touches the army, he talks it over with the Chamberlain and the Secretary of the Army (*kātib al-jaysh*), and on any other matter he commands what he thinks fit.

[24][127]

<103> Account of his routine on other days

This present Sultan's practice on Mondays is as has been described. On Thursdays too the same routine is followed, except that then he does not undertake to hear petitions, nor are any of the judges present, and neither the Army Secretary nor the clerks, unless there should arise some need for one of them to be summoned. He continues to hold these sessions all the year round, while he is in residence at the Citadel, Mondays and Thursdays, other than during Ramaḍān.[128]

On other days he leaves his inner apartments for the large outer state-room, which has windows overlooking his stables and, in the place of honour, the special throne of state. He sits sometimes on this and, at other times, before it on the floor, while the emirs stand as has been described, but not the Emirs of the Council, nor those of the "outer service", for ordinarily they do not attend this session, nor do any of the magnates, unless their presence is particularly required. At the third hour of the day the Sultan rises and enters his inner apartments, then his harem, to see his womenfolk. Towards the end of the day he appears in his inner apartments to deal with matters of state business, and his "inner service" officials call on him there on matters of business that concern him, as and when necessity dictates.

[25][129]

<103> Account of his routine on journeys

How he rides forth on feast days and Hippodrome days has already been described.[130] On journeys, however, he does not trouble to show all that pomp and circumstance. In his retinue when he is on the move, as visible evidence of his royal rank, are his body of mamluks with their officer in charge, and a major-domo (*ustādh-dār*) and before them go the "chests", the reserve mounts and the dromedaries. He himself rides accompanied by a large number of senior and junior emirs, both of the outer and inner service, and by a select troop of his personal mamluk servants. When travelling he rides with no housing and no banners, but reserve mounts do follow behind him.

Generally, he aims to delay his coming to camp till night-time. On arrival many lanterns and torches are borne before him, and on his approaching his tent, he is met by candles mounted in plated candelabras. The heralds cry out before him and all dismount, except for the arms-bearers and the grooms behind him, and the Axe-bearers march on, formed up around him, until he enters the first passage. He dismounts and proceeds into the *shaqqa*, a spacious circular tent, and from there into a smaller *shaqqa*, and then into an inner tent. Each tent is surrounded on all sides within by a [felt] tent wall. At the heart of the inner tent is a small wooden "fort", erected for the Sultan to sleep in. Opposite the *shaqqa* is placed the bath with lead cauldrons and a basin, after the fashion of a permanent bath constructed in a city, except that it is reduced in scale.[131]

When the Sultan sleeps, the mamluks patrol around him in concentric circles, and the guard patrols beyond them all. Twice nightly rounds are performed about the vestibule tent, firstly when he retires to bed and secondly when he rises. Each of the rounds is led by the Emir Jandar,[132] <104> a high-ranking emir, surrounded by lanterns, torches, drums and the night-watch. At the door of the vestibule sleep the marshals and the duty eunuchs (*al-khadam*).

On his journeys the present Sultan is accompanied by most things likely to be needed. Indeed, he practically has a hospital with him, so great is the number of doctors, oculists, surgeons, potions, drugs and the like he takes along. If a doctor visits anyone and prescribes something appropriate, it can be issued from the buttery or the pharmacy carried in the royal baggage-train.

[26][133]

The present Sultan customarily provides a meal at the beginning and end of each day for the emirs as a whole, except for those of the outer service, and they are few in number. In the morning a first meal is set out at which the Sultan does not eat, then comes a second, called "the special", at which the Sultan may or may not eat, then a third, called "the supplementary". This is when the Sultan eats. At the end of the day two meals are provided, the "first" and the "special", as the second is called. If a "supplementary" is called for, it is produced, otherwise not. Roast meat is a separate matter, because there is no regularly observed custom about producing it, but it depends on what instructions are given. At all of these meals, after eating, gifts are distributed, and then drinks are provided of chilled oxymel made from sugar and aromatic herbs with rose water.

It is the custom of our Sultan to provide each night near his resting place dishes containing various fried foods and cold collations, boiled sugar, boiled milk, and cooked cheese, bananas, unleavened white bread,[134] and dishes with oxymel and iced water, for the use of the night guards during <105> their watch over him, so that, occupied in eating and drinking, they do not fall asleep.

The night is divided up into watches by the hours of the sand clock. As one watch finishes, it wakes up the next and then retires to sleep till the morning. This is the constant practice both at home and abroad. Copies of the Koran are provided for those who can read, and chess too, to keep them from sleeping.

[27][135]

On Fridays our present Sultan attends the mosque adjacent to his palace in the Citadel,[136] accompanied by the inner service emirs. The remaining emirs come in by another door of the mosque. The Sultan performs his prayers to the right of the mihrab in a private enclosure.[137] The senior members of his inner circle sit with him, but the other emirs, both of the inner service and the ordinary complement, pray with him outside the enclosure, ranged to the right and the left according to rank. When he has heard the sermon and has completed the Friday prayers, he retires to his apartments and the chambers of his eunuchs and womenfolk, and all disperse, each one to his own place.

[28]

Account of how intelligence reaches him.[138]

It is the Sultan's practice to require his vicegerents in his realm to report to him any important new developments in their sphere or similar matters. His orders are received and his replies are returned to them containing his decisions.

Connecting the Sultan's court with all the lands of his realm are staging-posts, separated one from another by some "miles",[139] each having a number of post horses. At court and in every city the Sultan has at his disposal couriers, army personnel, to carry the dispatches and to return with the official replies. When a courier from any city in the realm arrives, or on the return of one dispatched from the court, the Emir Jandar, one of the emirs of a hundred, and the Dawadar <106> and the Privy Secretary usher him into the Sultan's presence, where he kisses the ground. The Dawadar takes the dispatch and passes it over the courier's face, then hands it to the Sultan, who opens it. The Privy Secretary takes a seat and reads it to the Sultan, who gives the necessary instructions.

Some of the intelligence that is submitted to him is written on thin, small-sized paper[140] and brought by carrier pigeons. The pigeons also have their staging-posts, but the stages between them are the equivalent of three or more post-horse stages. That is the range of the carrier pigeon, which it may not exceed. When a pigeon bears a dispatch, they mark it with a sort of distinguishing sign,[141] so that it may be recognised for what it is and not interfered with. The pigeon is then launched, and on arrival at the post prepared for it, the dispatch is taken further onward by another pigeon from that post, from place to place to the Sultan's court.

It is the practice of this realm for those in charge of city affairs, namely the police officers, to inform themselves of the daily occurrences in their areas of authority from the people who hold office under them in the various districts. Then the chief of police writes a report which comprises such material as he forwards for information, and this is brought to the Sultan, containing reports of the latest incidents such as any homicides, large fires or the like. There is no close watch kept on people's personal affairs.[142]

[29]

<107> An excursus[143]

One of the customs of the forces of this state is to ride on Mondays and Thursdays in the Parade.[144] This is a spacious open place, found in every city that maintains standing troops. They exercise there, then the troops halt before the vicegerent, or the chamberlain, if there is no vicegerent, and a sale of horses takes place by auction, and sometimes a large amount of military equipment is put up for sale, campaign tents, larger [Turkish-style] tents and weapons. Not infrequently a large amount of landed property is auctioned. If they are in Egypt, they then go up to attend the Sultan's levée in the Citadel, which proceeds as we have already described. Permission to retire comes after the eating of the meal. If they are somewhere other than Cairo, they formally attend upon the vicegerent at his residence, Government House. The vicegerent sits in state, petitions are read to him, and he delivers justice to the suppliants. Then a meal is provided and all emirs and troopers eat together before dispersing.

The Syrian forces have an extra parade on Saturdays, in addition to the two days mentioned, and the vicegerents are in session for the reading of petitions Mondays, Thursdays and Saturdays. Sometimes they sit for that purpose twice, both early and late, on those days.[145]

[30][146]

One of the things the present Sultan habitually does is to sign with his own hand all his orders. On the diplomas[147] of emirs, troopers and all who receive an *iqṭāʿ*, he writes his motto signature,[148] which in the case of our reigning Sultan, the Sultan al-Malik al-Nāṣir Nāṣir al-Dunyā waʾl-Dīn Abū al-Maʿālī Muḥammad ibn al-Malik al-Manṣūr Qalāwūn (may God perpetrate his rule) is "God is my hope".

On the letter of appointment of vicegerents and the warrants of officials, such as judges, viziers <108> and secretaries, and the rest of the office holders, and the warrants for allowances and pensions he writes his name and his father's name, Muḥammad ibn Qalāwūn.[149] He also writes his name on post dispatches and orders for the payment of dues and the satisfaction of claims.

He may at times honour his correspondent. Then for any man of the sword he honours, he signs himself in his letter "His father, Muḥammad ibn Qalāwūn". For those who wear the rounded turban, judges or viziers, to honour them he writes "His brother" in place of "His father".

In *iqṭāʿ* documents the form is to say "The noble command has gone forth", whereas in the case of letters of appointment, allowances and pensions the form is "It has been decreed by noble command". However, this is not the place to give an exhaustive treatment of the forms of diplomatic. If we were to start on this, it would be a lengthy business indeed. Yet we will give just a snippet touching on diplomas, letters of appointment and warrants, since these are basic in providing for people's livelihood.

The highest form of exordium[150] is with the formula "Praise be to God . . . ", and next comes the exordium with a formula beginning "Then after praising God . . . ", both preceding the wording "The command has gone forth" in diplomas, or "It has been decreed by [noble] command" in warrants. Then comes the lowest rank and this commences, in diplomas, with "The command has gone forth", or, in warrants, with "It has been decreed by command". The diplomas that open with the formula "Praise be to God . . . " are distinguished by a calligraphic superscription (*ṭughrā*) in black, <109> containing the Sultan's name and titles.[151]

[31][152]

In the matter of *iqṭā*ʿs for troopers, it is the practice of the present Sultan to be personally responsible for taking them into service. When those seeking a vacant *iqṭā*ʿ stand before him, and his choice falls on one of them, he orders the Secretary of the Army to issue the necessary papers. The latter draws up an abbreviated document, called the "authority" (*mithāl*), which contains the wording "The *iqṭā*ʿ[153] of so-and-so consisting of such-and-such".[154] Above it he writes the details of the person to whom it has been assigned, and then hands it to the Sultan, who writes on it in his own hand "Let it be written". The Chamberlain then gives it to the person in whose favour the order has been made, who kisses the ground. The document is then returned to the Army Bureau and filed for reference.[155] In the next stage a "square warrant" is produced,[156] complete with the endorsements of all the staff of the *Iqṭā*ʿ Bureau, otherwise known as the Army Bureau, and their motto signatures. The endorsement of the Sultan is then secured on this document, which is afterwards taken to the Bureau of Chancery and Correspondence. There the diplomas[157] are engrossed and the Sultan adds a motto signature, as we have mentioned already. The diploma is completed by the signing of all the staff of the *Iqṭā*ʿ Bureau, after checking it for correctness against the original order.

To turn to the recruitment of personnel in the provinces, the vicegerents have no authority to appoint an emir to replace one deceased. Indeed, if an emir dies, whether he be of high or low rank, the Sultan is informed of his death, and promotes a man of his own choice to take his place, either someone at court, whom he sends out to the place where he will serve, or someone already on the spot where the vacancy is, or someone transferred from another town, according to whatever he thinks best.

When any trooper of the Ḥalqa dies, the vicegerent enrols a replacement, and, very much as the Sultan does, he draws up an "authority", then a "square certificate", and the latter is dispatched by the post service to court. The *Iqṭā*ʿ Bureau checks it over, and if the Sultan passes it, <110> he endorses it with "Let it be written". From the *Iqṭā*ʿ Bureau a [second] "square certificate" is produced based on the first, and the Bureau of Chancery proceeds to use that one to draw up their document, as has been explained in the case of the troops serving in the capital. If the Sultan does not pass it [the provincial "square certificate"], he issues it to someone of his own choice. In that case, the administrative procedure is the one which has been explained already.

If an emir or a trooper dies before the completion of his period of service, his heirs are brought to account on the basis of his precise entitlement. A repayment may either be demanded from them or waived at discretion, depending on how much influential support they muster.[158]

The *iqṭā*ʿs of emirs and troopers may either be lands, which the beneficiary may exploit in whatever way he wishes, or money which he draws from certain sources of revenue.

[32][159]

The salaries of Men of the Pen are paid monthly, a total made up in cash and in kind. Those of some standing receive daily allowances of meat with or without seasonings, bread and fodder. The senior officials receive sugar, candles, oil and clothing-material annually, and animals to sacrifice at the Festival, and sugar and sweetmeats at Ramaḍān. The very highest of these, such as the Vizier, receives each salary period[160] 250 "army dinars", and also the equivalent value to this in the above mentioned commodities and produce when they have been detailed and added up.[161] Then the salaries become progressively lower and lower. Those who serve in the central administration are secure[162] in this respect.

Let us consider the judges and the ulema. The judges draw their salaries from the Sultan, which are mostly fifty dinars a month. They also have the madrasas, which are abundantly rich from their charitable trusts. <111> In Damascus the salaries of the judiciary derive from a trust for the general good and benefit of the Muslim community, attached to the property of the Great Mosque. As for the ulema, not one of them receives anything other than what derives from the trusts of their madrasas, except for those who benefit from a pension or some grace and favour allowance, but that amounts to little and is uncommon, and there is no regular pattern for it to make it worth a digression.

[33][163]

The Sultan keeps up charitable donations and gives abundant pensions, some of which is land in a certain region, and some a charge on certain revenues, in the form of cash, grain, bread, meat, oil and clothing-material. The meat, oil and clothing allowances are few and rare, for those who obtain such through application. The land, the cash, grain and bread are very abundant and decidedly[164] ample.

In general, sons inherit this from fathers, brother from brother, and cousin from cousin, so that it often happens that a person dies and his pension is cancelled and set down to someone unconnected, and subsequently a relative comes, presents his petition, in which he puts forward his prior claim to what his kinsman enjoyed, and it is restored to him.

In this realm the proper rites of Islam are performed in the mosques, and the sermons delivered in all settlements. No pensions and no charitable allowances, whether large or small, are taken without the warrant of the Sultan.

[34]

The realm contains a number of citadels, castles and forts, in each of which is a vicegerent, a judge of Islamic law, a preacher, a muezzin, oculist, surgeon and garrison troops. The members of the garrison receive pay and not *iqṭā*'s. Weapons for defence are stored there, and there is a complement of workmen and craftsmen, masons, carpenters and blacksmiths, and whatever materials are needed for the like.

[35][165]

<112> The dress of "those of the rounded turbans"

To begin with the judges and the ulema, they dress in a wide *dilq*-gown without a front vent but opening on the shoulders, and wear a large turban-scarf from which a long tail-piece hangs down between the shoulders. Those of lesser rank wear a long-sleeved *farajiyya*-gown without a front vent, and also have a tail-piece. Ascetics shorten the tail-piece and encourage it to hang down to their left shoulder as the Sunna recommends. None of them wears silk or any garment with silk in it. A few wear the *ṭailasān*-hood.[166] The *tarḥa*-shawl is regulation dress for the Shāfiʿī Chief Judge and distinguishes him from others.[167]

The leading members of this class ride mules with saddles devoid of any silver decoration, and in place of the *ṭamankiyyāt*[168] on the saddles sweat-pads are used, which are something like the saddle-covering, an abbreviated version of it, <113> made of coarse cloth, although it may be of various leathers. It is split and put between the saddle and its padded covering (*mīthara*).[169] Judges use instead of the *kunbūsh*-caparison the *zunnārī*,[170] which is made of coarse cloth and something like a cloak open at the breast, encircling the rump of the animal and showing neither tail nor crupper. Sometimes they ride with *kunbūsh*-caparisons, and the bits they use are large and of considerable weight.

Viziers and secretaries dress as follows: *farajiyya*-gowns, open at the front, and made of wool or of striped textiles made in Alexandria and such like, or of a silk and wool mixture or *bayāḍ*.[171] The very great form fluted ruches[172] on their sleeves and wear *bughluṭaq*s under their *farajiyya*s. Sometimes they wear jubbahs open behind. Their riding equipment varies, but mostly it resembles that of the troopers, or comes very near to it.

Men of this class in Egypt are less flamboyant than they are in Syria in their personal appearance, dress and mounts, apart from the stories that are put about concerning the affluence and free-spending of the Copts of Egypt in their own homes, even that one of them may wear the meanest clothes in the office, and eat the lowliest food and ride a donkey, but, when he comes home, he is transformed <114> from one state to another and emerges from poverty into plenty. However, people may sometimes exaggerate the things like that which they say about them, because their experiences are so disparate and their ways of life so greatly different.

The merchant class and the assorted elements of the common people wear clothes that vary considerably. The dervishes (*fuqarāʾ*), for example, although they are all united by the practice and habit of poverty, and share the garb of the sufi, their circumstances are clearly distinguishable in their clothes and their grades in the modifications they make.[173]

[36][174]

Remarks on the office-holders of this realm

Of all the offices of state at the court of the Sultan we shall mention only the important ones. The junior posts are subsumed under the senior ones and we have no need to refer to them. Every [post] we mention that is at the capital has its counter-part in each of the main cities of the realm, and the difference between them remains [proportionate to] the difference between the places

The great offices of state are filled firstly by the Men of the Sword, the Arms-bearer, the Dawadar, the Chamberlain, the Emir Jandar, the Major-domo, the Grand Hosteler, the Marshall of the Army and the prefects; secondly by the Men of the Pen, the Vizier, the Privy Secretary, the Inspector of the Army, the Inspector of Finance, the Inspector of the Chest, the Inspector of the Household Departments, the Inspector of the Treasury and the Inspector of the Stables, and thirdly by the learned class, the judges, the preachers, the Steward of the Treasury and the *Muḥtasib* (censor).

The present Sultan has abolished the positions of Vicegerent and Vizier at his court. When the vicegerency was still operative, the Vicegerent was formerly a sultan in miniature. He it was who distributed the *iqṭā*ʿs and appointed emirs. When one has said that, one has said enough. The Vizierate was filled at hap-hazard either by Men of the Sword or of the Pen. <115> The Vizier was second to the Vicegerent in status. But now the Sultan alone enjoys both the pomp that attaches to the sultanate and the executive power that belonged to the vicegerency. The Vizierate has also been abolished and during this present reign a post has been created, the holder of which is called the Inspector of the Privy Purse. The basic role of this post is for its holder to be responsible for what particularly concerns the Sultan's personal finances. He also has a responsibility overall for the Sultan's personal affairs, acting on his own initiative and undertaking to take note of the will of the Sultan. His responsibility in this remains, and thus his position is tantamount to that of Vizier, owing to his closeness to the Sultan and the enlargement of his authority.

Let us give an account of the function of each of the offices which we have mentioned.

[37]

Account of the offices of state

Vicegerent[175]

We have already said, speaking of the position of Vicegerent, that he is a sultan in miniature in any area distant from the capital. The Vicegerent is the wielder of absolute authority in any matter which refers to the army, finance or intelligence, namely the post service. No holder of any office in any vicegerency can act without his order, nor resolve any difficult situation without reference to him. He enlists troops and appoints to offices. In the case of those that are of some importance, such as the positions of the Vizier, the judge, the privy secretary and the secretary of the Army, then he may submit a suitable nominee to the Sultan, and it is rare indeed that he is not accepted. The greatest of these vicegerents are sometimes entitled "Prince of the Emirs", but if there is any dispute, then the one in Damascus alone merits that title, because there is no princely seat of power in Syria apart from it.

<116> The holder of the supreme vicegerency, namely that at the capital, is called "Protector of the Realm". We have previously indicated his high status. He is the second Sultan, and all the Vicegerents of the realm correspond with him on most of the matters concerning which he corresponds with the Sultan, and they consult him about them just as he does the Sultan. Entirely on his own initiative he enlists troops, and he also makes promotions to the rank of emir but in this case in consultation with the Sultan. It is his custom to ride with the army on parade days, and all dismount to bow before him. When he appears at the Sultan's court, he stands in the corner of the audience chamber. On completion of the levée he leaves for his own residence, accompanied by the emirs, and spreads a meal for them, just as the Sultan does. He also holds public sessions, which the officers of state attend. While the chamberlains stand before him, petitions are read out to him and complainants are presented, before finally all withdraw.

When the vicegerency was functioning in this fashion, the Sultan used not to undertake to hear petitions in person, nor to attend to complaints. He relied on the Vicegerent. So, when the Vicegerent had heard the petitions read over, if an order from him was sufficient to deal with any matter, he would issue one. However, to deal with anything that required the issuing of a royal decree, he would order the drawing up and issuing of it on behalf of the Sultan. It would be engrossed along with an indication within the document that it was at his behest,[176] and then issued. Any problematical business, which it was imperative for him to bring to the knowledge of the Sultan, was either communicated to the Sultan by the Vicegerent when he met with him, or the Vicegerent would send a person to inform him of it and receive his commands.

When there was a Vicegerent, the *Iqṭāʿ* Bureau, that is to say, the Army Bureau, attended only on him <117> and met with no one else. They had no access to the Sultan on any matter. The Vizier and the Privy Secretary might consult him on some matters but not on others. The Vicegerency subsequently dwindled away at court and its functions declined, and now it has been abolished.[177]

Chamberlain[178]

The function of this official is to dispense justice in relation to the emirs and the troopers sometimes on his own authority, sometimes in consultation with the Sultan, and sometimes in consultation with the Vicegerent, if there is one. It is his task to present audience-seekers and visitors,[179] to review the troops, and perform comparable duties. Now that no vicegerent exists, the Chamberlain is the acknowledged authority at court, who fills the place of the vicegerents in a good many matters.

Emir Jandar[180]

This official has the palace in his keeping, as it were. He has a staff of ushers, groups of equerries, "Khurasanians",[181] and orderlies (*jāndāriyya*). In conjunction with the Dawadar and the Privy Secretary he presents the postal dispatches, as we have explained previously.[182] If the Sultan wishes to interrogate or execute anyone, this is carried out by the holder of this position. In addition, he has the Armoury in his keeping, which, when used as a place of confinement, is more honourable than the common prison. <118> No prisoner stays there long; he is either quickly released or quickly executed. We have already mentioned that each evening and morning this official performs rounds of inspection about the Sultan's quarters when he is travelling.

Major-domo[183]

The Major-domo supervises all the branches of the Sultan's household, such as the kitchens, the buttery, the *ḥāshiya* (personal entourage) and the pages. He sees to the Sultan's requests and exercises jurisdiction over the pages and within the palace. He also has responsibility for the tasters, although their chief is his equal, having the rank of an emir of a hundred. He has absolute authority and enjoys complete freedom to ask for anything any individual in the Sultan's household needs in the way of expenses or clothing and the like.

Arms-bearer[184]

This person is in charge of the company of arms-bearers,[185] and he is the one entrusted with the bearing of the Sultan's arms in general assemblies. He is responsible for the Arsenal, what is to be ordered for it, what is presented to it and what is issued from it. The position is filled by one of the emirs of a hundred.

Dawadar[186]

His function is to convey messages from the Sultan, to keep him informed of affairs in general, to present petitions to him, to act as intermediary for whoever comes to court and to present the postal dispatches along with the Emir Jandar and the Privy Secretary, as has been mentioned.[187] He takes the Sultan's signature on the general mass of diplomas, warrants and letters. When he brings a decree from the Sultan, it is duly engrossed and his intermediary role[188] is expressly noted.

<119> Marshal of the Army[189]

This official is like one of the junior chamberlains. It is his task to record the personal particulars of the troops during reviews. He has a staff of marshals. When the Sultan, the Vicegerent or the Chamberlain require an emir or trooper,[190] they say to him, "Send for him and bring him here". When they order the arrest of any one of these, they order him to carry it out, and he is one of those responsible for the Chest during parades or on expeditions.

Prefects[191]

These are the chiefs of police and their duties are well-known and understood.[192]

[38]

[Vizierate][193]

Of the offices of the Men of the Pen the most exalted is the Vizierate, because he who holds it is second to the Sultan, if he receives his due and his rights are recognised. However, in recent years, the Vicegerency has come to overshadow it and the Vizierate has dwindled and taken a lesser position. We have already mentioned that certain persons from both the Men of the Sword and the Men of the Pen have filled the office with salaries agreed *ad hominem*.[194] The Vizier's function is too well known, because of his commanding word and complete administrative freedom for the encumbent's role to be set forth here. Yet, in recent times, there was a decline with the result that the Vizier became a sort of financial overseer, with no responsibilities beyond finance and no longer any broad sweep of administrative competence. His authority no longer stretched to appointments and dismissals because the Sultan aspired to comprehend the minutiae of affairs. Later the Sultan abolished the office[195] and deprived the state of its brightest jewel.[196]

The duties of the vizier were distributed to three persons; to the Inspector of Finance or Intendant of the Bureaux went the responsibility to collect revenue and control expenditure and meet current charges; to the Inspector of the Privy Purse the general administration of affairs and the nominating of functionaries, <120> and to the Privy Secretary the minuting of decisions in the Palace of Justice, those that the Vizier had minuted either in consultation or independently. None of these three officials could act independently without referring the Sultan or without his contacting one of them.

Office of Privy Secretary[197]

The holder reads incoming letters to the Sultan and writes the replies, on which he obtains the Sultan's signature before dispatching them. He deals with administrative orders, both incoming and outgoing, and holds sessions to read petitions in the Palace of Justice and to minute decisions on them. It is now his task to minute what used to be dealt with by the Vizier's pen, in accordance with instructions from the Sultan.

Inspectorate of the Army[198]

A sufficient indication of the role of the holder of this post has been given in the sections on the *iqṭā*ʿs and the Vicegerency.

[Comptroller of the Presence]

Alongside the Inspector are accountants[199] who look after the affairs of the realm, general and detailed. Their chief is the Comptroller of the Presence, <121> who has responsibilities for the whole state, Egypt and Syria, and who issues orders, which are countersigned by the Sultan, sometimes concerned with fiscal arrangements for agriculture, sometimes with payments, and sometimes with the employing of clerks on minor matters, and other similar business. It is an exalted office which comes next after the Inspectorate. The rest of the accountants have a strictly limited sphere of responsibility, which does not extend beyond a certain region of the realm. This bureau is the most important financial bureau. Royal warrants and decrees are registered[200] there and all other financial departments are branches of this one, to which their accounts are submitted and where ultimate authority lies.

Inspectorate of the Chest[201]

Initially the Chest was of great standing because it was the depository of the wealth of the realm. However, when the Privy Purse establishment was introduced, it weakened the importance of this one, called the Chest. It began to be referred to as the Great Chest,[202] but this is a case of the title exceeding what it describes. Nowadays it retains nothing except robes of honour which are distributed by it or casual revenues which are received and disbursed. For the most part the Inspector is a judge or some associate of a judge.

Inspectorate of the Household Departments[203]

This is an inspectorate of importance, though one dependent on the Major-domo. For everything which is in the competence of the latter the Inspector shares <122> the responsibility. We have explained in detail the duties of the Major-domo above.[204]

Inspectorate of the Treasury[205]

This is an important, highly esteemed office, the function of which is to transfer the state revenues into the Treasury and make disbursements from it, sometimes by actual cash transactions and sometimes by book-keeping exercises. Only a person of signal probity may fill this office.

Inspectorate of the Stables[206]

This is an important bureau which functions in the Sultan's Stables. It has responsibility for all the various stables, camel parks and the fodder, and for the pay of those employed there, and for the Stables' financial arrangements and distributions,[207] and all that is bought for them or sold in them.

As for the offices of the learned class, we have said already that they are those of the judges, the preacher, the Steward of the Treasury and the *Muḥtasib* (Censor). They are well-known and the functions of those who hold them are fully understood, because an Islamic state can hardly do without them.

[39]

<123> Excursus[208]

In this realm and its dependencies are found all three of the mosques "which are the goal of all pilgrims", the Holy Mosque [in Mecca], the Sacred House [in Jerusalem] and the Mosque of the Prophet (May God bless him and give him peace) [in Medina]. We shall start with what is a firmly recognised part of the state and situated within its borders, namely Jerusalem.

Jerusalem is the site of the Aqsa Mosque and the Dome of the Rock, which was the first of the two Kiblas;[209] and the Prophet (may God bless him and give him peace) made his Night Journey thither from the Holy Mosque; in the words of God Almighty: "Glory be to Him who took His servant by night from the Holy Mosque to the Aqsa Mosque, around about which We have spread Our blessings."[210]

On its right [i.e. eastern] side is the mount where Moses (upon him be peace) spoke with God,[211] and there or in the vicinity are most of the tombs of the prophets (may God bless them and give them peace).

Al-Tīfāshī in his work, *The Soul's Delight in the Perceptions of the Five Senses*,[212] wrote:

> It has been related that the land over which and around which God spread His blessings, is forty "miles" in length and forty in breadth with the Sacred House as the focal point. Its ancient name was Aelia. God's Word confirms that the Sacred House is at the centre of the square of the Holy Land, which was blessed by God Almighty.
>
> In the Aqsa Mosque,[213] in the Dome of the Chain, was the Judgement Seat of David (upon him be peace). There also is <124> the spot from which the Prophet (may God bless him and give him peace) was carried up to Heaven. It is covered by the Dome of The Ascension. The place where Job (on him be peace) prayed with the angels, at a dome called the Dome of the Angels, is found there too, as is the rock on which Joshua, the son of Nun, sacrificed as successor to Moses, the son of Imran. There too are the Prayer Niche of Mary and the Shrine of Zacharias, which was built by David and Solomon (peace be upon them).

There is also, I may add, the tomb of Abraham, the Friend (*khalīl*) of God, which, it is true to say, is located within the wall which encloses the place known as "the town of Abraham", but now commonly called al-Khalīl, although the tomb nowadays specified as such is not authentic.[214] The Glorious Koran and Traditions from the Prophet (God bless him and give him peace) contain sufficient mention of his merits and virtues.

The Jews [till] now pray towards the Rock and make their pilgrimage to Jerusalem, which also contains the Holy Sepulchre – the goal of Christian pilgrimage from all regions of the earth far across the sea. Next to Jerusalem is the city of Nablus, considered part of the Holy Land and within its limits. Its mount is the place of pilgrimage of the Samaritans, a sect of Jews, whose leaders maintain the prophethood of Aaron (peace be upon him). Thus Holy Jerusalem is revered by all Muslims, Jews and Christians, and is a place of pilgrimage for them all. They disagree only on the sites to be visited. We have only brought attention to this because it is beneficial to show all agreeing to revere Jerusalem and make it the object of their pilgrimage.

[40][215]

<125> The two holy sanctuaries, Mecca and Medina (may God increase their glory and renown), are in the Hijaz. The princes of Medina the Noble have generally and for the greater part of their time, with rare exceptions, remained subject to the ruler of Egypt. Some have rebelled at times, without, however, acknowledging the suzerainty of any other.

The princes of Mecca the Revered have in some cases taken "secret sips of the milk",[216] satisfying the ruler of Egypt by protestations of obedience and loyalty to him and then saying the same to the ruler of the Yemen. They tend more towards the latter and their true sympathies are with him. Later they recognised the sovereignty of the ruler of Iraq because of the strength of his authority.[217] Our present Sultan over a period of time imprisoned and freed various of them, setting up one after another in power, and dispatching armies time after time to try to bring them to an unclouded allegiance to himself, while retaining their honoured rank. At the present time he has established firm control over them; their refractoriness has yielded to him and their stubborn minds have relented despite some resistance and devious dealings. This came about after the death of Abū Saʿīd Bahādūr Khān ibn Muḥammad Khodābendeh,[218] the Sultan of Iraq, when [Ilkhanid] unity was subsequently destroyed, and up to the time of my writing this book they have not yet recovered nor have matters gone smoothly for them.

The princes of Medina, descendants of al-Ḥusain ibn ʿAlī (may God be pleased with them) are the family of Jummaz ibn Shīḥa, and the princes of Mecca the Revered, descendants of al-Ḥasan ibn ʿAlī (may God be pleased <126> with them), are the family of Idrīs ibn Qatāda. In both cities are a number of noble descendants of the Prophet, relatives of both princely houses. These princes of Mecca and Medina, whether they are loyal or rebellious, must, in the case of each person who seizes power, show themselves compliant towards the ruler of Egypt to acquire a diploma[219] for his position, because they fear the Sultan's proximity[220] and the constant expeditions sent against them from Egypt and Damascus. We have dealt with this to fulfil the expressed aims of the book but we have not broached the subject of the *Virtues and Merits* of the two cities. What need of that for the two sanctuaries when they hold the House,[221] the cherished goal of pilgrimage, and [the tomb of] the Prophet and Intercessor of this community, our Lord Muḥammad (may God bless him and give him peace). That they are the places where God's House is and where His chosen prophet lies is for them sufficient honour, before which the vaults of the heavens bend their necks and which encompasses the ends of the broad expanses of land and sea.

[41]

[Hama][222]

Within the limits of this realm is a place which nominally retains full authority and independent sovereignty, namely Hama, a city between Homs and Aleppo, held by the remnants of the Ayyubid house. The ruler of Egypt appoints and deposes his nominee at will. The city was wrested from them after the death of al-Muẓaffar Shādī [Maḥmūd][223] ibn al-Manṣūr Muḥammad ibn al-Muẓaffar, and it was put under the control of vicegerents <127> like the rest of the vicegerents of this realm. Subsequently, the present Sultan restored Hama to the Ayyubid house, and al-Muʿayyad ʿImād al-Dīn Ismāʿīl[224] ibn al-Afḍal ʿAlī ibn al-Muẓaffar, the cousin of the person after whose death it had been taken away, became prince there, and then after him his son, al-Afḍal Muḥammad, the present ruler,[225] who independently assigns emirates and *iqṭā*ʿs, appoints judges, viziers and his privy secretary and all officials, and from whom diplomas and warrants are issued. However, in such matters as assigning an emirate or a major office, he effects nothing really important without consulting the ruler of Egypt, who only ever replies that his decision is the right one. This or something like it is normal.

This city of Hama is built on the River Orontes and is one of the fairest cities of Syria.

[42]

[Cilicia][226]

One place which one must mention here is the land of Sīs, situated between Aleppo and Anatolia (Rūm). Long ago it was conquered by the Armenians and for a very long period it has been ruled over by the house of Leo, son of Mleh [sic].[227] Its lands are in part lowlands near the sea coast and in part mountainous regions. It is situated in the general zone of the old frontier fortresses of Islam. The king[228] is subject to the ruler of Iraq and Persia, being one of his chain of dependants. No force of his suzerain marched into Syria to wage war on the ruler of Egypt without his accompanying it. Great is the host of his men and extensive the damage he has caused Islam and its adherents; yet all the while he cajoles and flatters the Egyptian ruler and annually pays a sum of money as a fixed tribute. The forces of Egypt and Syria constantly raid him in the territory of al-Bīra, and his land has been overrun <128> and women and children taken captive. In the year of my writing this work, that is 738 A.H. [1337–8 A.D.], the Sultan dispatched a body of troops to Sīs.[229] In fear and trembling the king ceded a part of his territories adjacent to Muslim lands, from the River Ceyhan to the border. Thanks be to God, this passed into Muslim possession, under the control of the Sultan, who imposed on the king the [agreed] tribute for the remainder of his lands.

[43][230]

One special attribute of this realm is an emerald mine, situated on the same side of the river as Aswān, for which there exists on behalf of the Sultan a department and staff of notaries. The workers are paid and have their provisions supplied in return for digging and extracting emeralds. The mine is in hills of friable rock, and thus, when mined, sometimes collapses on and kills groups of workers.

Everything extracted is collected and sent to the Sultan and then widely distributed as exports.[231] I have seen one piece, the centre of which was of an extremely handsome green colour. The outside layers were all white and the layers between the centre and the outside passed in gradation from white to green. The nearer the centre, the greener it was, and the nearer the edge the more the tendency to white, until the edge itself was quite white. The centre had been perfectly matured by nature, but the edges were still not completely matured. Glory be to God, the Creator of all things!

Balsam is found in the realm, that is to say, small trees in Maṭariya, the suburb of ʿAin Shams (Heliopolis), near Cairo, which are irrigated from a well there and only grow on that spot. The well is revered by the Christians, who come to visit it and bathe in what they assert to be its curative waters. When the time is ripe a special official acting for the Sultan comes out to press the balsam, <129> take charge of it and deliver it to the Exchequer. In due course the balsam is transported to the citadels of Syria and the hospitals to treat those whose "temperaments" have been chilled.[232]

Christian princes, Abyssinians, Greeks and Franks, heap gifts on the Sultan for the sake of it and beg him to present some to them, since no-one is genuinely a Christian in their eyes unless he has been immersed in the water of the baptismal font and in their view it is essential that some balsam oil should be in the baptismal water. I have been informed of this by several Christians. It certainly has an obvious superiority in the treatment of hemiplegia, slackness of the sinews and other illnesses.

The ground-pine is found there too and "Solomon's idol" and "sesban"[233] from a place known as Dair al-ʾIzba near Old Cairo, a most efficacious cure for dropsy. There is opium too, an extract of the dark Egyptian poppy, and likewise the methel-nut, which grows in Damietta. The various plants and herbs, specified in the medical books, which grow in the mountains of Jerusalem and in Palestine and Jordan, are very numerous, such as the milfoil, with its thousand leaves, which is one of the most excellent antidotes effective against deadly poisons. I only mention all this in passing; it is not really apposite here.

[44]

<130> Account of the practice of this state concerning robes of honour and their various grades[234]

There are three sorts: for the Men of the Sword, the Men of the Pen and the religious classes.

First, the Men of the Sword. The robes of the senior emirs of a hundred are red Rūmī satin, and beneath, yellow Rūmī satin. The top robe has gold-embroidered edging, and is lined with grey squirrel and has a fringe outside with a covering of beaver. The *kalauta*-cap[235] is gold-embroidered with gold clasps, and the turban-band of fine muslin has attached to both ends white silk embroidered with the Sultan's titles, along with dazzling decorations in coloured silk [all finished off] with a gold belt.[236] The type of belt varies according to the rank of the emir. The highest grade has, placed between the belt's upright pieces, roundels, a central one and two flanking, studded with rubies, emeralds and pearls. The next grade has only a single, studded roundel without any gems.

Men of this rank who are appointed to some great office are given in addition a sword with gold embellishments and a horse, saddled and bridled and complete with a gold-decorated caparison.

The honorary gift of the lord of Hama is one of the most exalted of this group. <131> In place of the muslin turban-band he received one made in Alexandria of silk, similar in length and worked[237] with gold, known as *muthammar*.[238] Two horses are presented, one of them as described above and the other having, instead of the caparison, a red satin *zunnārī*-saddle cloth. The same is now standard for the Vicegerent of Syria, although with the addition of a gold embroidered appliqué panel, encircling the top coat.

Below this [top] grade comes a type called *ṭardwaḥsh*,[239] which is produced in the Fabrics Manufactuary (Dār al-Ṭirāz) in Alexandria, Fustat and Damascus, and consists of panels, some of which have script giving the Sultan's titles, others the "hunt" motif or birds, and yet others various colours, [the whole] being worked with gold thread. These panels are separated by areas of decoration. The edging of this [i.e. such a *ṭardwaḥsh*] is of gold thread, but sometimes when certain individuals rise high, an edging band of gold brocade is appliqued on. It is trimmed with squirrel and beaver, just as mentioned above. Below is a coat of the open-fronted variety, made of Alexandrian *ṭarḥ*[240], and a brocade cap with clasps and a shawl are as described before, and there is also a belt of gold, sometimes with a roundel, sometimes without. This outfit is for junior emirs of a hundred and others who attain equal status.

<132> The next grade below is *kanjī*[241] which has decoration in a contrasting colour, or possibly self-coloured but of a different shade, with squirrel trimmed with beaver. The rest is as described above, except that the belt and the turban-band are without decoration on the ends. Rather, one [the band] is in panels of green and gilt-yellow and the other [the belt] has no roundel.

Below this grade is *kanjī* of one colour with squirrel trimmed with beaver, and the rest as above. The *kalauta*-cap is sparse in gold; indeed, its sides are almost totally devoid of it. There is no belt.

The next below is a single colour *muḥram*.[242] For the rest it is as we have described, except for the cap and the clasps.

Below this grade is *muḥram* and beaver. Underneath this is worn a coloured coat in panels of red, green, blue or other colours, and squirrel and beaver. Underneath again is a cambric robe, either blue or green. A white turban-band has ends similar to what has been described before.

The lower ranks are of this sort, although with some necessary scaling down.

[45][243]

For viziers and secretaries the highest robe of honour is white *kanjī*, bordered by a plain silk inscription band, and squirrel and beaver (the beaver is lined with the squirrel <133> and the sleeves filled out with it). Worn beneath is a green *kanjī*. They wear an embroidered linen *baqyār*-turban[244] of Damietta manufacture, and a *ṭarḥa*-hood.[245]

The next rank down is marked by the absence of the beaver lining and by the fact that the sleeves are empty of it too. For the next rank below, one leaves off the hood, lower again the under-coat is *muḥram*, and yet lower the top-coat is a sort of *kanjī*, but not white. Below this rank the top-coat is white *muḥram*, still lower, *muḥram*, but not white. Subsequently the under-coat is a tabby garment of *ṭarḥ*, or something comparable. For lesser grades it is just as we have said in the case of the robes of the Men of the Sword.

The robes of honour of the judges and men of the learned class are of wool without any decorative band of inscription. They wear the *ṭarḥa*-hood. The highest grade is white, with green worn below, and then the lower grades follow on roughly as has been described.

[46][246]

The ceremonial dress of the preachers[247] is black, as this is the distinguishing colour of the Abbasids. They wear a round-necked *dilq*-gown, which has been described before in the account of the dress of the learned classes, a black turban-band and a black hood. Two black banners with inscriptions in white or gold are raised over the pulpit.[248] The "reciter",[249] one of the muezzins, comes forth preceding the preacher, dressed in black like him, but without the hood. He carries a sword in his hand, which the preacher takes from him when he mounts the pulpit. Having climbed to the pulpit and uttered the formula of benediction, the one in black makes the call to prayer below the steps of the pulpit and the muezzins follow him. Then he recites <134> the tradition "When, on a Friday, you say to your companion, 'Give ear!' as the Imam is preaching, 'you are prattling'."[250] Next the reciter repeats, after the preacher, the blessings on the Prophet, the prayers for the departed and for the Caliph and the Sultan, he first and then the muezzins. When the preacher descends to perform the prayer ritual, he takes the sword from his hand. These ceremonial robes are issued from the Royal Chest and are kept in the mosque storerooms to be worn during the hours of Friday prayer. When threadbare, they are returned to the Chest and replacements are issued.

[47]

Account of the two festivals[251]

The ceremonial with which the Sultan rides out on festive days has already been mentioned. There remains something else that must be added here, namely that, when he proceeds from the door of his palace in the Citadel of the Mount and descends to his passage from the Stables area into the Festival Square adjoining it, he is received in a pavilion (*dihlīz*), erected there for him in the most perfect splendour imaginable. He prays and listens to the preacher, then mounts again and returns to the Great Hall, described above. There he spreads a banquet and bestows robes of honour on the Parasol-bearer and the Arms-bearer, and the Major-domo and the Taster, and many of the officers of state, who wait upon him on the occasion of the festival, such as the major-domo deputies, the junior tasters, the chief Marshal of the Army, the Inspector of the Household departments, and others such as these.

At every festival it is the custom of our present Sultan to have prepared for himself a robe of honour as though for his own wearing, something <135> comparable to the robes bestowed on the senior emirs of a hundred, which, however, he does not in fact wear himself, but with which he favours some senior emir of a hundred by bestowing it upon him. In this sort of way the ruler of Egypt is extremely open-handed, and so his court has become a lively market for every sort of import. From every quarter people flock to it, with the result that this almost ruins the state and destroys its revenues utterly. For the most part this has probably been established by the present Sultan, who may well embarrass those who succeed him by this abundance of liberality.[252]

Our Sultan keeps up traditions, all excellent, of bestowing robes at the times he plays polo on various persons who normally expect to receive them from him at that time, such as the Keeper of the Polostick,[253] the Prefects and the like, among those who customarily perform service connected with that, normally from what he bestows and distributes.

When anyone brings him something he has "bagged" on his hunting trips, he rewards him. Moreover, when he goes to the chase and they hunt gazelles or ostrich, anyone who brings him some game is rewarded with a robe lined with beaver in an appropriate manner for the robe of honour of his rank, something grand for a great man and something modest for a junior, each according to his position. Likewise the falconers and hawk-handlers and similar personnel at each hunt are the regular recipients of his bounty, and his servants of the [Royal] Scullery, Buttery and Wardrobe[254] and the like, receive annual gratuities at the hunting season. All these are current customary [payments] which are maintained.

For all who come to wait upon our Sultan, whether visitors from abroad or those from another state seeking asylum, there are various pensions, salaries, gifts and presents[255] which are not open to residents in this country or those already secure under his aegis. In like manner, <136> merchants, who come and sell to him, receive on-going allowances of bread, meat, garnishings, sweetmeats, fodder and financial concessions, [in value] equal to all the slaves, mamluks and slave-girls that are sold to him, not to speak of other concessions allowed them in the shape of other dues waived. For all of these, if they sell him even one single slave, there are full robes of honour for each one according to his due, quite apart from the price and the gifts that some of them are given or the Sultan's capital that is supplied for their trading expeditions on [interest-free] loan.[256]

The Bedouin importers of horses from the Hijaz, Syria, Bahrein, Cyrenaica and the Maghreb receive an ample portion, indeed, the lion's share, of all this. Its not unknown for the Sultan to give ten times the price or more for a horse, apart from robes, allowances, rations of fodder, provision of lodgings and money for expenses during their stay, leaving aside the matter of the valuation of the horses and the written exemptions they are issued with from duties levied on any goods they trade with, such as what they received from the sale of the horses.[257]

[48][258]

This realm contains all the kiblahs of the religions. That of Islam is the House of Mecca the Revered, which, as we have said, is within the realm. The Jews pray towards the Sacred Temple (Jerusalem), which was the initial kiblah of Islam, and is also within the realm. The sect of the Jews known as the Samaritans have as their kiblah the Mount of Nablus. Again it is situated within the realm, and they maintain that it is Ṭūr Sīnā (the Mount of Moses). The Christians have no special place towards which they pray. They face the east, not any particular kiblah, but our realm contains all the shrines they hold in reverence, such as the Holy Sepulchre[259] in Jerusalem, to which they come on pilgrimage from all regions of the earth, flocking to it across lands and seas, <137> and also Bethlehem, the birthplace of Jesus the Messiah (on Him be peace), and the Church of Saydanāyā[260] in the country around Damascus, and the church at Tyre. The coronation of certain of their kings is not valid until they are blessed there[261] and the Church of St. John at Alexandria,[262] which is the central shrine of the Jacobite sect and is the seat of the Coptic Patriarch, whom the Abyssinian kings hold in honour and refer to with respect. When they receive a letter from him, they act on it implicitly without deviating in the slightest from its terms. Successive metropolitans are appointed over them by the Patriarch. On the death of one he sends another to be his representative amongst them. Each metropolitan exercises full authority in Abyssinia on behalf of the Patriarch. The whole population submits to his control, without disputing his commands in any matter.[263]

A trustworthy source[264] told me that a certain merchant in Egypt sent some money of his by an agent to Abyssinia. The agent died and the owner despaired of recovering his money, which was a considerable sum. His patience exhausted, he complained to the government. A word was said to the Patriarch, who wrote a letter to the King of Abyssinia, ordering him to restore the man's money. The merchant dispatched a person he relied on and he did not have long to wait before the latter came back bringing a letter expressing obedience, and accompanied by all the very money he had lost, the basic amount and the interest on it.

As an illustration of the Abyssinian reverence for the Patriarch's letters, it is related that the moment that letter crossed their frontiers and they learnt of it, the provincial officials came to meet it and raised it high on a lance and carried it, its bearer and his retinue, on superior steeds, and provided lodging and upkeep for them. The envoy was in this manner conveyed by the inhabitants of each province to the next <138> until he reached the court of the king who welcomed him with extreme honour and lavish hospitality. When Sunday came round, the letter was handed over and read to the king by the metropolitan in the church. The king stood bare-headed until it was finished, then ordered the money to be brought and handed over. He would not move from where he was until the money had been conveyed to the envoy, to whom he subsequently gave a handsome gift, before sending him back with honour, the recipient of regular provision of hospitality in his progress from one province to another until he had left the king's territory.[265]

This is why all the princes of Christendom, Melkite and Jacobite, send gifts to the ruler of Egypt and maintain a correspondence with him; they find it essential, to make it possible for the thronging pilgrims from their lands to visit the Sepulchre and the rest of their holy sites. The Jacobites are most dependent on him, because their Patriarch is a resident subject of the Sultan. They have no pope, unlike the Melkites, for whom there is the Pope at Rome. The Pope is their chiefest leader in error. They hold that he alone defines what it is right or wrong to do and that no-one may legitimately delay or anticipate his commands.

[49]

Excursus

The reigning Sultan counts among his supporters a sect called the Ismāʻīlīs, who dwell in Masyaf and the neighbouring fortresses of the "Mission", seven fortresses[266] on a line parallel <139> to the Homs–Hama line, close to the Mediterranean Sea in the Tripoli direction. These are the same people who, in Persian lands, are sometimes called the *Bāṭiniyya* (Esoterics), sometimes the *Malāḥida* (Dissenters). The essence of their creed is metempsychosis. They designate themselves "the Followers of the Rightly Guided Mission", and are the sect of the former Caliphs in Egypt, the Fatimids. The leadership of the sect came into the hands of Rāshid al-Dīn Sinān,[267] a former magician, who used his magic to beguile their minds, for example, by conjuring up the images of persons who died in obedience to their Imams, enjoying the delights of Paradise, or the images of those who died in rebellion against their Imams, suffering in blazing Hell-fire. They believe that every ruler of Egypt is a sanctified figure for them; thus this sect submits itself to him and they think it right to lose their lives in his obedience for the very great bliss that is the resulting reward. By the adherence of these people the ruler of Egypt acquires an advantage that makes him feared by his enemies, for from such men he may send out assassins who are heedless of their own possible death.[268] If one is sent by the ruler of Egypt to kill an enemy and fails through cowardice, his own people kill him when he returns, or, if he flees, they hunt him down and kill him.

I questioned their leader and authority, Mubārak ibn ʿAlwān, about their creed and I engaged him in discussion of this <140> several times. It became clear to me that the sect considers that souls are imprisoned in earthly bodies with the duty to obey the one whom they claim is the Sanctifed Imam. If the soul passes on in a state of obedience, it is released and migrates to the celestial lights, but if it passes on in rebellion, it falls into the lower darknesses. They hold that ʿAlī (may God be pleased with him) was the Sanctified One, then that this role was passed on from him, but this is not the place to go into this at length.

[50]

The great cities of note in this realm are the capital, Cairo (it has already been said that that means Cairo proper, the Citadel and Fustat, three cities now become one), Qūs, Alexandria, Damietta, Damascus, which is the second capital, Baalbek, Homs, Hama, Aleppo, Tripoli, Safed, Jerusalem, Kerak and Gaza. We have already mentioned the revered cities of Mecca and Medina and the way they became part of this realm, as explained above.

The Citadel of the Mount[269] is on an elevated site, called the Red Mountain, one of the outcrops of the Muqattam Hills, and was built by Qarāqūsh[270] for al-Malik al Nāṣir Ṣalāḥ al-Dīn [Saladin] Abū'l-Muẓaffar Yūsuf ibn Ayyūb (God have mercy on him). The latter never dwelt there, but it was first inhabited by his brother, al-Malik al-ʿĀdil Abū Bakr,[271] when he came to power. Built on its elevated site, it is nevertheless high at one point <141> and low at another. A stone wall encircles it with towers and salients until it reaches the Striped Palace, newly built by [our Sultan] al-Nāṣir.[272] From that point it is connected with royal apartments which are not constructed on the pattern of fortress towers.

There are two entrances to the Citadel; one, the main gate, faces Cairo, and the other leads into the Qarāfa. Between the two is a broad court surrounded on its south-east and north-west sides by residences, and on the south side is a market for foodstuffs. Across the main part of the court one arrives at a grand lobby where the emirs sit until permission is given for them to enter. At its centre is the Qulla Gate which leads one through wide passages to palaces, residences and houses, and to the Friday Mosque. It used to be hardly a mosque at all because it had been built so cramped, but the present Sultan reconstructed it on an ample and lofty scale, with its floor paved in marble and its roof lined with gold, and with a high dome in the middle, next to which is the enclosure, which is screened, as are the arcades, with iron grilles of masterly construction. The courtyard is surrounded by arcades on all sides.

From the passage of the Qulla Gate mentioned above one walks through entrance-ways into <142> a spacious square, at the heart of which stands the

Great Hall designed for sessions on ceremonial days and for holding [sittings of] the Palace of Justice. At the side of the square are splendid buildings. Alongside the Hall is a lane leading to the door of the Striped Palace, next to which is a small square where the inner group of emirs sit before they enter for their "continuous attendance" on the Sultan.

From the door of this palace one walks through passages into a palace of vast construction that towers high in the sky, containing two vaulted halls, the larger being the north one, with a view out over the Royal Stables area. One's gaze extends out to the Horse Market, Cairo and its suburbs, to the Nile and the adjacent fields and villages of Giza. In the other, the south hall, there is a private door through which the Sultan and his intimate retinue enter the Great Hall on ceremonial days.

From within this palace one gains access to three suites of inner apartments, one on the same floor level as this great palace and two raised above it, reached by a stairway. All these have iron grille windows which open up a view such as the one from the great palace.

These palaces have running water, lifted up from the Nile by water wheels turned by oxen, from one basin to another until it reaches the Citadel. It then enters the Sultan's apartments and the residences of the senior emirs, the inner circle that resides close to the Sultan, flowing through their houses and supplying their bathhouses. This is really a construction miracle because of the height to which it is raised, something approaching 500 cubits from place to place.[273]

From the inner apartments one enters the sanctum of the Harem and the doors of the private rooms <143> of the Sultan. All these palaces are externally of black and yellow stone,[274] and clothed internally with marble and decorative panels, gilded and with vegetal designs, in mother-of-pearl, stucco,[275] rare stones and various coloured (glass) pieces, and their roofs are decorated with gold and lapis lazuli. Light penetrates the walls through windows glazed with coloured Cyprus glass like gems stones set in necklaces, and all the floor area is paved with incomparable marble imported from all over the world. The Sultan's private quarters, as I am reliably informed, possess gardens, groves of trees, enclosures for rare and wonderful animals, and cattle, sheep and domestic fowl.

The rest of its interior, meaning the Qulla, is given over to the Royal mamluks, the "inner" emirs with their wives and womenfolk, their mamluks and their administrative officials, their separate pantry, wardrobe, buttery and kitchen establishments and their staffs.

Within the Citadel are dwellings for the great emirs, and the senior emirs of the *ṭablkhānah* or of ten, or those who have left the status of the inner service (*al-khāṣṣikiyya*) for the grade of the outer (*al-barrāniyya*). There too are the residences of the Vizier and the Privy Secretary, the Bureau of the Chancery and of the Army, the Financial Bureau, the marshals, the Armoury, the prisons with their inmates, and similar sorts of building, all in separated residences. It also contains within its purlieus mosques, shops and markets. This is the totality of the construction.

<144> Let us complete our account of the Royal Palace by saying that the Sultan may descend thence from alongside the palace hall to the Royal Stables,

then further to a Hippodrome[276] made leafy by verdant palms, which divides the Stables from the Horse Market to the west, and offers a broad prospect to the eye as it travels over its expanses. The Sultan rides down steps near his inner palace and so comes to the private stable, and then to this place, on horseback with the "inner-service" emirs in attendance, to review the horses when it is time to issue them or to receive new arrivals and purchases, or at the times when the hawks are fed.[277] Sometimes he remains on horseback and sometimes he dismounts there, even if no tents have been erected, but they may be, if he stays there a long time, or if the weather is hot or cold. At times a meal may be provided there. Then he rides back up to his palace. In this Hippodrome are all sorts of wild animals, beautiful to look at, and his own private horses are kept there for exercise. This Hippodrome is where the Sultan, his "inner service" staff and his body servants, who never leave his side, pray at the two festivals. He descends to it and ascends on return through a private gate to the palace entrance-hall, different from the one by which he normally descends, which we have mentioned above. The Sultan has a number of private gates to the Qarāfa and elsewhere, which it is not necessary for us to mention.

These palaces and the Great Hall, the Green Hippodrome, the mosque and most of the imposing buildings in the Qulla and the Citadel are the work and construction of the present Sultan.[278] <145> They are decorated with bands containing his titles and his name, which make one avert one's gaze, wearied by their brilliance, and set hearts fluttering at the scent wafted from their floral inscriptions. Princes acknowledge them to be evidence of his high aspirations, the amplitude of his spending and his generosity. One's eyes are riveted on the buildings and whoever sees them recognises that here is a man who despises both the [ultimate] enemy and the dinar.[279]

[51][280]

Cairo (al-Qāhira) is a city built in a low-lying area some distance from the high point of the Mount, and has damp alluvial soil (*sibākh*). Consequently the buildings decay quickly. Fusṭāṭ [Old Cairo], which in popular speech is now called Miṣr, is a city built on the east bank of the Nile. Just opposite, on the island[281] where the Nilometer[282] stands, many buildings have been erected, which form, as it were, a section of Miṣr, divided from it by a channel of the Nile. The view of the river at this point when the moonlight is spread over all or the lamps are lit at night is one that pulls at the heartstrings.

Both Cairo and Miṣr and their extensive suburbs have high apartment blocks, some of which reach four stories. Each story contains complete living units with all appurtenances and conveniences, and a roof-terrace of its own, separate from the one above, stoutly constructed and amazingly built, seeing that the apartments are built over one another. In this respect the likes of the builders of Egypt are not to be seen anywhere else. These two cities and their suburbs have towering palaces, large mansions, comfortable dwellings, extensive markets, madrasas, Sufi convents, hospices and *zāwiyas*. <146> All, notwithstanding the growing area of construction and the breadth of the streets, is crowded with humanity both in living-space at home and in circulation-space outside. All the nations of the world have been squeezed in and peoples[283] of all sorts have flocked thither. I have been told by more than one informant who has seen the great cities and huge settlements in the East and West, in remote and neighbouring lands, that never have they seen a city in which so many people have gathered as have gathered in Miṣr, Cairo and their suburbs. His Honour Majd al-Dīn Ismāʿīl al-Sallamī,[284] when I asked him about Baghdad and Tabriz and whether they have a population comparable with that of Egypt, told me that Egypt has as many people as all the countries from here to Tabriz combined.

The majority of the population are the common folk, shop-keepers, tradesmen and artisans; as al-Qāḍī al-Fāḍil ʿAbd al-Raḥīm al-Baisānī (may God have mercy on his soul) said: "The people of Egypt, despite their great number and the abundance of wealth that is attributed to their land, are wretchedly poor, toiling in the water, and exhausted, labouring in the fields." I believed him to have aimed at an elegant turn of phrase,[285] since every land has those who are exhausted in their labours. This remained my opinion, without any further thought about it, until I came to live in Egypt and travelled, in the company of the Sultan, over most of the country and saw a great number of people, those in whose name some piece of land was registered, land only the low-lying parts of which were naturally irrigated and the upper levels not at all. They stood two by two in stagnant, muddy water with a basket in their hands, holding it by a cord tied to its handles and emptying the water, with strong backward swings of the basket, <147> into a basin, that had been dug out, where the scooped up water was gathered and then distributed in channels to those higher parts which the water did not [otherwise] reach, to irrigate them. This was for them exhausting labour and great hardship. I realised that these were the people al-Qāḍī al-Fāḍil had in mind when he wrote "exhausted, labouring in the fields", for no one in the country is more hard-pressed than they. They are obliged to produce their fixed dirhem and ardebb. If they do not work, they are hounded without respite and cannot find the means to pay up.

The countryside of Egypt consists of an area of cultivated land extending between two barriers of hills and sandy wastes, punctuated by settlements, which are built of mud brick, black in external appearance, and surrounded by palms, here few in number and there abundant, but which are all on a single pattern; to see one is to see them all.

[52]

[Qūs][286]

Qūs is a city on the east bank of the Nile, deep in Upper Egypt, situated within the second clime. It has splendid mansions, fondacos,[287] apartment blocks, bath-houses and madrasas. It is where the elite of the merchants, learned classes and the wealthy reside, and is the first stage for the caravans of the merchants of

India, Abyssinia, Yemen and the Hijaz who come by sea and cross the desert from Aidhab. A profitable commerce is carried on there. The city has orchards, gardens and horticultural nurseries, but it is excessively hot and overrun with scorpions and geckos.

There is <148> a variety of deadly scorpion there, and consequently the local expression used when anyone is stung is "The scorpion has eaten him", because there is no hope of his recovery. I was informed by ʿIzz al-Dīn ibn Abī al-Majd al-Ṣafadī,[288] a notary in Cairo, that one day in summer he counted seventy geckos[289] in a row on the wall of the mosque. It is widely reported that, when any citizen of Qūs goes for a stroll anywhere, or is walking home, or setting out somewhere, in one hand he carries a lamp and in the other a sharp stick with which to stab the scorpions.

In Upper Egypt are survivals of ancient magic, and various stories are told about them. The most authentic one I heard was a story told me by a man I trust on the authority of Tuqṣubā,[290] the governor of Qūs, in these words:

> I arrested a sorceress and said to her, "I wish to see some of your sorcery." She replied, "One of my best tricks is to bewitch scorpions." "How can you do that?" I said. "By magic I set one on to a particular person by name", she replied, "and the scorpion relentlessly pursues that person until it stings and kills him." "Show me", I said, "set a scorpion on to me." So she took a scorpion, bewitched and then released it. It pursued and followed me whenever I kept dodging it. I then sat on a dais erected in the middle of an ornamental pool. The scorpion came to the pool and tried to reach me but could not launch itself into the water. It retired to <149> the wall, which it climbed as I watched it, right up to the ceiling and then came across it to a point directly above me. It dropped down to the ground and came at me. I struck it with a staff I had in my hand and killed it. Then I seized the sorceress and killed her because of her dreadful magic I had seen.

Many such stories are told but this is not the place to repeat them.[291]

From Qūs one goes on to Aswān, which is the gateway to the land of Nubia. From Aswān there is also a road which branches off through the desert to Aidhab on the coast, from where one may cross to Jidda, the port of Mecca the Revered. There are also trade routes by sea to Aden, and thence to any destination in India, Yemen and Abyssinia. We have singled out Qūs for mention rather than any other town in Upper Egypt just because it is the main city there and a staging post for all parties of travellers and caravans, whether moving up or down the country.

[53][292]

Alexandria is an ancient city, great and glorious, but formerly larger than it is now, more populous and more densely built up. It was built by Alexander, the Two-Horned One,[293] on the Mediterranean coast. It is said that it was his capital and his mother's permanent abode. Construction throughout is with stone and lime-mortar, and the houses are whitewashed inside and out, as white as doves. Its thoroughfares are broad and ample, and each quarter in itself is like <150> a chessboard square. The city is ringed with strong walls and impregnable towers, on which are protective screens and batteries of mangonels, and there is a permanent garrison for its defence. In Egypt there is no city, apart from Alexandria, whose ruling authority has the official rank of vicegerent.[294] The population is constantly on watch for developments at sea and raids by the enemy.

The city contains splendid houses and mosques, both great and small, hospices, Sufi convents, shrines, fondacos, apartment blocks, extensive markets, cotton factories and [manufacturies for] textiles and for the incomparable *ṭirāz*-bands. Merchant convoys flock there by land and sea from every distant hill and dale. In the whole world nothing can match its gauzy linen (*sharb)*, or the *ṭirāz* manufactured there and exported east and west to all corners of the globe. It produces, for example, the *ḥafīr* woven with gold and silver, the *muqassab* with gold thread, various *ṭardwaḥsh*, *jarr*, embroidered stuff (*manqūsh*), mixed stuff (*mumazzaj*), the *madfūn*,[295] tightly woven linen (*dabīqī*), plain stuffs (*sādhij*), the *muqtaraḥ*,[296] linen and cotton mixtures <151> (*maqāṭi*ʿ), *mumarrash*, the untreated linen, the "cut" (*maqsūr*), and suits of *maqāni*ʿ(?), and sorts of silk head-bands, and "coloured" stuff with gold and silver, wraps, and kerchiefs, all unrivalled for decoration and peerless in their beauty. Every day there is sold material worth thousands upon thousands of gold dinars, but the merchandise does not run out, nor does the stock dwindle.[297]

In Alexandria black dirhems[298] are legal tender, but they are confined there and are not issued anywhere else, and may not pass beyond its walls. Within the city two black dirhems equal one ordinary Egyptian dirhem. Actual black dirhem coins exist corresponding to the nominal unit, whereas, as we have explained, in the rest of Egypt it exists as a nominal unit of accounting but not in fact, three black dirhems equalling one ordinary Egyptian dirhem.

Alexandria is the port for trade with the West, Spain, the islands of the Franks and the Greek Empire. Their galleys come, import their goods and export the merchandise they seek.[299] Damietta (to be dealt with below) cannot bear comparison with Alexandria, although she is her partner in this sphere.

A canal cut from the Nile puts Alexandria in touch by boat with Old Cairo and vice versa.[300] At the time of the Nile flood the canal fills and flows over into cisterns within the city designed for water storage to ensure the city's drinking supply. The cisterns are interconnected from one <152> house to another, enabling a person to descend into one cistern and come up in any house he may choose. Beneath these cisterns are wells fed by springs with brackish water. There are therefore three levels: the wells, the cisterns above them and then the buildings.[301] The population of the city have no care to construct upper stories on the tops of their buildings owing to the heavy rains and the hollow foundations. Alexandria is set about with charming gardens and broad groves. The chief men of the place have comely palaces and tall pleasure pavilions, all fortified with solid construction and high walls for fear of Frankish raiders and Bedouin pillagers.

There are choice fruits in Alexandria. Indeed for its handsome fruits and their cheapness it surpasses Cairo. No wheat or barley is cultivated there, nor any of the grains and pulses or at least only a little. Most of the city's provisions are imported from the Egyptian countryside.

[54]

Excursus

In the preceding pages we have remarked that it was Alexander who built Alexandria. This is true in the sense that he re-built it. Its ancient foundation had come about in a way which al-Tīfāshī[302] described as follows in his work, *The Soul's Delight in the Perceptions of the Five Senses*:

> Aḥmad ibn Muṭarrif <153> in his *Placing in Sequence*[303] relates the following. The original builder of Alexandria was Jubair al-Muʾtatikī who was led to build it in the following manner. He marched against one of the queens of Egypt, called Ḥūriyyā, daughter of al-Thurayyā.[304] After a long period of war between them, she sent a messenger to say that she wished him to marry her, for their rule and their palaces to be one, that her person and her kingdom would be his, which was better for him than continued war and consequent exhaustion of his wealth and destruction of his men, and that, if he conquered her, then he would gain no advantage, because defeats would have wasted her wealth, and if he failed, he would pass away and so would all his wealth. Pleased with her suggestion, he agreed and a marriage was arranged according to their rites. He sought then to consummate the marriage, but she said that it was bad for them to be united other than in a city built by them for the purpose, in a most beautiful position and on a magnificent site, where no building but theirs had ever been. This was nothing but a stratagem to exhaust his resources and attain her ends by subtlety and guile, but he agreed and sent architects to her, giving her the choice of sites. Her choice fell on the site of Alexandria and she marked out the city. The architects then drew up the plans for it. She kept him informed and he agreed to all her requests.
>
> Having arrived with his army, he camped at the site and began to build. As soon as he erected a building, <154> the beasts of the sea came and wrecked and demolished it. For some time he remained there, until his money was spent and his resources reduced. He had the good fortune to be directed to a certain sorcerer, to whom, when he had summoned him, he complained of his position. The sorcerer devised some talismans and placed them in glass receptacles like caskets. These were lowered into the water before the buildings. When the sea beasts came and saw the talismans and the caskets, they shrank back and so the buildings stood firm.[305] After a long time the construction of the city was completed. He wrote asking her to come, which

she did with all her royal pomp and her troops. Camped opposite his army, she communicated her desire to ease the burden of the expense for suitable food and drink for the two armies. She had prepared, she said, robes of honour and gifts for his emirs and commanders, to lighten his commitments in building the city. She wished that he would agree. He did, so she made the necessary arrangements. In another message she expressed her desire to see him and his army in various martial exercises in the arena, and afterwards would they be at her disposal for presentation of the food and robes of honour, she enquired. In conformity with her wishes, he ordered the army to mount up, take their arms and perform. Afterwards, when all were bathed in perspiration, they went to her, to be met by her men with poisoned robes. The officers donned theirs, as did King Jubair. His was less poisoned than the others to ensure that he lived on for a while for her to have words with him. After only a short moment in the robes they were overcome and died. Seeing this, the rest of the army realised where their best course lay and hastened to seek terms. By proclamation they were assured of their own safety.

There was still a spark of life in the king, when she ordered him to be carried into her presence. When she looked on him in his death throes, she said, "A king who spends all his wealth, wastes his time and neglects his rule in pursuit of a desire, ignorant whether he will attain it or not, is a foolish king." Her last word coincided with the expiring of his spirit, and thus he died. She entered the city, where she remained for a time before returning to Misr.

[55]

<155> Subsequently Alexander came to power and enlarged the city, heightened the Pharos,[306] and fitted a mirror to it by which enemy ships could be sighted at a distance. When they come opposite it and its rays strike them, they set them on fire, just as a crystal glass in sunlight burns any rags that face it, without coming into direct contact with them. From that time onwards the city was called Alexandria, having previously had the name Raqūda, by which name it was known to the Copts in their ancient books.

For a time the mirror remained in that state, much to the discomfiture of the Greeks. One of their wise men worked out a scheme that involved their ruler agreeing to send sums of money with friends of his, who buried them in widely scattered places within the Islamic lands. On their return, after burying them, he put together a *Book of Buried Treasures*, in which he gave an account of the various sites. He finished the book with the statement that beneath the mirror on the Pharos of Alexandria lay a treasure of immeasurable wealth. He then gave the book, which he had "antiqued", to a sharp-witted man and bade him take it to one land after another, seeking out the sultan of each and informing him of the treasure in his land. When it was recovered, he was to take a small portion. This he did in the first land he came to. What he said proved true.

The money was brought forth and he took a small share of it. His fame spread to other lands. The sultan of each land in turn sent someone to secure his services after witnessing his extraction of the treasure of the land he was then in. So he continued <156> until he came eventually to Alexandria, where he told the king of what the book said concerning the mirror and added that, if the king removed the mirror and took the treasure, he would put the mirror back, better than it was at the time. The proposition agreed to, the mirror was removed and a start made on demolishing the structure below. The man then slipped away, leaving the money which he had received from previous treasure hauls, to allay their fears so that they would not start to hunt for him very intensively, and so he got away. They dug and found nothing, and realised that all this had been a trick to get the mirror demolished. They were not able to put it back because its builders had been wise men who had erected it under favourable planetary auspices. There is some dispute about this story; some authorities repeat it but others have a different story.

However, I have read in some history books that there are four wonders of the world: a copper horse in the furthest west of Spain, past which no-one ventures without being swallowed up in the sand; a copper tree in Rome, on which is a copper bird, called the Starling (al-Zurzūr), and when it is time for the olives to ripen, every single bird of that species (and it is a common bird) brings an olive in its beak and two in its claws and drops them by the said copper bird – the citizens of Rome press from this enough oil for their cooking and their lamps for the current year, because there are no olives in Rome; a copper beacon surmounted by a copper horseman in the land of ʿĀd, which, in the sacred months, flows with water, though it flows at no other time; a mirror on the Pharos of Alexandria, by which enemy fleets could be sighted when they set sail from Constantinople the Great. The people of Alexandria could see the people of Constantinople, though the whole wide sea was between them.

The measurement of the Pharos, which is a three-storied construction, is, according to the account of a certain scholar, 233 cubits. <157> The first floor is square and is 121 cubits high, the second is octagonal and 81½ cubits, and the third circular and 30½.

I point out that this account of the Pharos, having been verifiable, has now become a tradition, since its structure has fallen and it is completely destroyed. The Pharos stands only up to a height of less than 20 cubits. The Sultan has ordered it to be repaired but he has not really devoted great care to it. Nowadays the look-out is only maintained on a beacon newly built on a high mound within the city wall, known as the Mound of Muʿalla, which has no firm foundation nor high-built wall. The Column of Columns (Pompey's Pillar) still survives intact, an impressive but useless relic.[307] About half a day's journey to the west of Alexandria is the barren wasteland that connects with Barqa (Cyrenaica) and on to the Far West.

The Alexandrian rotl, called the *jarawī*,[308] is the equivalent of 2 rotls and 2 okes of the Egyptian standard. The local ardebb is divided into 8 *waiba*s and is the same as 1⅓ Egyptian ardebbs. Prices there generally tend to be low, and were it not for the controls, they would be even lower. Imports are very considerable in amount.

[56]

[Damietta]

Damietta (Dimyāṭ)[309] is a city on the coast at the mouth of one of the branches of the Nile. <158> At the present time it is not a solidly built place. A dike surrounds the city and follows the Nile as far as its outlet into the sea. It is a place subject to sudden enemy raids from the sea. For a long time the power of infidel [Christendom] fastened on the city, until by God's help they were overcome at the end of the Ayyūbid dynasty.[310]

I have been told by those who have seen Damietta that it is a small city with one madrasa and some markets that are not large. From there one may reach the lake of Tinnis, a city renowned in the past for its beautiful layout and the excellence of its textiles and goods. The lake is now only a salt-water lagoon or something like that. In Damietta and the vicinity banana trees are numerous and supply the needs of Miṣr, Cairo and their surrounding area.

A useful note

In *The Soul's Delight* al-Tīfāshī wrote:

> It is said that Tinnis, Dimyāṭ and al-Faramā were three brothers who ruled these three cities. Each one named <159> his city after himself. Tinnis used to be referred to as Tinnis of the Shacks. It is maintained that [Jesus] the Anointed One (peace be on Him) came to Tinnis and was hospitably received by the inhabitants. He prayed that God might bless them and that the city might draw its livelihood from all over the world, since he saw it situated in the middle of a lake.[311]

However, he did not visit Damietta.

The district of al-Jifār[312] consists of five towns, al-Faramā [Pelusium], al-Baqqāra, al-Warrāda, al-ʾArīsh and Rafaḥ. The whole of al-Jifār is sand and was so named owing to the difficulty experienced by both men and mounts in walking there because of the great quantity of sand and the distance between the stages of the crossing, and the hollows (*jifār*) in which camels and other beasts exhaust themselves[313] and perish. Thus the area was given the name Jifār. Similarly, the rope by which a camel is tethered (*yuhjar*) is called a tether (*hijār*), and that by which it is restrained (*yuḥjar*) is a restrainer (*ḥijār*). A horse is hobbled (*tuʾqal*) with a hobble (*ʿiqāl*) and girthed (*yubṭan*) with a girth (*biṭān*), and likewise for a *ḥiṭām* (noseband), a *zammām* and such like. Al-Baqqāra is derived from *al-baqar* (cattle), al-Warrāda from *al-wurūd* (coming to water), and al-ʿArīsh from *al-ʿarsh* (trellis). It is said that the latter marks the frontier with Syria and that it is the furthest the herdsmen of Abraham, the Friend of God (peace be on him), used to come with his flocks, that he built himself a trellis shelter to sit in, while his cattle were being milked before him, and the place was named accordingly. Rafaḥ is the name of a man, to whom the place has been attributed.

This is all I have to say about the cities of some note in Egypt.

[57]

Two ranges of hills set out to choke its cultivable land. They press close to one another where it starts in the furthest part of Upper Egypt. Later they begin <160> to allow some breathing space towards Giza. The hills then diverge and the distance between them widens until it is terminated by the Mediterranean Sea at the end of Egypt's districts. At its broadest the distance is about two day's journey and at its narrowest about an hour's. For the most part it is about two or from one to two hours' journey.

This is the true breadth of Egypt, unless you consider the desolate wastes where the Jinn fear to tread and evil-doers dread to venture. For the width we have mentioned is on both sides devoid of tillage, propagation, sowing and planting; empty of any human society, apart from the lone night-traveller or one who has lost his way. The thriving populated part is a third of that width, but that third is large and moreover produces a plentiful yield and a large harvest.

[58]

In Egypt there are so many different types of snakes, vipers and serpents, scorpions, rodents and other insects that, if some were not destroyed by the inundation of the Nile each year, or if some did not flee the Nile, while the people stand in wait for them on the roads with clubs and sticks in their hands to kill those that come to infest them, Egypt would be uninhabitable, no part of it could be settled and no-one could establish any permanent residence there.

[59]

Springtime in Egypt and the lakes and pools left behind by her Nile, the blossoms of clover and flax which embellish her robes, and the hosts of birds assembled in her land in all their winged assortment, all this[314] fills one's eyes with charm and beauty, and delights one in form and fancy. It is as if her vegetation were green emerald, the stretches of water blue turquoise and the blossoms have in each pendant a white pearl. Over her the birds form cloud shadows, and tents have been erected on her carpet of brocade.[315] When I beheld this wonderful sight in springtime and the still pools of water amongst its darkling bosky folds like stars in the heavens, I wrote:

<161> O Egypt, bless'd and bright, where life is sweet and all delight,
On meadows' slope the water of life and verdure do unite.

[60][316]

Egypt is divided into two provinces, a southern and a northern, which together have a total of fifteen governorates.

The Southern Province[317] is the bigger of the two and consists of nine districts, namely, the district of Qūs, east of the Nile and the largest of all (it includes Aswān, the southernmost limit of the realm, and also the bedouin[318] of Qammūla); the district of Akhmīm, also east of the Nile; the districts of Asyut and Manfalūṭ, and that of Ashmunain, which includes Ṭaḥāwiyya; the district of Bahnasā, which includes al-Gharābī, a term for villages along the margin[319] of the Manha Canal which extends to Fayyum; the district of Fayyum itself, which is separated from the others; the district of Atfih, east of the Nile; and the district of Giza.

The Northern Province[320] has six districts: the district of Buhaira, the area of which adjoins Alexandria and Barqa: the district of Gharbiyya (the Western district), an island comprising the land between the two rivers – <162> the tidal branch of the Nile, which flows into the sea at Damietta and is called the Eastern branch, and the other branch with its outlet at Rosetta, called the Western: and the district of Manufiyya. Manf, which gives this district its name, was in past times [the capital of] Egypt.[321] Within Manufiyya is Ibyar, called the Island of Abu Nasr.[322] It is indeed an island in the middle of the western arm of the Nile. [The other districts are] the district of Qalyub, a town east of the Nile; the district of Sharqiyya (the Eastern district), which stretches out to Syria, Qulzum and the Hijaz; and similarly the district of Ashmum, known as Ashmum Tanah,[323] which includes [the regions of] Daqhiliyya and Murtahiyya. In this province are situated the strategic towns of Burullus, Rosetta and Mansura, the latter built during the seige of Damietta. In this province are Alexandria and Damietta, two commercial cities on the sea, which do not themselves possess a district.

[61][324]

<163> The Oases are quite cut off beyond the Southern Province to the west. They are not counted as part of the governorate or district structure, nor are they administered by any governor appointed by the Sultan. The *iqṭāʿ* holder for the area is responsible for the administration. The linked chain of oases lies between Old Cairo, Alexandria, Upper Egypt, Nubia and Abyssinia.

In the words of al-Bakrī:

> It is a territory standing by itself, unconnected with any other and self-sufficient. In this area are found alum and vitriol and wells with sour water which is used

as vinegar, and wells with various tastes, acid, astringent and salt. Every sort has a use and a special property.[325]

[62]

Description of Cyrenaica, an appendage to this realm[326]

To quote Ibn Saʿīd:[327]

> This is an extensive realm, although it cannot have any independent existence as a polity, because the bedouin have seized control of it. In former times the city of Tobruk was its capital. <164> There is no regular government there. Indeed, the only inhabitants are the tent-dwelling nomads. It is in fact closer to Ifriqiya (Libya) than to Egypt, but everything up to Aqaba[328] belongs to the ruler of Egypt and comes under his control.

I was informed by his Excellency the Emir Nāṣir al-Dīn Muḥammad ibn al-Muḥsinī[329] that it is a land with plenty of water and a healthy climate. The terrain consists of plateaux and rugged slopes for the most part, but there are meadows and many trees. There are ancient cities whose buildings still survive to this day, but which are devoid of inhabitants. The remains of lofty palaces indicate their former magnificence, but today they are in the hands of the bedouin, owners of cattle and numerous grazing beasts, camels and sheep, some of whom *do* sow crops in certain parts of the area and obtain abundant yields, and yet they are nomadic people and do not take a great interest in building or cultivating.

From more than one member of the Egyptian forces, who had been in those parts on expeditions sent there, I have heard that it is similar to the outlying parts of Syria and the hills of Nablus in the varieties of trees that grow and in the configuration of the land and its general appearance, and that, if only it could be peopled and settled by farmers, it could be a great province, something like half Syria.

Cyrenaica had been assigned as *iqṭāʿ* by diplomas of the ruler of Egypt to Ibn al-Muḥsinī, who would journey there and collect what was his due from the bedouin. Later it was assigned to the emirs of Sulaim, Egyptian bedouin Arabs, and they are now responsible for collecting the required levy[330] from the bedouin of Cyrenaica.

<165> I was told by the Emir Fāʾid ibn Muqaddam al-Sulamī,[331] to whom it is now assigned, that Cyrenaica is one of the best countries for riding animals and has some of the most nutritious pasture. Indeed, the horses of Cyrenaica are among the strongest in build. Just to say "a Cyrenaican horse" is recommendation enough. They are round [i.e. barrel-chested], not too tall, but broad, stocky and firm of hoof, and unite the speed, powerful charge and perfection of line of the Arab with the solidity of hoof, sure-footedness on mountains and in rugged country, and the endurance of the hack. In appearance it comes between the Arab and the hack, bearing marks of resemblance to both types, though inclining more towards the beauties of the Arab. The stallions of the Cyrenaican breed are

superior to the mares. The troopers in Egypt think very highly of them and they are sold for high prices, and yet do not fetch as much as the horses of Bahrein, the Hijaz and Syria.

The width of Cyrenaica, measured in journey time, is two months. The capital was the city of Antapulus [Pentapolis], and Tobruk, mentioned above, is one of its cities, which include Tolmetha and Labda [Leptis], the latter possessing abundant marble, <166> columns and slabs. It is still there, some standing erect and some lying flat. Sirte is another of its towns of note.

The Qadi Abū Isḥāq Ibrāhīm ibn Abī Sālim informed me, when speaking of Labda, that it is full of excellent white marble, even the streets and the pedestrian walk-ways in the markets, and that nothing is lacking to restore it to prosperous life except people. Another informant, the Sheikh Sharaf al-Dīn ʿĪsā al-Zawāwī,[332] said to me, "I passed through the country of Cyrenaica and I saw everything ruinous, desolate and deserted. No-one was there but nomadic Arabs. Palaces still stand, containing nothing but the grain the bedouin store there." He also told me, "In the mountains of Cyrenaica are trees that bear fruit, olives and many others, but there is no thriving city worth mentioning. The inhabitants are exclusively nomadic, whose only means of exchange is barter. Indeed, those who do at times acquire coins, offer them for sale, saying, 'Who will buy these dirhems from me', for they do not look upon them as a currency or a medium of exchange."

[63]

Account of the second realm,namely, the realm of Syria[333]

The capital is the city of Damascus. Syria used to be called the Land of Canaan, but these people were killed or expelled after the coming of the Israelites, in whose hands the country remained until <167> the Romans conquered them and took it away from them.

In *The Soul's Delight* al-Tīfāshī wrote:

> According to the Sharīf al-Idrīsī,[334] when discussing the boundaries of Syria, on the east it is bounded by the Jezira (Mesopotamia), which lies between Syria and Iraq, and is so called because it is between the two rivers of the Tigris and Euphrates. It is the "land hard by", mentioned in God's Book in the Chapter of the Greeks (al-Rūm).[335] Nineveh, the city of Jonah (peace be on him) is in the Jezira. The present day capital is Mosul, and there too are found Raqqa, Nisibis, Diyar Rabia and the Taghlib tribe. Jezira forms a zone separating Syria from Iraq, delimited by the two rivers, the Tigris and Euphrates.
>
> To the south, Syria's boundary is the Valley of the Villages, to the west Ascalon and the mountain barrier between the two seas, where the cities of Lot (peace be on him) are located. From north to south is a month's journey or thereabouts, and it lies partly in the fourth, and partly in the third, clime.

The direction of its Kiblah, in order to face the Spout[336] and the "Syrian" corner of the Kaaba, is towards the east. Most of the population are southern Arabs, though there are northerners (Maʿadd).

He continued:

The author of *The History of Syria*, al-Ḥāfiẓ Ibn ʿAsākir[337] Abū'l-Qāsim ʿAlī ibn al-Ḥasan, with his chain of authorities going back to al-Shaʿbī, related: "When Adam fell from Paradise, and his children spread throughout the world, his sons dated events from Adam's fall. That marked the era, until God sent Noah. Then events were recorded from the date of his Mission till the time of the Flood and the destruction of all on the face of the earth. After Noah, his offspring and all with him <168> in the Ark alighted on dry land, he divided the earth between his three sons. He assigned Shem the centre of the earth, where was the Sacred House, the Nile, Euphrates, Tigris, Ceyhan and the Oxus, that is all between Pishon and the River Nile and between the South Wind's portal and the North Wind's. Ham he gave that portion of the earth west of the Nile and beyond it to the Portal of the West Wind. Japheth's portion was in Pishon and beyond to the Portal of the East Wind. Then the children of Noah separated and left Babel to go forth in all directions and each group reached its own region."

According to Ibn ʿAsākir through another chain [of authorities], from Hishām ibn Muḥammad and his father:[338] "From amongst those who were assigned commands, that is the sons of Noah (peace be on him), the sons of Shem settled in Magdal, the navel of the earth, lying between Sātīdamā[339] and the sea and between Yemen and Syria. God gave them prophecy, scripture, beauty, dark and fair complexions. The sons of Ham settled where the South and West Winds blow, the area called Darum, and God gave them dark skins and little of the fair. He made their land fertile and lifted from them the burden of plague. In their land he placed the tamarisk, arak, calotrope, bay, laurel and palm. The sun and moon crossed their skies. The sons of Japheth, the Unbeliever, [settled] where the North and East Winds blow. They have reddish and <169> bright complexions. God emptied their land and the cold there became intense, and God emptied their skies, and thus none of the seven planets moves above them because they are directly below the Great Bear and the Little Bear, the Pole Star and the 'Two Calves'.[340] They are also sorely tried by plague."

Later ʿĀd came to Shihr and there they perished in a valley called Mughīth. ʿAbīl came to the site of Yathrib, and the Amalekites to Sanaa before it bore that name. Some subsequently moved to Yathrib and expelled the ʿAbīl. They settled where Jaḥfa is. A torrent came and swept them away,[341] and thus the place received its name. Thamud came and settled in Hijr and the vicinity, only to perish later.

In due course, Ṭasm and Judais migrated to the Yemama, which is in fact named after a woman of their kind. They too passed away. Amim moved into the Land of Abar, where they perished in time. That land is between the Yemama and Shihr, and today no-one may go there. The Jinn rule it. It derives its name from Abar ibn Amim. The Banu Yaqtan ibn ʿĀbir came to Yemen, which was called "Yemen" [South Land] when they turned right to go there. A tribe of the Banu Canaan ibn Ham migrated to Syria (*al-Shām*) [North Land], which received its name when they turned left towards it. Previously, Syria had been called the land of Canaan. Later the Israelites came, killed the inhabitants and expelled them from the land. So Syria belonged to the Jews, but they were invaded by the Romans, who slew them or dispersed them into Iraq, except for a few of them. Finally the Arabs came to conquer Syria.

Abū Bakr Muḥammad ibn al-Qāsim al-Anbārī[342] said: "There are two ways of looking at the name for Syria (*al-Shām*). It may either be derived from *al-yad al-shuʾma* meaning 'the left hand', or that could be an adjectival form from <170> *al-shuʾm* meaning 'evil omen'. One may derive verb forms from the following proper nouns, Nejd, Iraq, Amman, Syria (*al-Shām*), Misr and Kufa, meaning in each case 'to travel to . . . ' that particular place. In the Glorious Revelation is the phrase 'those of the left-hand' (*ashāb al-mashʾama*),[343] and 'a Shaʾāmī man' means 'a Syrian'. Yemen was so called because it is on the right hand of the Kaaba, and Syria was called al-Shām because it is on the left hand (*shimāl*) of the Kaaba. It is said that first of all the name for al-Shām was Sūriya."[344]

[64]

Account of Damascus and its foundation[345]

The following tradition is related on the authority of Kaʿb al-Aḥbar.[346] The first walls built on the face of the earth after the flood were those of Harran and Damascus, then Babylon. In another tradition it is said that when Noah alighted on the mountain top, he looked out and saw the mound of Harran between the two rivers of Jullab[347] and Daisan and went and built there the enceinte of Harran. Then he went off and built Damascus, before returning to build Babylon.

According to another tradition, Jairūn ibn Saʿd ibn ʿĀd ibn ʿAws settled at Damascus and built the city there, <171> and called it Jairūn, which is to be identified as Iram the Colonnaded[348], for there is no place that has so many stone columns as Damascus. Ibn ʿAsākir said: "I found in a certain book that Jairūn and Barīd were two brothers, the sons of Saʿd ibn Luqmān ibn ʿĀd. They are the two after whom Jairūn and the Barīd Gate in Damascus are named."

There is a tradition stemming from Wahb ibn Munabbih[349] that the servant of Abraham, the Friend of God (on him be peace), built Damascus. He was an Abyssinian, whom Nimrod, son of Canaan, had given to Abraham, when he walked out of the fire. The servant's name was Dimashq [Damascus] and he had full control of Abraham's wealth.

Ibn ʿAsākir told that he found in the work of Abū ʿUbaida ibn al-Muthannā, entitled *The Virtues of the Persians*,[350] that Paivarasp,[351] the Chaldean king, built the cities of Babylon, Tyre and Damascus. Ibn ʿAsākir said:

> I have heard from another source that when the Two-Horned One (Alexander) had returned from the east, having made the Wall between the people of Khurasan and God and Magog, he set out on his march to the west. Having come as far as Syria, he climbed the pass of Dummar and caught sight of the place where the city of Damascus now stands. The valley where the river of Damascus runs was a cedar forest. (It is claimed that the cedar that existed in the year 313 A.H. [925–6 A.D.] was a survivor of that forest.) As Alexander looked on it – and the water which <172> today is separated into various streams was then united in one bed – he took to thinking how he could build a city there. What he thought about and enthused about most was that he saw a mountain encircling the site and all the forest.
>
> He had a servant, called Dimashqus, in charge of all his realm. After descending from the Dummar pass, Alexander proceeded to the site of the village of Yilda, near Damascus, just three miles away. There he ordered a hole to be dug, which, when complete, he ordered to be filled in again with the earth that had been taken from it. When the earth was put back, it did not fill the hole. So he said to his servant, Dimashqus, "Leave this place, for I had intended to found a city here, but, now that I have had this demonstration, it is not a suitable place for a city." "Why?" he said. Alexander replied, "If a city is built here, then it will not grow enough food to support its inhabitants." Alexander marched on to Bathaniya and Hauran. He looked out over that broad expanse and gazed at the red earth there. He ordered some of the earth to be picked up, and when he held it in his hand, it pleased him greatly, for he was looking at earth that was just like saffron. He camped, and on his instructions a hole was dug and the earth put back again. It filled the hole with much earth to spare.[352] Then Alexander said to his servant, Dimashqus, "Return to the place where the cedars are. Cut down those trees and build a city on the bank of the river bed. Name it after yourself. That is a fine site for a city, and this place will sustain and provision it."

Ibn ʿAsākir added:

> The mark of the genuineness of this is that the population of the Ghuta (Oasis) of Damascus cannot produce sufficient food without having recourse to Bathaniya and Hauran. Dimashqus went back, built the city and gave it a fortress, <173> the inner city. He provided four gates, Jairūn, the Barīd Gate, the Iron Gate in the Cobblers' Market and Paradise Gate, the latter being the inner gate. When these gates were closed, the city was shut

> fast. Outside the gates was pasture ground. Having built the city and taken up residence, Dimashqus later died there, but before that, he had built on the site of the present Great Mosque a shrine where, until his death, he worshipped God.

It is told that the builder of Damascus built it with the seven planets in mind. Jupiter was in the ascendant at the foundation. The city was given seven gates, on each of which one of the seven planets was represented. The image of Saturn was on the Kaisān Gate. The images which were on all the gates have been destroyed, except for the Kaisān Gate, since Saturn shown there is extant to this day. On the authority of Abū ʾl-Qāsim Tammām ibn Muḥammad Ibn ʿAsākir wrote: "I read in an ancient book that the Kaisān Gate was devoted to Saturn, the East Gate to the Sun, Thomas' Gate to Venus, the Little Gate to Jupiter, Jābiya Gate to Mars, Paradise Gate to Mercury, and the other Paradise Gate, which was blocked up, to the Moon."

From Abū Mushir, Ibn ʿAsākir reported: "The ruler of Damascus built the citadel of Damascus, which is around the mosque within the city, according to the ground plan of the temple of the Sacred House (Jerusalem), and brought the doors of the Jerusalem temple and used them for the citadel's doors. The doors now at the citadel are those from the mosque of Jerusalem."

[65][353]

<174> The names of certain places in Syria

Ibn ʿAsākir quoted a tradition which goes back to the Prophet to the effect that Ishmael, the son of Abraham (peace be upon both), fathered twelve sons, one of whom was called Duma, and that Dumat al-Jandal was named after him.

There is another tradition that Lot had four sons and two daughters: Moab, Ammon, Jallan and Malkan, and Zughar and al-Rubba. These gave their names to ʿAmmān, the city of the Belqa, Moab, again in the Belqa, and the Spring of Zughar and al-Rubba.[354]

Al-Sharqī ibn al-Quṭāmī said: Sidon was called after Saidūn ibn Sadūqā ibn Kanʿān ibn Ḥām ibn Nūḥ (Noah), and Jericho (Arīḥa) after Arīḥa ibn Mālik ibn Arfakhshud ibn Sām (Shem) ibn Nūḥ, and Belqa after Ablaq ibn ʿAmmān ibn Lūṭ (Lot), who ruled and lived there.

It is said that Kiswa derives its name from the fact that it was there that Ghassan slew <175> envoys of the Byzantine Emperor who came to them demanding tribute. They killed them and took their clothes (*kiswa*).

Here ends the material I have taken from al-Tīfāshī.

[66]

Damascus is the place where Jesus (on Him be peace) will descend and it is the rallying point for Muslims on the Day of the Great Slaughter. It has been mentioned before that al-Khwārizmī[355] said, "I have visited the four paradises[356] of this world, and the Ghuta of Damascus is superior to all, just as they are superior to all else. It is like Paradise formed on the face of the earth."

Very numerous indeed are the descriptions of Damascus, but these are ones that I like. From Ibn ʿUnain:[357]

Damascus – I long for her intensely,
Despite constant calumny and importunate censure.

A land where the pebbles are pearls and its soil is
Perfume, and the breath of the north wind cool wine.

Her waters flow there unrestrained;
The breeze from the meadows is healthy, yet languid.

From ʿArqala:[358]

Between Saṭrā and Muqrā lies a paradise
Whose rivers flow broadly through myrtle and willow.

The wallflowers here lie strewn on the earth,
As though they are fashioned from pearl and coral.

<176> Birds chant in the branches at dawn.
This is the life – though it endures not.

After his exile from the city, Ibn ʿUnain also wrote:

Damascus, its two valleys and the sanctuary, are watered by
[Clouds] continuously thundering, but broken,

So that one sees the face of the meadows with a dark-brown cheek,
And the temples of the tall trees bright and glistening.

It brought back happy days I passed
Between the lava field of ʿĀliqain and ʿAshtarā.[359]

These are the haunts! – not the ravines of ʿĀlij,
Not the sands of Kāḥima nor the Valley of the Villages![360]

A land such that, when the East Wind passes through,
It wafts from its branches odiferous musk!

I left it unwillingly and abandoned it
Not through dislike, and journeyed not from choice.

From al-Buḥturī [361]:

Life is in the shade of Dārayyā when it is cool;
And our wine we shall mix[362] with the wine of Baradā.

When you wish, you may fill your eye with a city
So delightful and with sweet moments to match.

Damascus has revealed all her charms.
He who praised her has been true to his promises.

Clouds gather on her hills in groups at evening,[363]
And in the morning verdure is scattered over her countryside.

You see nothing but a green valley,
Or a juicy red ripeness or a trilling bird.

It's as though the summer heat, once come, had retreated,
Or the spring returned, having gone far away.

The wine there is celebrated throughout the world and known wherever the vine is grown for the nobility of its vintages. Its goblets unfurl red banners and light red coals on cheeks' surface. Some is <177> red like blazing fire, some tawny like gilded glass and some white like a droplet of a stream or silver. Rosy bottles overflow, their gleaming mouths smiling on the red-lipped cup-bearers.[364] Purity mingles there like a white cheek imbued with a redness, shining like a lamp in the blackness of the night. Its bouquet is a gift of fragrant apples for the guests. In the Shouf there is a wine which is clearer than glass and too delicate to mix. It is suspended above the water in the goblets, and its redness rises above it like twilight over the lamp of the heavens. Beams dart about it and the ear delights in the laughing music of its singers. Saydanāyā is the mine where its gold is found and the region of its bright star. Ibn ʿUnain alluded to that when he wrote:

And wine from Saydanāyā, whose wafted scent is
Amber and whose garment sandalwood;

Musky of fragrance, its origin is
Too noble for Babylon, too grand for Qutrubbul.

Al-Qāḍī al-Fāḍil has been the exception in writing critically of Damascus, when he remarked: "I entered Damascus quite distracted due to the change of weather and climate, the different buildings, changed people and the new scene. Who will bargain with me for Egypt for I would sell the Baradā for a drink from its water. The relics are impressive but useless.[365] Those excellencies we have heard of are elusive." He also wrote of the city after a snowfall: "Damascus' houses today are moulds for snow. It has begun to melt, so the streets are in need of boats."[366]

[67][367]

In Damascus are the counterparts of all the departments that are found in Egypt – though this is not so for the rest of Syria – such as four Chief Qadis for the four schools of law, a Judge of the Army, <178> a Treasury from which payments and robes of honour are issued, weapons stores, armouries and household departments comprising an abbreviated royal establishment, so that, if the Sultan were to arrive there with no baggage train, he would find there all the departments to sustain his royal estate. Every emir that is promoted there and in any other city in Syria, any official charged with any office, the holder of which is customarily given a robe of honour, or anyone who does a service connected with some matter of state or some other business, for which he deserves a robe or some gift of favour, but neither the one nor the other is issued from Egypt, will receive his robe or gift from Damascus. From there are also issued the banners of emirates, their standards and their ceremonial drums and other instruments (*ṭabl-khānah*).

In the Armouries are factories for mangonels, weapons and chain-mail. This material is carried all over Syria, and the whole area and the fortresses are kept well supplied. From the Damascus citadel soldiers and artificers are despatched to all the fortresses of Syria and sent on expeditions and state missions.

[68][368]

Damascus is a fine city. Its citadel[369] stands at ground level and is surrounded, both itself and the city, by high walls, which are in turn surrounded by a moat, the waters of which encircle the citadel. When the need calls, the water can be let into the whole moat that encompasses the city to complete the encirclement. The city lies in a level plain, raised above the river bed which descends from where the skirt of the mountain ends, and is exposed on all sides to the passage of the wind, except to the north, for it is screened there by Mount Qasyun. People find fault with it on this account. It is described as being unhealthy, and were it not for the mountain to the west, clothed <179> in snow summer and winter, it would be even worse off in that respect and its situation more hard to bear. The mountain is the antidote for that poison and the medicine for that complaint.

It is a well laid-out city with splendid buildings in stone and timber. Bricks are strengthened between their courses by resinous timber baulks. This timber is among the best in the world, and is called poplar. It is planted in the gardens there, nurtured and then cut down when fully grown, still producing resin. If any beam of this wood breaks, it remains fast and firm in position for several years or more, even though it may be hanging on by one fibre.

The city has broad suburbs on all four sides and is most firmly and securely dominated by water in all its parts, as we shall explain when we come to describe the river. The city is divided into quarters relative to the Great Mosque, not because it is thought of as the geographical centre of the city, for the distance from the mosque to the south and east ends of the city is further than the distance from the mosque to the city limit on the two other, north and west, sides. The most distinguished parts of this city are those near the mosque, in which are magnificent houses with gilded ceilings and marble pavings. Some have their walls clad in variegated marble panels framed by mother-of-pearl and gold and there are pools of running water. Water may flow through a house in several places. There are also high upper stories, broad courtyards, pleasantly arranged markets and strong warehouses. <180> The city possesses artisans skilled in every craft, masons, weapon-smiths, gold- and silversmiths, embroiderers and others. Exquisite products of all kinds are made and the local craftsmen pride themselves on their superiority over all the other craftsmen of this realm, except for the case of some few products that are made in Egypt.

Her fine products are supplied to Egypt, Syria, Iraq and Rūm (Anatolia), particularly bows, inlaid copperware, gilt glassware and lamb skins tanned with acacia, which are a bye-word.

Damascus is one of the world's four paradises. Al-Khwārizmī said, "I have seen the four paradises on earth and the Ghuta of Damascus is the best of them, just as they are together superior to all other places."[370] It is as though it is the heavenly Paradise on earth, as we have said. There are delightful gardens with bubbling streams, and tall shady trees with swaying branches, where birds sing, and in the pleasure gardens stand imposing buildings and lofty pavilions, and there are deep pools and lakes along which shady pergolas stretch with vaulted arbours fronting one another, and which are surrounded by plantations and groves, bordered with cypresses, tightly cloaked, and poplars, their frame so slender, and blossoms, sweetly scented, and fruits from Paradise, deliciously appetising, and wonders which are too celebrated to need description.

<181> At the foot of Mount Qasyun is Ṣāliḥiyya, a city extending along the base of the mountain, facing Damascus all along its length, with houses, gardens, madrasas, hospices, magnificent mausolea, imposing buildings, a hospital and magnificent markets abundant in cloth among other things. In the upper parts of the city along the skirt of the mountain are the public cemeteries. The whole of Ṣāliḥiyya overlooks Damascus, its Ghuta, all its gardens, its two mounts,[371] the hippodromes, the course of its river and the villages around it.[372]

The site of the famous monastery of Murrān[373] is now part of where the Muʿaẓẓamiyya Madrasa[374] stands over towards the Pass of Dummar.[375] There are some traces of it still extant.

[69][376]

The suburbs of Damascus

As we have said, there are magnificent suburbs on all sides of the city. The most magnificent are those to the west and north. On the western side they spread widely from beneath the Citadel and possess an extensive open space, the Horsemarket, on the bank of the river. Military equipment is brought there from the different parts of the city and sold on parade days. Where it comes close to the river, it ends in two prominent features, enclosing it [the river] to the south and north. Skirting each of these is a hippodrome, green with herbage. The river valley divides them. In the south hippodrome stands the Striped Palace,[377] which was built by al-Malik al-Ẓāhir Baibars al-Bunduqdārī <182> al-Ṣāliḥi.[378] The facade from ground level to the very top is in black and yellow stone in alternate courses, an unusual design but wonderfully well-built. One enters through a gatehouse on a bridge, which rides over the course of the river on an arch, into an outer hall, which looks out on to the south hippodrome. This hall was added by Āqūsh al-Afram during his vicegerency in Damascus.[379] Then one enters the palace proper through an extensive lobby which comprises princely chambers which arrest one's glance and borrow from the rays of the sun the bright lights in the coloured marble, upright or flat, on the paved floor or on the back walls and the high and low friezes, embellished with gold and lapis lazuli and gilt mosaics, and on panellings of marble up to the cornices of the ceilings. In the Great Palace are two facing halls; the windows of the eastern hall give on to the extensive Green Hippodrome[380] and those of the western on to the luxuriant river bank, where the stream is like molten silver. The palace has high loggias, which flirt with the clouds and look out on all four sides upon the whole city, the Ghuta[381] and the river valley. It offers the perfection of convenience with its princely chambers and royal stables, its bathhouse and complete facilities for all other purposes. Opposite the door of the palace is a gate that leads from the courtyard to the northern hippodrome.

On the two eminences mentioned above are some fine buildings, private residences, <183> belvederes, mosques, madrasas, hospices, Sufi convents, *zāwiya*s and baths, extending along both sides which run along the river. In recent years the Vicegerent has built on the southern rise a marvellous mosque and near to it an imposing mausoleum and a princely residence. Facing the mosque he has laid out a neat market and an outstanding bathhouse, which has made the area even more beautiful and remarkable.

The northern suburb is called ʿUqaiba and forms an independent city in its own right, with mosques, large and small, madrasas, hospices, Sufi convents and *zāwiya*s, splendid markets and baths. Many houses belonging to emirs and troopers are found there.

[70][382]

The river of Damascus

The river Baradā flows from two springs; the distant one is just before a village called al-Zabadānī and the nearer is a spring at a village called al-Fīja at the foot of Mount ʿAzzatā.[383] The water issues from a cleft at the bottom of the mountain slopes. A vaulted chamber of Roman construction has been raised over the source of the water. Along its course it is fed by other springs. Eventually the river divides into four, two to the right and two to the left, the latter two raised above the main stream in the bottom of the valley, which continues to subdivide regularly. Along the river on both sides are dense orchards until it passes a place called al-Rabwa (The Hill). There al-Malik al-ʿĀdil, the Martyr, Nūr al-Dīn[384] Maḥmūd ibn <184> Zankī (may God have mercy on him) built the shrine known as the Cradle of Jesus. It is said that Mary sought rest there with her child, Jesus (on Him be peace), and that this hill is the one referred to in God's Holy Word, "We gave them rest at a hill, peaceful and watered by a spring."[385]

The view of this valley is one of the most pleasing to be found, because of the intermingling of shade and waters, the constancy of sunshine and breeze, and because the two surrounding mountains carpet[386] the ground there with violets beneath the trees that incline over the branches of the willows, between which the cheeks of roses spread fragrance, the smiling mouths of jasmine are revealed and the lilies' tongues uncoil, and where the murmuring antiphon of stream and dove is heard and the steeds of the breezes meet, one winging from the north over the sprigs of wormwood and [the other] from the south over the aromatic orchards.

To the side of this valley, to the north of its southern portion, is a flat expanse along the margin of Mezza, like a section of bleak desert, where wormwood and citronella grow and the East and West winds sport. It is known for its healthy air and its wide-open space. It has a beneficial and salubrious effect on the immediate vicinity.

Let us return to our account of the river and name the seven courses, the main stream and the six subdivisions.[387] The main stream is the Baradā – this name is firmly attached to it and it is known by no other. <185> To the west of the line of the Baradā the highest, branching away to the south, is the Dārayyā river and then in order come the Mezza channel, the Qanawāt and the Bānās. Left of the Baradā, on the eastern side, the highest, branching northwards, is the River Yazīd and then comes the Thawra. The Qanawāt and the Bānās are the two city rivers; they dominate it and hold sway over the buildings there. The Banas enters the Citadel, then divides into two, one part for the Mosque and one for the Citadel. Then each of these two parts subdivides again into channels which branch off into "fingers" about the city according to fixed proportions and established rights. Likewise, the Qanawāt is distributed about the city, but it has no way into the Citadel or the Mosque. Its waters flow in underground pipes until they reach the beneficiaries, and after serving the wide range of uses, the waste water, the overflow from pools and the effluent from ablution places and conveniences pour into pipes and vaulted drains which are constructed beneath the drinking water conduits. The effluent is gathered into one stream and then leaves the city to irrigate the plantations.

The rest of the rivers, apart from the main stream of the Baradā, pass on into the orchards and plantations. Along them are fine residences and buildings, particularly the Thawra, for it is the Damascus Nile, on the banks of which are the most magnificent buildings and the inhabitants' promenades, to which they most frequently resort and wend their way. Seeing it, one would imagine it to be a green emerald, so dense are the shadows over it and so compact the tall trees on both sides. The Yazīd flows on the outskirts of <186> Ṣāliḥiyya and cuts through a part of its built-up area.

The main course of the Baradā has a separate channel alongside the city, which runs inside the city wall and provides the power for its mills. The out-flow of that channel then joins the main river and eventually passes beyond the built-up area and the series of mills erected along its banks to the conclusion of its course where it is encompassed by densely planted groves of quince and white poplars and orchards. Then it flows on beyond the villages of Damascus to irrigate the land where it holds sway, finally to flow into a lake there next to the desert.

These are the mother-streams, that is to say, the Baradā and those that are branches of it. However, each of these streams is further divided into others, great and small, and from these multiply further channels which are then distributed through the orchards and groves to irrigate the lands and to turn the mills, which can hardly be counted, so many are they.[388]

[71]

The Great Mosque of Damascus[389]

Its renown is world-wide. First it was a temple for star worshippers, then a Christian church, till Damascus fell at the hands of Abū ʿUbaida ibn al-Jarrāḥ and Khālid ibn al-Walīd (God be pleased with both).[390] The building was partitioned; the eastern half fell to the Muslims, while the western half remained in the hands of the Greeks until the caliphate of al-Walīd ibn ʿAbd al-Malik, who appropriated it and completed it as a Muslim mosque. It has been a house of worship from ancient times. In a previous passage we have spoken of it.[391]

[72][392]

<187> The districts of Damascus

They are twenty-eight in number, as follows:

- The district of the immediate environs, called the Hinterland Governorate, and consisting of the Ghuta, the Meadow (al-Marj), Jubbat ʿAsāl[393] and Iqlīm, all this forming one district.
- The Southern Coastal Lands and their dependencies, which is a way of expressing the territory of Gaza and its neighbours, both the plains and upland country. This amounts to nine districts: the particular area of Gaza provides three of them, the district of Gaza itself, that of Qartayyā and the district of Bait Jibrīl.
- The Coastal Plain has three, that is to say, the districts of Ramla, Lydda and Qāqūn.
- In the Uplands are three districts, those of Nablus, Jerusalem the Noble and the town of Khalīl [Hebron]. That is all in this region. The famous places are to be mentioned [each] in its place under its district, except for Nablus, which we will mention here, simply to say that it is a developed city, which is needed [by others] but which itself is self-sufficient.
- The Southern Region, namely, the Ḥaurān, the Ghawr (the Jordan Valley) and associated lands, forms ten districts, namely:
    - The district of Baisān. Baisān possesses a small castle of Frankish construction, and is the chief city of the Ghawr.
    - The district of Banyās, the chief city of the Golan, where is situated the castle of Subaiba.

- <188> The district of Shaʾrā.
- The district of Nawā, an ancient city, where is the tomb of Job (on him be peace).
- The district of Adhraʾat, that is, the city of Bathaniyya. Al-Balādhurī said: "When the Muslims conquered Bosra, the ruler of Adhraʾat came to them and the same terms were agreed as those that the population of Bosra had made, that Bathaniyya should be subject to a tax on the produce of its lands. Yazīd son of Abū Sufyān proceeded to occupy that area."[394]
- The district of ʿAjlūn, which comprises Ṣuwait. The castle of ʿAjlūn lies between the Jordan and the land of al-Sharāt.[395] The castle is a recent construction, small in size, though strong, situated on a hill overlooking the Jordan Depression, known as Jebel ʿAwf. It derives its name from some troublesome members of the Banī ʿAwf, who lived there. When al-Malik al-ʿĀdil Abū Bakr ibn Ayyūb assigned this mountain (as an *iqṭāʿ*) to ʿIzz al-Dīn Usāma, the latter built this castle[396] to protect his deputies from them after they had shown themselves refractory and stubborn. On its completion he spread a banquet to which the chiefs of the Bani ʿAwf came. He seized them and locked them up. Where it stands there used to be a monastery where lived a monk called ʿAjlūn, who thus gave the castle his name. On the site of Bāʿūtha there was also a monastery where there was a monk of that name. When the town was built it took its name from him.[397]
- The district of Balqa, which includes the town of al-Ṣalt.[398] Al-Balādhurī said: "To Balqa belongs the rural district of <189> al-Sharāt, in which is al-Ḥumaima. That is where ʿAlī ibn ʿAbd Allāh ibn al-ʿAbbās lived."[399] Also in Balqa are Moab and Amman. The former was conquered by Yazīd son of Abū Sufyān and the latter by Abū ʿUbaida (may God be pleased with him).[400] The citadel in al-Ṣalt was built by al-Malik al-Muʿaẓẓam ʿĪsā[401] ibn al-ʿĀdil, and the reason why he built it was that some serving women of his household passed that way and were attacked by some men known as the Banū Raḥmān, who lived in the village of Kafr Yahūdā. They insulted them and carried off a number of the women. So he built the citadel on the summit of a mountain known as the Emir's Head. The site had been dense scrub land.[402]
- The district of Sarkhad. The town is ancient, although its citadel is relatively modern. It was built a little before the Martyr Nūr al-Dīn Maḥmūd ibn Zankī (may God have mercy on him). At the close of the Ayyubid regime it was in the hands of the deputies of al-Ẓāhir ʿAlī ibn al-ʿAzīz.[403] The man who held it for him was Masʿūd ibn Qilīj, the Marshal. When the army of Hulegu[404] came after taking Damascus, they demolished the battlements, and then left it in his hands. Al-Malik al-Ẓāhir Baibars al-Bunduqdārī again fortified and embellished it. Ṣarkhad is the main town of upper Ḥaurān.
- The district of Bosra. Bosra is the main town of lower Ḥaurān, rather of the whole Ḥaurān, or even <190> the whole of this region. Al-Balādhurī

said: "Bosra, the chief city of the Ḥaurān, is on the edge of the desert. It is mentioned in the Traditions of the Prophet (God bless him and give him peace). Before his mission began he visited the city, as a merchant on behalf of Khadīja[405] bint Khuwailid al-Asadiyya (God be pleased with her), and there he met Baḥīrā, the monk, whose tomb survives there to this day."[406] Further from al-Balādhurī: "When Khālid ibn al-Walīd had arrived, the Muslims concentrated at Bosra and took it on terms. They remained a while in the Ḥaurān and completed its conquest."[407] Having mentioned Bosra, Ibn Jarīr [al-Ṭabarī] added: "In this rural district (*kawra*) is the citadel of Ṣarkhad, not an ancient foundation. It was held by a series of rulers."[408] It has been the practice of our age and of the recent past that it should be held by those dismissed from the rank of Sultan or an office almost as high.[409]

- The district of Zuraʿ.

This is the total of districts [for this region].

- The Northern Coastal and Upland Region consists of four districts:
  - The district of the Biqāʾ of al-ʿAzīziyya.
  - The district of the Biqāʾ of Baalbek.
  - The district of Beirut, a port on the coast, is encompassed by a wall of stone. <191> There is a hill where iron is mined and a forest of pine trees, twelve square "miles" in extent, which reaches to the Lebanon chain. The local water supply comes from wells and the city is the outlet for the overseas trade of Damascus.
  - The district of Sidon, a walled city, is named after one of the descendants of Canaan, son of Ham. Its local area is densely wooded and abounds in rivers. It comprises 600 or more village settlements. The people of the city drink from water brought to them by a conduit.

This is the total of this region's districts.

- The Northeastern Region, namely the territory of Homs, has four districts in all:
  - The district of Homs.
  - The district of Qāra.
  - The district of Salamiyya.
  - The district of Tadmor [Palmyra]: Tadmor is a Syrian-Iraqi city because it is in contact both with the land of Iraq and that of Syria. It is a fine city, built by Solomon, where there are magnificent gardens and prosperous trading-houses. The inhabitants are affluent. From here merchants travel the whole world.

This is the sum total of the Damascus "realm".

[73]

Baalbek[410]

Baalbek is a city built in ancient times to the north of Damascus. It is said that it was built by Solomon, the son of David (peace be upon them both). There is a large citadel there, which is on the same level as the surrounding ground, <192> like that of Damascus. Both the citadel and the city are encompassed by a strong, impregnable wall, massively built with large, heavy masonry cut from hard, resistant rock. There are three large pieces of finely dressed masonry beneath a tower and two salients, which survive whole and are of great length and breadth and of massive thickness, like huge blocks of fallen rock. Also in the citadel are large lofty columns, of very extensive circumference and outstanding height, and it contains princely remains of some magnificence and manifest beauty from the buildings of those Ayyubid princes who ruled there independently, such as, for example, the Palace of al-Amjad[411] and the Pool.

The city is an abbreviated version of Damascus in the perfection of its beauties, its excellent layout and construction and in the various charitable institutions flourishing there, such as the main Friday Mosque, the other mosques, the Hospital, the Hadith College, madrasas, hospices, Sufi convents and *zāwiya*s, and the neat markets which contain all sorts of items for sale, and in the way the water flows through the houses, streets and market places of this city. In Baalbek is produced an excellent butter in pots. It is highly prized and exported to many lands.[412] The city is ringed by a large and charming oasis (*ghūṭa*) where orchards of entwining trees yield fine fruits of many different sorts.

Outside Baalbek is a free-flowing spring, extensive in circumference, widely known as al-Zaina [the Fair One], the water of which is exceedingly pure. Amidst green pasture and charming orchards it is clothed in the splendour of beauty. A mosque stands nearby and alongside it there is a new Friday Mosque,[413] perfect in its <193> gilded finery and its amazing beauty. From it extends a river, which breaks over the pebbles in its course through the meadows like the blade of a sword being sharpened on a whet-stone, until, having entered the city, it is distributed through its houses and institutions. The stream is called Ra’s al-ʿAin [the Head of the Spring].

Baalbek also possesses another spring, further away than this first one. It is called the Spring of al-Lūjūj and is situated at the edge of the city’s distant orchards. The water is light and carminative. It is the only source of drinking water used by the great and the wealthy of Baalbek. A branch from it joins the north side of Baalbek and flows through it in a conduit there, and serves the citadel. It is an excellent and renowned supply of water.

Baalbek is a small, pleasant town, flourishing and prosperous, where prices are generally lower than in Damascus. Its luxury items are numerous. The *malban*-sweet is made there in different varieties, the likes of which are not often found, but in Damascus scarcely anyone can do without them.

In the Baalbek area is the famous Mount Lebanon, a blessed plot, the home of saints, pious men and wandering ascetics, where many take refuge who have dedicated themselves to the worship of Almighty God. It is the first step on the Sufis' Way and the pivot of the Saints' orbit. Those who know it will acknowledge this and those who are ignorant of it cannot deny it.

Despite Baalbek's beauties that we have recounted, al-Qāḍī al-Fāḍil criticised it in these words:

> My letter comes from a wretched little hole, no, an oubliette, called Baalbek, where I am encamped at a source whose roaring waters deafen me, high on mountains whose [snowy] bluffs blind my eyes, beneath a sky <194> that has unveiled a dubious early morning, facing a combat in which the master-of-ceremonies will pass around the cup of death, and with mangonel stones behind me. When the towers, like letters, see their diacritical points,[414] their lines are erased. God save me from what they describe.[415]

[74]

[Homs][416]

Homs is an ancient city that was formerly called Sūriyā. It was held in high repute by the Byzantine rulers as one of their seats of government and was always referred to honourably by them. It is situated in a plain lying alongside the river Orontes, which is to the north of it, and is built of small black masonry. It possesses a citadel which is not strong. A wall, stronger than the citadel and, in height, overtopping its towers, surrounds both it and the city. It has a water supply drawn from the Orontes, which flows to the residence of the Vicegerent and certain other places there. From the hinterland of Baalbek it receives various sorts of cloth.[417] The areas outside the town are better than those within, particularly in spring. The town's surroundings clothe themselves with the garments of springtime, bedecked with flowers as far as the eye can see, which delight one with the glances of the narcissus and the smiles of the daisy. At their centre is the lake of pure waters, abundantly productive, with fish brought there from the Euphrates to stock the lake, and waterfowl scattered along its margins.

Alongside the Friday Mosque in Homs is the Dome of Scorpions,[418] the like of which is nowhere else to be found. It is said that it is an ancient talisman, erected to keep scorpions away from the town. Thanks to it <195> not a single scorpion is found there. Any scorpion taken to Homs dies without fail. If anyone takes some earth from the ground at Homs, mixes it with water until it becomes mud and then sticks that mud lump to the inside of one of the walls of that dome, leaving it till it falls off by itself without anyone's knocking it, and then takes it and puts some of it in a room, no scorpions will ever enter there, or, if put in any of the household effects and furniture, no scorpion will come near. If some is sprinkled on a scorpion, it induces a sort of intoxication, or sometimes has a stronger affect, and kills it. This is something about the truth of which one does not need to enquire. People living in the furthest east or west are quite willing to credit this. Indeed, what is said is that this is not something peculiar to this dome but that it is a special property inherent in the Homs earth in general. No scorpion will come near a man's clothes or goods so long as he has on him some dust from its soil. A host of people have told me of this, and I have seen for myself and tested what property inheres in the mud that is stuck on the dome. This is something that al-Qāḍī al-Fāḍil alluded to when he wrote, announcing the tidings of the city's fall: "Mangonel scorpions crawled up to its walls, contrary to Homs' custom with scorpions; stone against stone was hurled and the hostility that is notorious between relatives was plain to see."[419]

Homs would follow Alexandria for its manufacture of fine fabrics of many different sorts and of excellent workmanship, were it not for the fabrics' lack of sheen and roughness of body.[420] Yet it fetches the highest prices, and even if Homs cannot overtake Alexandria in Egypt, it surpasses Sanʿāʾ in the Yemen.

[75]

[Hama][421]

Hama is an ancient city, lying in a red elongated valley with two <196> high prominences looking down on it, called the Horns of Hama. Imruʾl-Qais mentioned Hama, and Shaizar too, in his poetry, on the occasion of his passing by on the way to see the emperor. Hama is built on the banks of the Orontes very solidly in stone. It possesses a citadel of coloured stone, encircled by a wall, and princely mansions and palaces overlooking the river, with regal halls and private chambers, and mosques, madrasas, hospices, *zāwiya*s and markets, of which no variety nor any type, magnificent or humble, is wanting. Most of the lofty buildings and the extant charitable institutions derive from the overflowing bounties of the local Ayyubid regime. There are the large "noria" water-wheels erected along the Orontes, which turn on their own and raise water to the royal palaces, the residences of the emirs and the great, the gardens and plantations, in which are trees and groves of diverse kinds.

In Hama there is to this day the surviving line of the Ayyubid royal house. Were it not for them, this region would be devoid of any survivors of that line and exemplars of nobility, whom the learned wait upon with their compositions and the poets with their panegyrics, whom the Sufis and the wandering mendicants and the hosts of hopeful petitioners seek out, to whom the craftsmen offer as presents the products of their manifold subtle skill and to whom, before all, the merchants bring their marvellous curiosities. Their generosity surpasses hope and excels expectation, so that <197> everyone clings to Hama's rulers and seeks them out especially, in eagerness to benefit. They are more liberal than the spilling rain-cloud and more generous than the moist winds that blow.

To return to our account of Hama, it has not in the past had any great fame. Renown belonged rather to Homs, but later its fame grew with the Atabeg dynasty, and when the dynasty of al-Nāṣir Ṣalāḥ al-Dīn [Saladin] arose and Hama passed to the princes of the Ayyubids, they made the city into a metropolis with great buildings and sumptuous residences, by appointing emirs there and raising troops, and they enlarged the markets and added to its palaces and plantations. They attracted to the city all those craftsmen who excelled in their craft. All that its beauties possessed[422] continued to grow and increase, till now it has become perfect in its beauties and is considered a metropolis and one of the finest principalities. It has abundant fruits and copious blessings. Prices there are low and its character is princely, apart from the fact that it is torrid in the summer because the breezes are blocked and cannot blow through. In autumn there a change occurs which is attributed to unhealthy air. No snow survives there in storage until the summer, as it does in the rest of Syria, but it must be imported from neighbouring areas.

Around Hama are extensive meadows and broad open country where game birds are abundant and the hunting good. After Damascus, Syria has nothing to compare with Hama. No town, near or far, in its neighbourhood can approach it for its intrinsic charm.

Hama has no more than two [dependent] districts, the district of Bārīn and the district of al-Maʿarra.[423]

[76]

<198> Aleppo[424]

Aleppo is a great and ancient city, mother of provinces and territories, lowlands and uplands. In its area are most of the citadels, castles, forts and frontier posts of Syria. It is known as Aleppo the Grey, and itself has a wonderful, ideal citadel. It, I mean Aleppo, is situated in the middle of an extensive, red plain[425] and the citadel, which is on a high hill, was already great in the period of the Hamdanids[426] and raised them in eminence higher than the planet Saturn. Then came the Atabeg dynasty and it became yet more magnificent, took a belt and bracelets from the constellations of the heavens, and so it continued, always mentioned with respect and admiration. The population refused to grant that Damascus had any superiority over it, until Hulegu trampled it with his horses' hooves and beseiged it, while dispatching his detachments of cavalry and his infantry the length and breadth of Syria. Aleppo's walls were razed and the suburbs demolished. Those likely to gloat broke forth in lamentations and heedless triflers wept for the city. Yet, despite the trials that beset her and the vicissitudes that encompassed her, she remains a capital city and a sight to delight the eye, built in the yellow stone that has no rival anywhere. One might say that, [dressed] in this stone, she proudly paces in garments of brocade, picked out in the golden glow of evening.

In the city are great residences, the Friday Mosque, which has the superlatively high minaret, the hospital, mosques, madrasas, hospices, Sufi convents, institutions of perpetual charity and alms trusts. Into the middle of the city flows a branch of a water course, which divides throughout its houses and dwellings.

The water supply is exiguous and cannot slake the city's thirst nor satisfy its consumption. However, the city has <199> cisterns filled by rain water, spotlessly clean and providing cool water, which is the inhabitants' drinking supply. Ice is brought into the city from the hinterland, but the populace are not greatly interested in it because of the cool air and water they have, and the near balance of winter and summer climate. The River Fuwaiq is the old river of Aleppo and the Sājūr is the new one, which the present Sultan channelled into the city and which currently holds sway over it.[427]

Aleppo has the most extensive territory in Syria and the flattest areas for racing steeds to gallop over. It possesses broad meadows and a far-spread hinterland, both settled and nomad country, with encampments of Bedouin Arabs and Turks. Its army is sizeable and there are [auxiliary] groups from the Arab and Turcoman tribes.

It grows watermelons the likes of which are rare in Syria and various sorts of fruit, but most are brought from its lands bordering on Sīs and Rūm (Anatolia), the lands of Diyar Bakr and the desert of Iraq.

Counted amongst its districts are Wādī al-Bāb and Buzāʾa. This valley (*wādī*) is the famous one which the poet al-Manāzī[428] camped in and described as follows:

> A valley protected us from the heat of the parched ground,
> Itself protected by the luxuriance of its lofty foliage.
>
> We camped under its trees, which bent over us
> As mothers bend over the infant they wean.
>
> <200> We sipped cool water to quench our thirst,
> Sweeter than the wine of him who drinks with kings.
>
> Its pebbles startle the maiden all-adorned,
> Who feels for her neatly strung necklace!
>
> [The valley] repels the sun howsoever it confronts us;
> It bars the sun but admits the breeze.

[77]

The dependent area of Aleppo is a large one, containing castles and forts, and some places that have no castle. Altogether there are twenty-three districts,[429] namely:

- The district of Shaizar, the well-known town.
- The district of Shughr and Bakās, a castle.[430]
- The district of al-Qusair, also a castle.
- The district of Dairkūsh.
- The district of Ḥārim.
- The district of Antioch, the great and famous city.

- The district of Baghrāṣ, a strong castle on the frontier facing <201> the Armenians.
- The district of Darbsāk, a castle.
- The district of Ḥajar Shughlān, a castle.
- The district of Rāwandān, a castle.
- The district of ʿAintāb, a pleasant and splendid city.
- The district of the city of Behesnā, a fine city according to reports.
- The district of Karkar, a castle.
- The district of al-Kakhtā, a castle.
- The district of al-Bīra, a renowned and splendid castle.
- The district of Qalaʿat al-Muslimīn (The Castle of the Muslims),[431] a splendid castle.
- The district of Manbij.
- The district of al-Jabbūl.
- The district of Tīzīn.
- The district of ʿAzāz.
- The district of Sarmīn, including al-Fūʾa and Misrīn.
- The district of Kafarṭāb.
- The district of al-Bāb and Buzāʾa, mentioned above.[432]

[78]

Tripoli[433]

We have already remarked that it was built at the time of the conquest as a replacement for <202> ancient Tripoli. In former times it used to be called The House of Learning (*Dār al-ʿIlm*), and was ruled by a succession of princes of the Banū ʿAmmār,[434] who originally held the office of judge there. When this new city was built, it was an unhealthy spot and disliked as a place to live in. After it had been inhabited for some length of time and the population had increased along with the number of animals there, and the tainted waters which were surrounded by stagnant bogs had been drained away and gardens created there, where allotments and plantations of trees were laid out, the site became more tolerable and less disease-ridden.

Asandamur al-Kurjī (the Georgian)[435] was vicegerent there and he could never quite shake off a sickly lassitude. He complained to the honoured doctor, Amīn al-Dīn Sulaimān ibn Dāʾūd the Physician,[436] of the unhealthiness of the place and enquired of him whether there was anything that could alleviate this. The doctor advised him to increase the number of camels and other riding animals in the city. This he did and ordered the emirs and troops to do likewise. The situation improved and turned out as the doctor had suggested. I questioned many doctors about why this should have been so and [each one] said that he did not know.[437] Above every wise man there is One yet wiser![438]

<203> His Honour, Abū Bakr ibn Ghānim[439] (may God have mercy on him) said,

> The reason for the bodily ills that arise there is that, owing to its proximity to the sea, the city is torrid and hot. In those conditions during the first part of the night one cannot bear heavy coverings. So, if one sleeps with few bedclothes, the considerable cold towards the end of the night, coming from the neighbouring mountains, surprises one. The cold, following on heat, comes when the pores are opened and when the sleeper is unaware of the change, and so the inevitable happens.

There is a river which dominates the houses and apartment blocks. The water passes in at points high up on the buildings which can only be reached by tall stairs.[440] The city is encompassed by towering mountains, which have healthy air and light (soft?) water, and where trees, vines and meadows are found, and sheep and goats. Walnuts and bananas, sugar cane and dates all come together there. Sugar is manufactured too. Merchant convoys flock to it by sea and their ships stand at anchor there. It is a centre of agriculture and stock-raising. It is at present an extensive, teeming city with two hospitals, mosques, madrasas, *zāwiya*s, impressive walls and handsome, renowned baths. All the buildings are of stone and lime, whitewashed externally and internally. The city is surrounded by its belt of plantations (*ghūṭa*) and beyond that it is ringed by its fields, a marvellous sight and beautiful to behold when viewed from some commanding hill.

It is a principality with a standing army and Turcoman [auxiliaries] and, in particular, the local mountain folk have a skill in shooting the bow of heavy [draw-] weight with penetrating arrows.[441] <204> It contains forts and castles, and the well-known castles of the "Mission" (the *Ismāʿīlī daʿwa*) are situated close by. Their seat of power is Masyāf, and the castle of Qadmūs is one that belongs to them.[442]

There is a bathhouse at Qadmūs where all sorts of snakes emerge, so many that no-one can count them, and anyone sitting within washes himself while snakes pour out of the pipe along with the water, and as one prepares to leave the bathhouse one lifts ones clothes to put them on and snakes fall out in all directions. However, they are harmless. Not once have they ever been known to harm anyone.[443]

Near this castle is the castle of al-Khawābī. The writer, Badr al-Dīn Ḥasan al-Ghazzī told me that in its wall, that is the wall of al-Khawābī, is a particular place,[444] and if anyone is bitten by a viper or any other snake and is taken to see for himself that place in the wall of al-Khawābī, or if the person bitten is incapable and sends an "envoy" to represent him to that place, and if he duly goes there and sees it with *his* eyes before the death of the patient who has been bitten, the patient will survive and eventually be quite well again. This is a veritable marvel which is spoken of widely. I do not know whether this is due to a talisman there or to a peculiar property of that stone. Whichever is the case, this is something strange and remarkable and the most remarkable thing about it is the fact that <205> this is beneficial to the person bitten when seen by a substitute, if he does not see it for himself. Glory be to Him who holds the knowledge and to Whom all is attributable.[445]

Near the Castle of the Kurds [or Krak des Chevaliers], to the north west on the main highway is the Valley of the Gushing Spring (*al-Fawwār*). At that point it resembles a well raised above ground level. But below the well is a cistern, which extends to the north, where water gushes forth once a week and no more. Some land and fields are irrigated from it and the Turcomans camp there and water their animals. The rest of the time it is dry and produces no water at all. A rumble like thunder can be heard before it gushes forth. Behind the cistern is the building [of the Monastery of St. George]. Those who have entered the cistern say that at the end of it is a large river with a west to east underground course. It flows clear and there are waves and a strong wind. It is not known where it flows, nor where it comes from.[446]

At a stone's throw out in the Syrian sea at Tripoli by the Burj al-Jaṣṣāṣ is a spring of sweet water, which rises about a cubit or more above the surface of the water. When the sea is calm it is visible to all.[447]

[79]

[Safed][448]

Safed is a city on the slopes of a mountain, which enjoys a healthy climate and soft water. <206> The water is brought by pack-animals from the valley. There is a spring in the city, which, if it shed tears, would not moisten the corners of the eye, nor would the organs of weeping fill the pupils with them.[449] Mostly the inhabitants go to the baths in the valley there and the city baths are not thought satisfactory because of the shortage of water and their poor construction.

A standing force is stationed there, consisting of [local] troops and imported [mamluk soldiers].[450] Safed is two day's journey distant from Damascus and is subject to that city. Everything that is found in Damascus is found in Safed too, whether it comes from Safed and its own territory, or whether it is imported from Damascus. Safed is not far from Acre, and since the destruction of the latter city has remained the chief city of the littoral.

There is a castle there the like of which one seldom finds. It has, as it were, an overlay of evening gold. For love alone it longs for the clouds, only the twilight roams over it, a wine which sparkles where the starlight falls, and it remains close to earth only because, if it yearned for the sky, no bond would detain it.[451]

When al-Malik al-Ẓāhir Baibars conquered it,[452] its importance grew greatly, and indeed it deserves honour and merits its high position through the construction of its mighty building that God has raised there.

The secretary Ibn al-Wāsiṭī wrote of Safed: "The Castle of Safed was built by the Franks. Originally it was <207> an eminence on which was a flourishing village beneath the Orphan's Tower. The Templars built it in the year 495 A.H." [1101–2 A.D.] He added: "It is an impregnable castle on a hill surrounded by other hills and valleys."

It has eleven districts,[453] namely:

- The governorate of its hinterland.
- The governorate of Nazareth, the fountainhead of Christianity.

- The governorate of Tiberias, which contains the famous lake and the remarkable hot spring. Tiberias is at the foot of a mountain which overlooks the lake, the length of which is twelve "miles". People with "chilled temperaments" come to visit the hot spring to seek a cure. One can almost boil eggs and braize young goat in the spring. The water of the lake is sweet and it is the source of the Jordan river.[454] Qadas[455] is part of this district. Formerly the Sawād and Baisān also belonged but then they were detached.
- The governorate of Tibnīn [Toron], which includes Ḥūnain [Chateau Neuf]. These are both strong fortresses built by the Franks after the year 500 A.H. [1106–7 A.D.][456] They are in the area of Mount ʿĀmila[457] between Banyas and Tyre.
- <208> The governorate of ʿAthlīth.[458]
- The governorate of Acre.
- The governorate of Tyre; these last two are too famous to need description.
- The governorate of al-Shāghūr.
- The governorate of al-Iqlīm.
- The governorate of Shaqīf Arnūn [Beaufort]. On the bluff (*shaqīf*) itself is an impregnable castle, close to which is Shaqīf Tīrūn [Tyron], a fort, the main part of which is an inexpugnable cavern. The latter is not part of Safed.
- The governorate of Jīnīn.

These make up the districts of Safed. Places within the region of Safed that deserve mention are Haifa, a ruined town on the coast,[459] and the castle of Kawkab,[460] the castle which al-ʿImād al-Isfahānī[461] described as "anchored and firm, mighty and arrogant", and the castle of Ṭūr, isolated on the Mount of Ṭūr, which was built by al-ʿĀdil Abū Bakr ibn Aiyūb. Subsequently the Franks challenged him for possession of it, so he demolished it.[462]

[80]

Jerusalem[463]

The Holy Land comprises the city of <209> Jerusalem and the surrounding country up to the River Jordan (otherwise known as al-Sharīʿa) reaching longitudinally as far as Palestine (known as Ramla), and from the Syrian Sea [Mediterranean] to the cities of Lot latitudinally. This country is mostly mountains and river valleys except for the areas on its fringes.

The city of Jerusalem the Noble is situated on a high hill, a round city, in the centre of which is the wall encompassing the [Dome of the] Rock and the mosque now called the Aqsa. The Aqsa Mosque properly refers to everything enclosed by the above-mentioned wall, known as the Wall of Solomon.[464] The city is dominated from the east by a taller hill, which is separated from the city by the Valley of Gehenna and is known as al-Ṭūr [Mount of Olives]. There until this present day is a fine Roman building from which it is said that the Messiah (on Him be peace) ascended into heaven. In this valley is the Spring of Siloam,[465] which issues from a place on the hill on which Jerusalem is built, and flows into that hill for a distance greater, it has been estimated, than the height an arrow can reach, then issues from a cleft in the hillside into a small open space. Where it comes into the open on the hillside, it appears to be simply a running stream which originates at that cleft. Subsequently it flows on the surface and pours into the valley where it irrigates the vegetable plots. The water supply is meagre rather than plentiful.

The city of Jerusalem is built with stone and lime, and most of the stone is black.[466] The roads are very steep.[467] There were remains of an ancient ruined citadel, which was restored by the present Sultan in the year 710 A.H. [1310–1 A.D.] by the hand of Baktimur al-Jūkandār, when he was Protector of the Realm.[468] In fact, whether it exists or not makes no difference, since it is quite useless and cannot withstand a seige.

<210> Jerusalem possesses madrasas, a Sufi convent, hospices, zawiyas and mausolea. The Aqsa Mosque has many charitable trusts which currently maintain it in good order and support the muezzins, the staff that serve it and a number of learned scholars and Koran readers.

At the beginning of this book it has been said that Jerusalem is sacred for all the religions and a place of pilgrimage, for the Jews visit it and the Christians make their pilgrimage to the rubbish-heap.[469] The latter also visit the church of Bethlehem, the birthplace of Jesus (on Him be peace).

After the Frankish control of Jerusalem had been given up it fell prey to destruction and decay until this recent period when efforts were directed towards restoring places there and there was every incentive to do so. The present Vicegerent in Syria took abundant interest in this.[470] He constructed a conduit into the city which he linked to a pool, a source that could supply the city with water at times when water was short. The conduit flows into the city, enters the walled enclosure of the Aqsa Mosque and runs there. Alongside the Hospice of al-Manṣūr Qalāwūn the Vicegerent constructed a splendid madrasa,[471] which he donated as a trust to maintain a professor, canon lawyers and students of law according to the school of the Imām Abū Hanīfa (may God be pleased with him), and above it a Sufi convent, overlooking [the Ḥaram], and, as part of the complex, a school for orphans,[472] through which he acquired a full reward and the people at large a great boon (may God recompense him and accept his offering). He also built there two magnificent baths, of which the city was in very great need, because there were no acceptable ones there, and he erected bazaars and residential blocks,[473] so that Jerusalem became splendid to behold, its streets thronged again, and once more the flourishing city that it had been, after being rated less than <211> a village and passing through a lean period.

[81]

Hebron[474]

The city of the Friend of God (on Him be peace), where the fields of Abraham were, is an unwalled city about a half day's journey, at average speed, from

Jerusalem, closed in amongst mountains, not in any open plain nor yet in a valley. It is the chief settlement of a district; yet were it not the site associated with Abraham (on Him be peace), it would not be considered worthy of any special mention. The sanctity of that blessed sojourn has redounded to its credit. Its excellence has been recognised throughout the world and great cities have bid its people welcome.

Baktimur al-Jūkandār, before he became Protector of the Realm, brought water from a spring, situated at some distance, into the town.[475] I have seen the water flowing on a raised construction, reached by about twenty steps upwards.

Abraham is [buried] within a walled enclosure there. He lies within the wall but the precise site of his tomb is not accurately known. Within the wall there is the [underground] cavern of God's Friend, which bears his name <212> and where a lamp is kept lit. For this reason the common people refer to the Lord of the Cavern and the Lamp. This we have already alluded to in an earlier section.

[82][476]

[Kerak]

Kerak is a city with a citadel, known as Kerak of Shawbak, though Shawbak is an older settlement, while Kerak is a new foundation, for it was a monastery inhabited by monks, who became numerous, enlarged the monastery buildings and multiplied its "sons". Neighbouring Christians settled there under the aegis of the monks, markets sprang up, and by providing for the monastery they earned their living. The Franks then came and encircled the place with walls, and so it became a celebrated city. Later they built the fortress, a renowned citadel. The Franks held power there until it fell in the time of the Sultan al-Malik al-Nāṣir Ṣalāḥ al-Dīn Abū'l-Muẓaffar Yūsuf ibn Aiyūb (God Almighty have mercy upon him).[477] The fortress is on a site which it is difficult to scale, for its scorpion rocks do not yield to magic spells.[478] With its shoulders it has jostled Sirius in its passage, for it towers into the sky. The crescent moon threw the weight[479] of its rider, and has taken its seat amid this barren region on a high outcrop, which only the soaring eagle can reach and where the lamp of the dawn appears merely suspended from its battlements. This is why princes have adopted it as a refuge from what may befall them and as a storehouse for their treasures. For the sons of Sultans it has always been a place to retreat from politics and a haven from the blows of fate.[480]

Its water supply is provided by the rain, and it also has a valley where springs gush with water. It is a fertile spot and favoured, where crops grow and flocks graze freely.

Concerning it al-Qāḍī al-Fāḍil says:

> Kerak was an obstruction in our throats and a mote in <213> our eyes; it lurked above the highways and forced one to follow dubious tracks. It held our aspirations in a stranglehold and impeded the laying of our plans and the ways to achieve them. It became a debt to fate on that road and a pretext for anyone who neglected his duty to perform God's Pilgrimage. It dominated

Islam as a turban crowns the head. It stifled the Hijaz and allowed not a soul to come up from the Tihāma. Its valley stands at the confluence of the mountain fastnesses torrents and its shadow [falls] where the spears' star points rise. It and Shawbak (may God facilitate the conclusion)[481] are like the verse of the poet describing two lions:

No day passed without their having
Human flesh or a taste of blood.

To indicate that it is a site and centre of warfare for God,[482] a repository and seat of that duty, it is enough that it is in the vicinity of Tabuk, the raid on which was the last of the Prophet's raids.[483] The laudable steps of Muhammad came this far on the road thither. To act according to the last actions of our lawgiver and to take one's stand on that is a directive not hidden from sagacious minds. This citadel is encircled by a city, firmly enwrapped by the mountain.[484] No crow may find a foothold on the citadel's heights. The winding valley like a bracelet protectively surrounds the city's wrist and the brow of the beetling mountain guards its mass of people. Its shoulder is hard yet God will break it. Its mouth is suckled from the clouds' breast but the cradle of the mangonel shall wean it. They broke it down and behold, the town stands in ruins, no, is prostrate on its bier. The die[485] of its coins has been obliterated from the mints, so the people of error trade at ease there no more. Every altar in the church is now a stable, every tower-stair a precipice and every spot for a newborn head is in truth a place for a head to fall.

He also writes of it:

One of the conquests granted by God to our Sultan was Kerak. How can one grasp what it was – a citadel which was <214> for Islam such a hardship, or rather, for the Kaaba of Islam (may God increase its glory) such a torment.[486] Yet the favours of God are too numerous to be ever adequately described. God covered the night of Polytheism with the bright day of Islam, bidding it come quickly.[487] I do not doubt that alongside [the army's] archers the inhabitants of the Holy Sanctuary were archers employing the arrows of dawn prayers, who also fought, though in their life of devotion they did not march forth but were not absent from the campaign. "For all has God promised a goodly reward."[488]

[83]

[Shawbak][489]

Shawbak, which is attributed to Kerak by name, is a small city, sited further into the desert than Kerak and southwest of it. It possesses underground reservoirs formed from running streams, and throne-like towers raised on high, and fruits, as God Almighty said of Paradise, "never failing, never withheld".[490]

Shawbak was taken at the time that Kerak fell, after the latter had been beseiged for two years.[491] Al-Malik al-Nāṣir [Saladin] assigned both places to his brother, al-Malik al-ʿĀdil, who held them until he gave them over to his son, al-Malik al-Muʿaẓẓam ʿĪsā. The latter devoted his efforts to both, and left Kerak a self-sufficient city, to whose fortifications and beauties he added. He imported rare trees into Shawbak and left it a rival to Damascus for its handsome appearance and flowing waters, and superior in its pleasant air.

<215> Ibn Jarīr [al-Ṭabarī] mentioned the Region of the Mountains,[492] as follows "A new city has been created there, called Kerak." In his *Book of the Conquest of the Lands*, al-Balādhurī said that the main city of this region was al-ʿArandal.[493]

The districts of Kerak are four in number:

- Zughr, an ancient city, hot and adjoining the desert. Excellent indigo is found there.
- Maʿān, an ancient city, now in ruins, both itself and its district.
- Muʾta, which still survives and which is famous for the engagement fought there. It is the site of the tomb of Jaʿfār ibn Abī Ṭālib (on him be peace).[494]
- Shawbak, a new foundation, as has been mentioned.

[84]

<216>Gaza[495]

Gaza is a city between Cairo and Damascus, where Hāshim ibn ʿAbd Manāf is buried and where al-Shāfiʿī (God have mercy on him) was born.[496] It is a city most solidly built with stone and lime, situated on a rise about a mile from the Mediterranean coast. It has healthy air, carminative water, which aids the digestion but is not thought pleasant. The inhabitants take their drinking water from wells. There is also a reservoir to collect the rain, in which the winter rainfall is kept, but that [too] is considered unpleasant. Many fruits are grown there, the best being grapes and figs.

It possesses a hospital, built by this present Sultan (may God reward him), which was sorely needed by passing travellers at this spot. There are also madrasas and mausolea, which he has embellished.[497] It is indeed a noble vicegerency, one that has a detachment of regular troops, and Arab and Turcoman auxiliaries.

It has both land and sea outlets. To the south it is adjacent to the Wilderness of the Israelites, and is both a crop-raising and stock-rearing area, and a place where settled and nomadic populations meet. The permanent inhabitants are local tribesmen who are hostile to one another. Were it not for the respect inspired by the government, there would be a constant conflagration and no-one could close their eyes for a doze, for no-one could live there in safety nor settle there, neither outsider nor insider.

[85]

<217> One of the territories recently annexed to this realm is the Ceyhan region,[498] where the seat of the vicegerency is the city of Ayās, which is now a thriving, populous place. The new additions also include Kāwarra and Isfandakar, and half of Maṣīṣa, for what passed into Muslim hands includes all the territory up to this Syrian side of the river Ceyhan, and also half of Adana, while the other half, beyond the Ceyhan on the Armenians' side, is theirs.

The areas that the Muslims destroyed while they remained under Armenian control are Hārūniyya, Ḥumaimiṣ, Tell Ḥamdūn and al-Nuqayyir. All these are situated east of the Ceyhan towards the north. Other new possessions are Qalaʿat Jaʾbār east of the Euphrates, and the fortress of Daranda, which is beyond Behesna towards Rūm.[499]

This is the full tally of our realm.

[86]

A valuable excursus concerning Gaza

Authorities have said: It is possible that the name [Ghazza] is derived from *ghuzz*, meaning "jawbone", which name it acquired because it stands at the mouth of Syria next to the seaside, or that it is derived from the Bedouin expression *aghazzat al-baqara*, when the cow (*al-baqara*) is *mughizz*, that is, when it has a difficult pregnancy. Gaza was named accordingly, as men and animals find difficulty in getting there because of the sand that surrounds it. In the past it was known as Gaza of Hāshim, named after Hāshim ibn ʿAbd Manāf, the ancestor of the Prophet (may God give him blessing and peace). The Quraish caravans used to travel there, one of the two journeys mentioned in the Koran,[500] the winter and summer journeys, this being <218> the summer one. There was a strong fort guarding the town, of which traces survive to this day. The Qais [tribe] destroyed the fort when certain Yemeni tribes came there. In his ode called the *Dhāhiba*, which contains 300 verses of satire against the Yemeni tribes and rehearses all their shortcomings, culled from the Koran and Tradition, while recalling the virtues of Quraish, Abū ʿĀmir al-Sulamī[501] says:

> For we are those that set fire to Harūrā
> And we are the destroyers of the fortress of Gaza.

Gaza is the site of the tomb of Hāshim ibn ʿAbd Manāf, and that is why it is referred to as Gaza of Hāshim. Hāshim was the first of the sons of ʿAbd Manāf to die. They were four brothers: Hāshim, whom we have mentioned, buried at Gaza; the next to die, ʿAbd Shams, was buried in Mecca on al-Ḥajūn;[502] then Nawfal, who died on the way to Iraq at a place called Salmān, where his tomb is found; and al-Muṭṭalib, who died in the Yemen at a place called Radmān, where his tomb is found. These are the four sons of ʿAbd Manāf.

[87]

Supplement

Concerning the cause of their journeys that brought about the deaths of those who died abroad

There is in fact general agreement that ʿAbd Manāf had five sons, the leaders of all Quraish, namely, Hāshim, al-Muṭṭalib, Nawfal, ʿAbd Shams and Abū ʿAmr.[503] Hāshim and al-Muṭṭalib were known as "the two full moons",[504] and Nawfal and ʿAbd Shams as "the two radiant ones"; Abū ʿAmr died as a young boy, and nothing is recorded of him in connection with his brothers.

The whole of Quraish and the Arabs at large used to call these four sons of ʿAbd Manāf "the vessels of finest wood"[505] because of their nobility, their beauty and their splendour. <219> Now the Quraish were great traders, yet they used not to leave Mecca or the Hijaz. Foreigners would come to them with merchandise, and then they would trade. This was their practice for a long time, until Hāshim ibn ʿAbd Manāf rode out to Syria and visited Caesar, the Emperor of the Byzantines. At this time Hāshim's name was ʿAmr al-Muʿallā. Each day he would slaughter a sheep, make a large dish of sops (*tharīd*), and place the meat on it in joints. He would then invite those around him to eat with him. Hāshim was a very handsome man and of a most noble and generous disposition. The report came to Caesar that here was a man of Quraish who crumbled bread [Arabic verb: *hashama*], poured gravy over it and placed the meat on top. The foreign custom was to put gravy in bowls, add the meat to the gravy and dip their bread in that. They had not seen sops before and so, because he crumbled bread to make the sop, he was called Hāshim. In the words of their local poet at Mecca:

> ʿAmr al-Muʿallā crumbled gravy sops for his tribe,
> When the men of Mecca suffered drought and were thin.[506]

He was the first man, Arab or non-Arab, to do this. Caesar summoned him to his presence and, after seeing him and speaking with him, was greatly pleased with him. Hāshim said, "O Prince, my people are *the* merchants of the Arabs. If you think it fit to issue me with a document in which you guarantee them the safety of their persons, their money and goods etc., they will bring you spices and dates from the Hijaz which you consider rare, and other things which they acquire but which do not reach you from beyond your frontiers." <220> The Emperor ordered the drawing up of a comprehensive document for the Arabs, which Hāshim received, and then departed. From the chiefs of every Arab tribe he came to on the route to Syria, he took a compact (*īlāf*), an agreement for the security of Quraish merchants when staying with them or when in their territory, security for their persons and their possessions. Hāshim took this compact from all the tribes that lay on his route from Syria to his destination at Mecca. He brought home something the like of which no one else had ever brought them, and they rejoiced greatly. They set out with a great trading caravan. Hāshim went with them to look after them, act as guide and introduce them to the Bedouin chiefs all along their route, and in due course brought them to Syria and to camp at Gaza. During that journey Hāshim died and was buried at Gaza.

Subsequently, his brother, al-Muṭṭalib travelled to Yemen, and did what Hāshim had done in Syria and secured a written agreement from the rulers of Yemen for any of Quraish who might journey to their country. Then he set out to obtain compacts from any Bedouin on his route back to Mecca, just as Hāshim had done. Al-Muṭṭalib was the oldest of ʿAbd Manāf's sons, and he was known as "the Well-head" on account of his generosity. He died at Radmān in the Yemen during one of his travels.

ʿAbd Shams ibn ʿAbd Manāf journeyed to the Abyssinian king and obtained from him a document and an agreement for any of Quraish who went there, and on his return secured compacts from all the Bedouin tribes he encountered between Abyssinia and his final destination at Mecca, as Hāshim and al-Muṭṭalib had done. He died at Mecca, and his tomb is at al-Ḥājūn. He was older than Hāshim.

Nawfal, the youngest of the brothers, travelled to Iraq, and obtained an agreement from Chosroes and then arranged compacts on his return route to Mecca. He set out for Iraq again to trade, but died on the way there at Salmān.[507]

[88]

Explanatory note

There is some dispute about the aforementioned verse. The most correct tradition holds that <221> it is by Ibn al-Zibaʿra.[508] From lexicography we learn that *zibaʿra* means "a shaggy camel with very hairy ears and head, which is also short and thick-set". The verse is from an ode of his on Hāshim and his brothers, composed with the fault in the rhyme called *al-iqwāʾ* in the last verse.[509] The ode goes as follows:

> O man that changes [so frequently] his abode,
> Why have you not visited the clan of ʿAbd Manāf?
>
> May your mother be bereaved! If you would pass by their abode,
> They would protect you from hunger and misalliance.
>
> They are those that feed [the hungry] when the winds howl,
> And travel far for the "compact" journeys.
>
> They are those who secure agreement from their distant climes,
> And tear [meat] in pieces at the arrival of guests.
>
> ʿAmr al-Muʿallā crumbled gravy sops for his tribe,
> When the men of Mecca suffered drought and were thin.

[89][510]

This concluding section on Ramla has been suggested at this point by the closeness of that town to Gaza. It is said that the person who first founded Ramla was

Sulaimān[511] ibn ʿAbd al-Malik ibn Marwān, and that, before it was built, the chief city of Palestine was Lydda, where, as a youngster, Sulaimān ruled on behalf of his father. While Sulaimān held titular authority, he was accompanied by someone appointed by his father to direct and advise him.

Next to the church at Lydda was an orchard, a well-looked-after, pleasant spot where fruits abounded. Sulaimān frequently expressed his admiration for it and would sit there, enjoying its delights. One day he said to the elder, who was his adviser, named Rajāʾ ibn Ḥayāt, "I want you to buy this orchard for me so that I can build buildings here that are fit for the likes of us."[512] The orchard belonged to the priest, the encumbent of the church. Having summoned him, Rajāʾ told him the situation, and the priest said, "I hear and obey. <222> Take me before the judge and the notaries that I may certify my agreement and finish the matter straightaway." When he had summoned them, the priest came before them and said to them all, "You know, do you not, that this orchard is mine, that I possess and hold it without hindrance or dispute?" The judge and the notaries replied affirmatively, intending thereby to authenticate his ownership so that the sale might be valid. But he went on, "Bear witness now that I endow the church with it, finally and categorically, irrevocably and unconditionally, till God inherits the earth and all thereupon." All were astounded and [the success of] his trick was complete. All present were outraged, and Sulaimān would have killed him, but Rajāʾ restrained him, soothed and diverted him. "Come, let us go on a trip", he said, "and devise something that will be the ruin of this church and others." So off they rode, and Sulaimān ordered that none should follow them. When they were clear of Lydda, they saw a tent of goat hair pitched on a hillock, which is now the site of the oratory. It was very hot, so Rajāʾ said to Sulaimān, "Let us turn aside to this tent to see who is there and to rest there until the cooler part of the day." They drew near the tent, greeted those within, though as yet they could see none. Then a woman came out to them, wearing a veil, who returned their greeting in the sweetest accents and manner. She asked them to alight there with eloquent words and genuine purpose. This they did, and then she bade them to make themselves more comfortable and take their ease. Her reception delighted them, and Sulaimān forgot the affair of the orchard in admiration of her generosity and good sense. They asked her name, and she replied, "Ramla", and told them that she had a husband who was with the herds of Lydda. She offered them food and milk, saying, "I have sweet and sour milk, and hot and cold bread, because my preferences are different from those of my husband in the matter of food. I prepare for him what he prefers, and I prepare for myself what I desire." She offered them something of all that and made a dish of sops for them. They, meanwhile, were quite carried away by her beauty and charm, <223> her manners and admirable conduct in all she set her hand to. She entreated them to eat, saying, "Were it right for me to eat with you, I would do so. Food calls to itself those that are noble." So they ate, and observed the trees and the fields and other things besides around about the tent, and both approved the site and its position overlooking the surrounding cultivation. Rajāʾ said to Sulaimān, "If you were to order the building of a monastery here for the Christians and a mosque for the Muslims, and if you were to order it to be publicly proclaimed that any Muslim or Christian who wishes to be in a protected area (*ḥimā*) should build a house next to his mosque or his monastery, a city would grow up and the church [at Lydda] would be made otiose by the monastery. This place is more beautiful than the site of Lydda and superior to it." Sulaimān carried out that plan, and people, Muslims and Christians, hastened from all directions to mark out their houses and fine mansions according to their aspirations and means. Sulaimān planned a small mosque and a modest administrative building, but Rajā' said, "Alter this, for it will be a large city." So he planned a large mosque and an extensive residence, that is to say, the present mosque and the present residence known as Government House.

Sulaimān next intended to demolish the church and take its marble and columns for the mosque, but Rajā' dissuaded him from that and wrote to ʿAbd al-Malik, telling him of the treacherous and cunning action of the priest, and of what they both had done, the building of the city and the mosque. ʿAbd al-Malik wrote to the Greek Emperor – for at that time Islam was dominant over the Greeks – and the Emperor sent ʿAbd al-Malik someone to show him a place from which he obtained columns the like of which for well-proportioned beauty had never been seen. Along with them he extracted marble, both cut and uncut, sufficient for the mosque and with some to spare. It is said that this was in a village of Darum, Darum of Gaza, called ʿĀmūda. The most that the Christians suffered from this was that the Emperor obliged them to transport the columns and the marble from ʿĀmūda to the mosque. The city was called <224> al-Ramla, after the woman mentioned above, whom Sulaimān rewarded handsomely, as he did her husband.[513]

Notes

1 Ibn al-Dawādārī, ix, p. 128.
2 Ibn al-Dawādārī, ix, pp. 185–6.
3 The term "emir" (Arabic: *amīr*) denotes a member of the officer class of the military. Rank is differentiated by reference to the number of troopers an emir is obliged to maintain.
4 For a useful summary of the family fortunes, see Ibn al-Furāt, ix, pp. 391–2; *Khiṭaṭ*, ii, pp. 56–9; Hartmann, pp. 1ff.
5 Al-Yūsufī, p. 131.
6 Al-Ṣafadī, viii, pp. 252–70. See also Brockelmann, ii, p. 141, *Supplément*, ii, p. 176.
7 See de Goeje, v, p. 161: Cod. 670 Warn., 146ff, dated 956/1549. Perhaps al-Ṣafadī, viii, p. 257/16–p. 265, gives an idea of the content.
8 Brockelmann, *Supplément*, ii, p. 176, states that the manuscript at Leipzig identified as this work is wrongly attributed.
9 Al-Ṣafadī, viii, pp. 265–6.
10 *Ṣubḥ*, ix, p. 320, where a long investiture document for the Caliph al-Ḥākim Aḥmad written by al-ʿUmarī, possibly only as an exercise, is given, quoted from "the collection of his writings" which al-Qalqashandī had seen under this title.
11 Ṣafadī gives this title, but others have *Fawāṣil al-samar*, which would be *The Divisions of Conversation* etc.
12 This part of the book has been translated and studied by Hartmann, pp. 1ff.
13 *Masālik* (facsimile).
14 Al-Ṣafadī, viii, p. 255.
15 The term *ustādār* (major-domo) could apply to various levels of administrative personnel. Here it signifies one of the most important officials of the Mamluk state with responsibilities for taxation and the sultan's household.
16 A *madrasa* was the principally Sunni institution founded by rulers and other magnates for the higher study of theology and other religious subjects, in which the teaching staff and the students were maintained by endowments (*waqf*).
17 A complete edition has been produced by Kamāl Salmān al-Jubūrī and Mahdī al-Najm, (Beirut, Dār al-Kutub al-ʿIlmiyya, 2010) but was not available for the preparation of this translation.
18 See Blachère.
19 *Waṣf Ifrīqiyya*, p. 33.
20 *Masālik*, p. 172.
21 See *Masālik* (*Qabāʾil*), pp. 56–7.
22 See Meisami & Starkey, ii, p. 772.
23 The term *iqṭāʿ* denotes the "assignment" of government revenue from agricultural sources or from taxation in cash, most typically for the maintenance of the military but, on occasions, for civilian personnel. Someone so beneficed is a *muqtaʿ*. For the grades of emir and the value of their *iqṭāʿ*s, see Section 18 of the text.

24 A few lines are quoted in *Ḥusn*, ii, p. 196/21–3. Cf. Sections 38 and 47.

25 I.e. the sanctuaries at Mecca and Medina and the Aqsa Mosque at Jerusalem. For the tradition of the Prophet which is quoted in the text, see Kister.

26 Probably the Jabal al-Ṭūr in Sinai is intended, the mountain where Moses spoke with God (see *EI*, 1st ed., iv, s.v. al-Ṭūr).

27 For a twelfth-century man's puzzlement about this biblical tradition (Genesis, 2:10–14) and the difficulty of reconciling it with what he knew of geography, see Fulcher of Chartres, pp. 216–17.

28 Cf. *Khiṭaṭ*, i, p. 233; *Ṣubḥ*, iii, pp. 286–7, 309; al-Nuwairī, i, p. 356; Ibn Ẓahīra, p. 133; *Ḥusn*, ii, p. 194/6–7, p. 196/23–4. See also Section 42.

29 See Quatremère, "Memoire". The so-called Cleopatra's emerald mines were "probably the original and only source of beryl in classical times" (Lucas, p. 389). These mines are situated in the Jebel Sikait and Jebel Zubara area, in the mountains close to the Red Sea, north-east of Aswān. See also Floyer; Webster, p. 84.

30 I.e. *al-ʿadl*, meaning "one whose witness is acceptable".

31 Cf. *Khiṭaṭ*, i, pp. 194–7; *Ṣubḥ*, v, pp. 273–4; Paul.

32 A description of the Jebel Sikait workings (MacAlister) writes of them as "a network of long and tortuous passages just large enough to allow of the body being dragged through", and adds that "there is a fine galt, or reservoir, in a small tributary from Wadi Nugrus, near the ruins. It is five hours distant from Jebel Sikait . . . and contains enough water to last a party of twenty for the season."

33 Lit. camphor talc, i.e. talcose schist (?).

34 Lit. silver talc, i.e. muscovite schist (?).

35 See also *Ṣubḥ*, ii, pp. 103–4, where this section is further quoted, and the emeralds are said to be of three sorts (although four are in fact given); in order of superiority they are *dhubābī* (fly-green, "like the large flies in spring"), *raiḥānī* (verdant), *salqī* (chard colour) and *ṣābūnī* (soap-green).

36 Seton-Kerr, p. 97: "I found the Egyptians made splendid labourers and intrepid miners. I searched them in the middle of the desert and on my way back, but found no gems, as Caillaud did, concealed upon the persons of his Albanians. Yet the day after I quitted Aswān, as I was informed by some tourists, emeralds were offered for sale in the bazaar."

37 For passages on the balsam plant and the oil it produces, see *Khiṭaṭ*, i, p. 240/24ff; *Ṣubḥ*, iii, p. 287; *Ḥusn*, ii, pp. 193, 195; Ibn Ẓahīra, p. 133; ʿAbd al-Laṭīf al-Baghdādī, pp. 41–5. Cf. Section 42.

38 In general for each term consult Hinz; Balog. This section has been translated into French by Gaudefroy-Demombynes, p. 137.

39 The *dinār jaishī*, "army dinar", was an accounting unit used to calculate the value (*ʿibra*) of an *iqṭāʿ*. It was made up of payments in cash and kind. See Rabie, pp. 47–9.

40 For Egypt see *Ṣubḥ*, iii, pp. 442–4 (coinage), p. 445 (weights and measures: note that in this account the ardebb in the countryside can reach 11 *waiba*s); *Ḥusn*, ii, p. 191.

41 For Syria, see *Ṣubḥ*, iv, pp. 180–1 (for Damascus), pp. 215–6 (Aleppo: 1 rotl = 12 okes = 720 dirhems, compared with 600 in Damascus), pp. 236–7 (Hama).

42 Almost the whole of this section is given practically word for word in *Ḥusn*, ii, p. 196/ult.–p. 197/9. See also *Ṣubḥ*, iii, pp. 311–12; ʿAbd al-Laṭīf al-Baghdādī, pp. 47–79. For various prose and poetry extracts dealing with the flora of Egypt, see *Ḥusn*, ii, pp. 236–62.

43 For the Manha Canal, otherwise know as the "sea" of Joseph, see *Ṣubḥ*, iii, pp. 301–2; *Khiṭaṭ*, i, pp. 71, 247. For other references to the Canal and the Fayyum, see Maspero & Wiet, pp. 83, 142–3.

44 Two sorts of cucumber are mentioned: *khiyār*, "cucumis sativus" and *qiththāʾ*, "cucumis fluxuosus".

45 Quoted almost word for word in *Ḥusn*, ii, p. 197/9–12. In general, for the fauna of Egypt, see *Ṣubḥ*, iii, p. 314; ʿAbd al-Laṭīf al-Baghdādī, pp. 91–107.

46 Cf. *Ḥusn*, ii, p. 197/12–19 (some variation); *Ṣubḥ*, iii, p. 447/15–ult.

47 An extremely detailed description of the "battery-hen" techniques employed in Egypt is given in ʿAbd al-Laṭīf al-Baghdādī, pp. 79–89; see also *Khiṭaṭ*, i, p. 26. A "battery-hen" establishment formed part of the endowment of Sultan Ḥasan's Mosque-Madrasa (from a copy of the *waqf* document, courtesy of Mrs Shehira Mehrez). In June 1481 Rabbi Meshullam of Volterra saw the method in operation in Alexandria. One or two thousand eggs at a time were put in "ovens" and live chicks were produced within three weeks (see Adler, ed., p. 160).

48 Only the first sentence is quoted in *Ḥusn*, ii, p. 197/19–20, and there is a brief allusion to this passage in *Khiṭaṭ*, i, p. 163/13–15.

49 This is an adjectival form from Māḥūr, a village in Syria, according to al-Samʿānī, xii, pp. 7–8. Both editions of our text have "al-Mākhūrī". Note, however, the merchant who came to Cairo from Damascus, mentioned under the year 818/1415–6, whose nisba was al-Māḥūzī (*Sulūk*, iv, p. 323). Al-Idrīsī (p. 3) mentions a Māḥūz Jubail on the coast between Jubail and Juniya.

50 *Sharb* refers to an exceptionally fine linen, which is said by Marzouk, *History*, pp. 58–9) to have appeared from the Fatimid period on, perhaps in imitation of Byzantine *siklaton*, for which see *Khiṭaṭ*, i, p. 400/9ff. The type *mumarrash* is not identified. The basic meaning of the root is "to scratch"; perhaps the appearance of the texture is intended in some way. Possibly the same root appears in a list of stuffs from a winter clothing allowance of an official, given in *Khiṭaṭ*, i, p. 400/10: *shaqqa* [*ṭ.l.y m.r.sh*].

51 For this sense of *istaʿmala*, see Cahen, p. 166, note 2. One supposes that Jamāl al-Dīn was a rich merchant who operated in the lands of the Ilkhān. Official gifts of Alexandrian fabrics from the Dār al-Ṭirāz were sent to foreign rulers (see *Ṣubḥ*, xi, p. 426).

52 The last Ilkhānid ruler, Abū Saʿīd, died in Rabīʿ II 736/Nov.–Dec. 1335.

53 What does one make of the report in *Sulūk*, ii, p. 435, that in 738/1337–8 al-Nashū effected a forced sale of a thousand lengths of *sharb* linen, each for 300 dirhems (type?), when the market price at the time was between 150 and 160 dirhems?

54 The Egyptian textile industry and the institution of the Dār al-Ṭirāz may be studied in: Marzouk, *History*; Marzouk, "Tiraz"; Serjeant; Cahen, pp. 165–8.

55 Cf. *Ḥusn*, ii, p. 197, which erroneously reads *wa-mabānīhā biʾl-ḥajar* "its buildings are of stone", lacking the phrase "only a few". See Gil, pp. 158–9 (bricks); pp. 167–8 (*jarīd*). The term *naqiyy* is frequently found in property deeds from Egypt, see Richards, "Karaite Community", p. 118; Richards, "Sinai", appendices pp. 287–93, *passim*. *Ṣanawbar* is "pine" in the widest sense. Perhaps it could be translated by the broad term "redwood".

56 The terminology of religious institutions was imprecise. Generally one may understand that a *zāwiya* denoted an establishment for Sufi study and devotion or an area set aside within another building, in which studies also of a legal nature could be carried on. See Little.

57 This section with some abbreviation (and requiring some correction) occurs in *Ḥusn*, ii, pp. 197–8; cf. *Ṣubḥ*, iii, pp. 370, 374–5.

58 For the general history of Cairo, see *EI*, 2nd ed., iv, s.v. al-Ḳāhira.

59 *EI*, 2nd ed., s.v. the commander of the Muslim army that conquered Egypt c. 641 A.D.

60 *EI*, 2nd ed., s.v. Djawhar al-Ṣiḳillī (the conqueror of Egypt for the Fatimids).

61 *EI,* 2nd ed., s.v. al-Muʿizz li-Dīn Allāh: the first Fatimid Caliph in Egypt (358–65/969–75).

62 See further in Section 49.

63 *EI*, 2nd ed., s.v. Ḳarāḳūsh (Bahāʾ al-Dīn). A leading emir of the early Ayyubid period, he died in 597/1201. For the wall, see Cresswell, ii, pp. 190–212; *Khiṭaṭ*, i, pp. 377–80.

64 ʿAbd al-Raḥīm al-Baisānī (526–96/1132–1200), the celebrated minister of Saladin and renowned prose stylist, see *EI*, 2nd ed., s.v. al-Ḳāḍī al-Fāḍil.

65 Part of the complex of buildings built by the Sultan al-Manṣūr Qalāwūn (678–89/1279–90), see *EI*, 2nd ed., s.v. Ḳalāwūn; Creswell, ii, pp. 190–212; Northrup.

The text of two endowment deeds of Qalāwūn (dated 685/1286) and a brief study is given as an appendix in Ibn Ḥabīb, i, pp. 295–396.

66 Situated to the south-east of Cairo, between the Citadel and the Mausoleum of al-Shāfiʿī; see *Khiṭaṭ*, ii, pp. 443–5).

67 See *Masālik*, i, pp. 235–40. Cf. *Khiṭaṭ*, i, pp. 122–3, 204, 228; *Ṣubḥ*, iii, pp. 324–9, 376; *Ḥusn*, i, pp. 33–8 (for the Pyramids and the Sphinx). ʿAbd al-Laṭīf al-Baghdādī (pp. 107–77) has a perceptive chapter on Egyptian antiquities.

68 See Section 55.

69 For the "Green House" at Memphis, see the detailed description in ʿAbd al-Laṭīf al-Baghdādī, pp. 139ff.

70 Al-Qalqashandī makes the comment that all the observations could have been made over the long period necessary, recorded in books and then used by a single builder (*Ṣubḥ*, iii, p. 327).

71 This was Muḥyī al-Dīn Muḥammad ibn Zakī al-Dīn ʿAlī ibn Muḥammad, who died Shaʿbān 598/May 1202, see Abū Shāma, *Dhail*, pp. 31–2. He held the office of Qadi in Damascus and Aleppo. The letter referred to here was written by Muḥyī al-Dīn on behalf of Saladin, so that Saladin is the "he" in al-Fāḍil's reply. See British Museum Ms. Add 25756, fol. 63.

72 *Koran*, 79, v. 24; 43, v. 51.

73 There is a story that al-Rashīd, the Abbasid Caliph, to express his displeasure with Egypt, appointed an extremely foolish black slave called Khaṣīb (see Ibn Baṭṭūṭa, pp. 66–7; Sadi, ch. 1, apologue xxxix, pp. 181–2).

74 An allusion to *Koran*, 26, vv. 34–5, where Pharoah says: "This is truly a learned magician. He wishes to take you from your land by his magic."

75 In Arabic *khādimahu* "his servant", referring to al-Qāḍī al-Fāḍil himself.

76 Damascus' river, see Section 15.

77 This refers to the Frankish strategic threat to Muslim communications between Syria and Egypt. Cf. Section 82 where one reads "Kerak was an obstruction in our throats etc".

78 *Koran*, 12, v. 31; a reference to Joseph (Yūsuf) and hence to Saladin through his personal name.

79 Cf. *Ṣubḥ*, iv, pp. 86–7.

80 Cf. *Ṣubḥ*, iv, pp. 87–8, 182.

81 See also Section 69.

82 ʿUqaiba was a district outside the city wall to the north opposite the Faraj and Farādīs Gates (Elisséeff, *Description*, p. 153, note 8).

83 For the rose water of Jūr in Iran, see *EI*, 2nd ed., s.v. Fīrūzābād; and that of Nisibis, see Ibn Baṭṭūṭa, p. 251.

84 Cf. *Ṣubḥ*, iv, p. 93.

85 For historical and descriptive material on the Great Mosque at Damascus, see *Masālik*, pp. 178–203. See further in Section 71.

86 This section is quoted quite fully (although the texts need correcting) in *Khiṭaṭ*, ii, pp. 215–16; *Ḥusn*, ii, p. 93/7–19; *Ṣubḥ*, iv, pp. 14–16, 50. In general, see Ayalon, "Structure of the Mamluk Army",

87 It remains an open question whether Europeans, Greeks or men from Anatolia are meant.

88 The *ṭabl-khānah* signified the band of drummers and other instrumentalists that played at set times during the day before the residences of appropriate persons (cf. the Gate Music of Indian princes) and also the right to enjoy that distinction.

89 This was essentially, or originally, the non-mamluk element in the army. See *EI*, I, 2nd ed., ii, p. 99, s.v. *ḥalḳa*.

90 Sing. *manshūr*, the "patent" document which was the individual's authority to benefit from his *iqṭāʿ*.

91 Basically this was the assignment of some part of the state's income, typically from the taxes of specified agricultural areas but also from other cash sources, in payment for service, above all military service. See Rabie, ch. 2: "The *Iqṭāʿ* System".

92 An accounting unit of different values for different grades, paid in cash and in kind, see Cooper, and references there cited; also Rabie, pp. 48–9.
93 Unless the diploma (*manshūr*) of the emir specifies what proportion should go to his troopers, which he then may increase but not reduce (see al-Nuwairī, viii, p. 207).
94 Syrian *iqṭā*ʿs are dealt with in *Ṣubḥ*, iv, p. 50/17–19, p. 183/1–4.
95 A full account of the centralised control of the emirs' troops is in al-Nuwairī, viii, pp. 206–8.
96 Cf. *Khiṭaṭ*, ii, p. 216; *Ṣubḥ*, iv, pp. 51, 56. In general see Ayalon, "System of Payment".
97 Note the distinction implied in a Tunisian context between *malābis* (finished garments) and *kiswa* (lengths of material) in *Ṣubḥ*, v, p. 149.
98 Material not made up seems to be intended (see note 97). Ayalon wrote, "The mamluks were always given a special allowance to cover the cost of a *kiswa* [dress], but never received it ready made", and note the monetary sums he quotes for the fifteenth century ("System of Payment", p. 257).
99 Cf. *Ṣubḥ*, iv, p. 54; *Khiṭaṭ*, ii, pp. 200–1.
100 Āqūsh al-Afram paid any of his troopers or mamluks who had a horse die and then took its crupper to his kitchen 600 dirhems (al-Ṣafadī, i, p. 337), and Baibars recompensed *Ḥalqa* troopers or emirs' troopers with 50 dinars for the loss of a horse, and for the loss of a mule with 40 (Ibn Shaddād, *Taʾrīkh*, p. 297).
101 Cf. *Ṣubḥ*, iv, p. 55/9–11.
102 Cf. *Ṣubḥ*, iv, p. 55/15–18.
103 In the Arabic a *birdhawn*, meaning "a hack, non-thoroughbred for everyday use".
104 Here used in the sense of "the locality from which the alloted income is drawn".
105 Cf. *Ṣubḥ*, iv, p. 63/1–3.
106 For the first two paragraphs *Khiṭaṭ*, ii, p. 201, follows this text very closely; and for the second paragraph, see *Ṣubḥ*, iv, p. 46; *Ḥusn*, ii, p. 93. The royal regalia are dealt with in *Ṣubḥ*, iv, pp. 6–9, and one should consult Vermeulen.
107 The manuscripts are unclear. This reading assumes *yajīhā* (for *yajīʾuhā*), which could draw support from the parallel passage in *Khiṭaṭ*, ii, p. 201/12–13: "when the sultan rides out on the Feast Day or enters Cairo or any city of Syria". The Beirut edition reads *madīnat takhtihā*, "its capital city"; the Cairo edition has *madīna yuḥibbuhā*, "a city he likes".
108 The celebration of the end of the Fast of Ramadan. When "the two feasts" are mentioned, this and the celebration of the Day of Sacrifice during the Pilgrimage to Mecca are intended.
109 In Arabic *al-raqaba*. Cf. *Ṣubḥ*, iv, p. 8.
110 In Arabic *al-ghāshiya*. *Ṣubḥ*, iv, p. 7, describes it as "a saddle covering made of leather pierced with gold embroidery, which anyone who sees would imagine to be entirely made of gold. It is carried before [the sultan] when he rides in ceremonial processions. . . . The grooms carry it, lifting it high and swinging it left and right."
111 Sing. *janīb*: the leading of such horses in procession and other items of ceremonial mentioned here derived from Abbasid and Seljuq practice.
112 Cf. *Ṣubḥ*, v, pp. 457, 462.
113 This passage is reproduced with some differences in *Khiṭaṭ*, ii, p. 200/6–13; *Ṣubḥ*, iv, pp. 611–13.
114 Here, and indeed in the whole of this section, there are difficulties, and the translation is offered with more than the usual reserve. I have assumed that *ṭabl-khān* and *ṭabl-khānāt* here refer to the drums and other instruments and not to the emiral ranks for which they are a privileged adjunct. In two places the manuscripts of the *Masālik* clearly have *al-māl* (as does the text of the *Khiṭaṭ*) and it has been translated as "treasure". It seems to be differentiated from *khizāna*, which one might normally wish to translate as "treasure chest", but which here, if I am correct above, appears to contain the emir's "band". The *Ṣubḥ* text twice reads *al-alf* instead of *al-māl* (iv, p. 61/6, 9), for which I find no obvious meaning.
115 This is the reading of the edition (*bi-ʿinānihi*). *Khiṭaṭ*, ii, p. 200/13, and *Ṣubḥ*, iv, p. 61/ult., read *bi-ʿibāʾatin* ("with a blanket").

116 Cf. *Khiṭaṭ*, ii, p. 217 (also pp. 98–9); *Ṣubḥ*, iv, pp. 40–1. For the dress of the military aristocracy in general, see Mayer, pp. 21–35, although it will be seen that my interpretation frequently differs from Mayer's. Al-Suyūṭī (in *Ḥusn*, ii, p. 190, ult.) claims to deal with military dress in a "section on the sultan" but the passage has not been located. In addition he punctiliously declines to mention robes of honour of emirs and viziers because they contain forbidden silk and gold, and he has sworn not to burden his conscience by putting such things in his work.
117 See Dozy, i, p. 149: "genre de vetement porté dans l'Inde et en Egypte par les émirs".
118 The pouch, according to Maqrīzī, was made of black Bulgarian leather and could hold half a *waiba* of corn. The scarf (*mandīl*) was three cubits long, that is, a little more than 1½ metres (*Khiṭaṭ*, ii, p. 98).
119 In *Ṣubḥ*, iv, p. 40/14, this is expressly changed to "sometimes they are studded (*turaṣṣa*ʿ) with jade".
120 Details of the robes of honour for the military will be found in Section 43, and for the civilians in Section 44.
121 Cf. *Khiṭaṭ*, ii, pp. 208–9; *Ṣubḥ*, iv, p. 44; for the second paragraph onwards, see *Ḥusn*, ii, p. 92. This section has been translated in Gaudefroy-Demombynes, pp. xcviii–xcix.
122 See Section 49.
123 Later (at the end of Section 38) called the *Muḥtasib* (censor). Apart from his wide responsibility for public morality, his main function concerned the regulation of aspects of urban life, above all the control of markets. For a general view, based on Ibn Ṭuwair, see *Khiṭaṭ*, i, pp. 463–4, which passage is given in translation in Gaudefroy-Demombynes, p. lxxvii, note 4. See also *EI*, 2nd ed., iii, s.v. *ḥisba*.
124 See Dozy, ii, p. 212: wardrobe-masters.
125 Members of the corps of equerries, personal pages of the sultan (see Dozy, ii, p. 346).
126 The senior chamberlain (*ḥājib al-ḥujjāb* or simply *al-ḥājib*) controlled access to the sultan and had a judicial role in disputes among the Mamluk elite. See Sections 36 and 37.
127 Cf. *Khiṭaṭ*, ii, pp. 209–10; *Ṣubḥ*, iv, p. 45; *Ḥusn*, ii, pp. 92–3.
128 This is reading (with the Cairo edition) *ghair ramaḍān aiḍan*, and not, as the Beirut edition, *wa-ʿīd ramaḍān aiḍan*, "and on the Ramadan festival too". Cf. *Khiṭaṭ*, ii, p. 209/16: *mā ʿadā Ramaḍān*, "apart from Ramaḍān".
129 Cf. *Ṣubḥ*, iv, pp. 48–9; a good deal of this section is translated into French in Quatremère, *Histoire*, i, part 1, p. 192 (note).
130 In Section 20.
131 Joinville, p. 250, has left an interesting description of Sultan Tūrānshāh's camp in 1250 A.D.
132 Manuscripts P and T (like *Khiṭaṭ*, ii, p. 222/14) have *amīr bābdār* (officer of the Gate), but cf. the entry for the Emir Jandar in Section 37.
133 Cf. *Khiṭaṭ*, ii, p. 210/26–36; *Ṣubḥ*, iv, p. 49/10–13, p. 56/7–17.
134 Reading *kīmāj*, instead of the edition's *kīmākh*. Cf. Dozy, s.v *kumāj*: "une espèce de pain très-blanc, sans levain, ou cuit dans les cendres", and Clauson, p. 722: *kömeč*, "bread baked in ashes". *Khiṭaṭ*, ii, p. 210, has *sikbāj*, a sort of meat stew with vinegar.
135 Cf. *Khiṭaṭ*, ii, p. 212/23–7; *Ṣubḥ*, iv, p. 43/3–8.
136 The mosque in the Citadel was built by al-Nāṣir Muḥammad in 718/1318–19 to replace an earlier one and then again rebuilt in 735/1334–5 (*Khiṭaṭ*, ii, p. 212/18–23, 27–9).
137 There is a brief passage on the private enclosure (*maqṣūra*) in *Ṣubḥ*, iv, p. 7/5–9.
138 Cf. *Ṣubḥ*, iv, p. 59/6–ult.; *Khiṭaṭ*, ii, p. 211/18–27. On the post-horse system, see *Khiṭaṭ*, i, pp. 26–7; *Taʿrīf*, pp. 184–96; al-Ẓāhirī, pp. 118–20. On the pigeon post, see *Ṣubḥ*, iv, p. 60/1–3; xiv, pp. 389–94; *Khiṭaṭ*, ii, p. 231/16–p. 232/10; *Taʿrīf*, pp. 196–7; al-Ẓāhirī, pp. 116/ult.–117/16. In general, see Sauvaget, *La Poste*; Gaudefroy-Demombynes, pp. 239–54.
139 The *mīl* is not the English mile, but a third of a *farsakh* (parasang), or 4,000 "canonical cubits", approximately 2 kilometres (see Hinz, p. 63).

140 For the especially thin paper, called *waraq al-ṭair* (airmail paper!), see *Ṣubḥ*, vi, p. 192/1–3.

141 Apparently in the form of brand marks on the feet or beaks of the pigeons.

142 For this last paragraph, cf. *Khiṭaṭ*, ii, p. 211/27–9; *Ṣubḥ*, iv, p. 60/6–9. According to Ibn al-Athīr, the watchman (*ḥāris*) of each quarter in Baghdad had to write a report to the Caliph early each morning, including all manner of topics, such as who had been meeting with whom. The Caliph al-Ẓāhir, who succeeded in 621/1224, is said to have abolished this practice (Ibn al-Athīr, xii, p. 443). In 663/1264–5 Baibars meted out punishment to several subordinates of the Prefect of Cairo and to watchmen and heads of quarters for their inaccurate daily reporting to him in the so-called *waraqat al-ṣabāḥ*, "morning paper" (Ibn al-Dawādārī, viii, p. 106).

143 Cf. *Khiṭaṭ*, ii, p. 215/1–5; *Ṣubḥ*, iv, p. 62/6–11 (paraphrase in Gaudefroy-Demombynes, pp. c–ci).

144 The manuscripts and both the *Khiṭaṭ* and *Ṣubḥ* read *fī'l-mawkib* (normally meaning "in the parade, procession"), although the latter two sources refer to a context where one is not obliged to understand that a place is meant. The emendation *fī'l-maidān* "in the Hippodrome" is tempting.

145 For the ceremonial in Damascus, see *Ṣubḥ*, iv, pp. 194–7 (paraphrase in Gaudefroy-Demombynes, pp. 169–73).

146 Cf. *Khiṭaṭ*, ii, p. 211/7–18; *Ṣubḥ*, iii, p. 58.

147 For the restriction of the meaning of *manshūr* in Mamluk times to the document that issued an *iqṭā'*, see *Ṣubḥ*, xiii, p. 157.

148 On the "signature" in general, see *Ta'rīf*, p. 83; al-Ẓāhirī, pp. 101–2; also Stern, *Fatimid Decrees,* pp. 123–65.

149 The father's name was written only if he too had been a ruling sultan (*Khiṭaṭ*, ii, p. 211/10–11); see various examples in Ernst; Risciani, with illustrations.

150 For more on the different grades, see *Ta'rīf*, pp. 87–9.

151 Two examples (in negative), one of al-Nāṣir Muḥammad and the other of his grandson, Sha'bān ibn Ḥusain, are reproduced in *Ṣubḥ*, xiii, pp. 165–6.

152 Cf. *Khiṭaṭ*, ii, p. 217/15–33; partially *Ṣubḥ*, iv, pp. 50–1. The first part of this section is translated by Quatremère, *Histoire*, i, part 1, p. 161 (note). For fuller details on the issuing of *iqṭā'* diplomas, see al-Nuwairī, viii, pp. 208–10; *Ṣubḥ*, xiii, pp. 153–66 (with examples).

153 The actual word used here is *khubz* (lit. "bread, sustenance"). It was mistranslated by Quatremère (op. cit. supra), who understood *khabar*. In *Sulūk*, iv, p. 462, we read: "Each of them [the troops of the Ḥalqa] has an *iqṭā'*, called a *khubz*."

154 From the more complete description of later practice in *Ṣubḥ*, xiii, pp. 153–6, it may be understood that this formula gave the name of the previous holder who was giving up his *iqṭā'* for whatever reason.

155 A rare surviving example of Army Bureau paperwork is published in Richards, "Mamluk Petition".

156 Reading: *tuktabu murabba'atun*. The "square warrant" (*murabba'a*) was a document folded to produce four pages and not a scroll. Cf. the document published in Richards, "Mamlūk Emir's 'Square' Decree".

157 For the final *manshūr*, see the detailed account in *Ṣubḥ*, xiii, p. 157.

158 This process, the measurement of entitlement against actual service, is described in al-Nuwairī, viii, p. 211. See also *Ṣubḥ*, iv, p. 62, last para.

159 Cf. *Khiṭaṭ*, ii, p. 224/18–23; *Ṣubḥ*, iv, p. 51/15–ult.

160 Arabic: *fī'l-mudda*. The *Ṣubḥ* text has *fī'l-shahr*, "each month".

161 The second half of this sentence has a corrupt appearance in the manuscript. This translation owes a lot to the clearer, and possibly more correct, version in *Ṣubḥ*, iv, p. 51/16–17.

162 Reading *amīnun*, although there is no certainty in the manuscripts. Could one read *aimanu* "more fortunate"?

163 Cf. *Khiṭaṭ*, ii, p. 224/23–7; *Ṣubḥ*, iv, p. 51/18–ult.
164 The Beirut edition reads *muddatan*, and the Cairo edition *amrihi*. The manuscripts suggest *marratan*, which perhaps balances *jiddan* in sense, as a variant of *bi'l-marrati*, "absolutely".
165 Cf. *Ṣubh*, iv, pp. 41–3; *Ḥusn*, ii, p. 190. See also Gaudefroy-Demombynes, pp. xciii–xcv. For the various types of apparel, see Mayer, index.
166 Lane, *Lexicon*, s.v., describes it for his own day, worn by "professional learned men", as "an oblong piece of drapery . . . worn in such a manner that one end hangs down upon the side of the bosom, the middle part being turned over the head and under the chin, and the other end being thrown over the shoulder and hanging down upon the back".
167 When Baibars established the four Chief Qadis in 663/1265, he allowed all to wear the *ṭarḥa* (*Sulūk*, i, p. 540). Clearly this was not continued. The *ṭarḥa*, as described in the *Ṣubḥ*, covered the turban and hung down the back. Note too that in Section 45 the *ṭarḥa* is said to be part of the robes of honour for the highest rank of viziers and secretaries.
168 An unexplained term.
169 According to Maqrīzī, the saddles of judges and the religious classes were made of black Bulgarian leather (*Khiṭaṭ*, ii, p. 98/10). Hadith literature was generally hostile to the use of the *mīthara* (see Wensinck et al., iii, s.v. *w.th.r.*). There were also protective pads (sing. *bidād*) and sweat absorbers (sing. *murashshiḥa*) used beneath the saddle (see ʿAlī ibn Hudhail, p. 42). The vocabulary and general sense of this passage are obscure.
170 *Zunnār*, from a Greek word, means "waist-belt, girdle".
171 *Bayāḍ* literally means "whiteness".
172 Lit. "wind-catchers", the ducts that ventilated the interiors of houses.
173 For the garb of the sufis, see Trimingham, p. 184, note 3.
174 *Ḥusn*, ii, pp. 93–4.
175 I.e. the *nā'ib*. Cf. *Khiṭaṭ*, ii, p. 215/5–6, 19–26; *Ṣubḥ*, iv, p. 17/1–15 (also v, pp. 453–4); *Ḥusn*, ii, p. 93/25–ult. See Gaudefroy-Demombynes, pp. lv–lvi.
176 By the use of the phrase *bi-risālat fūlān*, "by the message of . . . ", for example, the vicegerent (see Stern, "Petitions from the Ayyūbid Period").
177 Al-Nāṣir Muḥammad did not fill the office again after the dismissal of Arghūn in 727/1326 (*Sulūk*, ii, pp. 279, 375, 547).
178 I.e. the *ḥājib*. Cf. *Khiṭaṭ*, ii, p. 219/29–31; *Ṣubḥ*, iv, p. 19/14–18 (also v, p. 450/9–12); *Ḥusn*, ii, p. 94/10–12. See Gaudefroy-Demombynes, pp. lviii–lix.
179 Reading *wa-man yaridu*.
180 *Khiṭaṭ*, ii, p. 222/10–14; *Ṣubḥ*, iv, p. 20/6–11. See Gaudefroy-Demombynes, pp. lix–lx.
181 This group is missing from the version in *Ḥusn*, while in the *Khiṭaṭ* it appears as al-*ḥarāmāniyya*, and in *Ṣubḥ* as *al-khāzindāriyya*. For the connection of "Khurasanians" with *jāndāriyya* (admittedly, mostly in the context of seige works), see Gibb, "Armies of Saladin", p. 84 and notes.
182 See Section 28.
183 I.e. the *ustādār*. *Khiṭaṭ*, ii, p. 222/14–18; *Ṣubḥ*, iv, p. 20/13–18 (also v, p. 457); *Ḥusn*, ii, p. 94/12–14. See Gaudefroy-Demombynes, pp. lx–lxi.
184 I.e. the *amīr silāḥ*. Cf. *Khiṭaṭ*, ii, p. 222/24–6; *Ṣubḥ*, iv, p. 18/14–17 (also v, pp. 456, 462); *Ḥusn*, ii, p. 94/5–7.
185 In Ibn Shaddād, *Ta'rīkh*, pp. 242–3, we read that the Sword-bearer Bektāsh al-Fakhrī had approximately a hundred *silāḥdāriyya* subordinate to him.
186 Literally "the pen-box holder", a military executive official. Cf. *Khiṭaṭ*, ii, p. 222/26–30; *Ṣubḥ*, iv, p. 19/3–7 (also v, p. 462); *Ḥusn*, ii, p. 94/7–19. See Gaudefroy-Demombynes, pp. lvii–lviii.
187 Ibn Shaddād, *Ta'rīkh*, p. 242, writing of the *dawādār*s in the plural, says: "They read to him private correspondence from other rulers, answer these letters, and act as intermediaries between the sultan and his viziers and secretaries."

188 Reading *risālatuhu* in the nominative, preceeded by two passive verbs. For the term itself, see Stern, "Petitions from the Mamluk Period".
189 I.e. the *naqīb al-juyūsh*. Cf. *Khiṭaṭ*, ii, p. 223/1–5; *Ṣubḥ*, iv, pp. 21/ult–22/2; *Ḥusn*, ii, p. 94/14–15. See Gaudefroy-Demombynes, p. lxii.
190 Emending *ʾaw khadaman* (a plural noun!) to *ʾaw jundiyyan*. The Cairo edition has the ingenious emendation *li-wajhin mā*, "for some reason or other". *Ṣubḥ*, iv, p. 22/1, reads *ghairahu*, "some other person'!
191 I.e. *al-wulāt*. Cf. *Khiṭaṭ*, ii, p. 223/9–16; *Ṣubḥ*, iv, p. 23; *Ḥusn*, ii, p. 94/15–16. See Gaudefroy-Demombynes, p. lxiv.
192 It is assumed that by "prefect" the author means the urban police chiefs of the three constituent parts of Cairo, i.e. al-Qāhira, Fusṭāṭ and Qarāfa. For *wulāt* in the sense of district governors of Egypt, see *Ṣubḥ*, iv, pp. 26–8.
193 Cf. *Khiṭaṭ*, ii, p. 223/16–20, 26–8; *Ṣubḥ*, iv, pp. 28–9; *Ḥusn*, ii, p. 94/16–24. See Gaudefroy-Demombynes, pp. lxvi–lxix.
194 This rather free translation represents *ʿalā qadr al-ittifāq*, although the reading is not unambiguous in the manuscripts. *Ṣubḥ*, iv, p. 28/15–16 (followed by the Cairo edition) reads *al-infāq* at the end, but trust in the accuracy of quotation in the manuscript tradition of the *Ṣubḥ* is lessened by the word *wa-qaṭīʿatuhā* that follows rather than *waḥīfatuhā*.
195 For the abolition of the vizierate after Mughultay al-Jamālī in 729/1329, see *Sulūk*, ii, p. 311–12, p. 547/7; Ibn Ḥajar al-Asqalānī, iv, p. 255.
196 Lit. "denuded the neck of the state of its necklace".
197 I.e. *kitābat al-sirr*. Cf. *Khiṭaṭ*, ii, p. 226/6–11; *Ṣubḥ*, iv, p. 30/3–12; *Ḥusn*, ii, p. 94/24–6. See Gaudefroy-Demombynes, pp. lxix–lxxi.
198 I.e. *naẓar al-jaish*. Cf. *Khiṭaṭ*, ii, p. 227/7–10; *Ṣubḥ*, iv, pp. 30/20–31/7; *Ḥusn*, ii, p. 26–7, 94.
199 Cf. *Ṣubḥ*, iv, p. 29/14–ult.
200 The Beirut edition has *bait,* which is unlikely. As in the Cairo edition, the present translation assumes *tuthbat*, which is how the sentence is quoted in *Ṣubḥ*, iv, p. 29/18. Possibly *thabat*, "inventory, list, record of", would remain closer to the consonantal outline found in the two manscripts that have this passage in full.
201 I.e. *naẓar al-khizāna*. Cf. *Khiṭaṭ*, ii, p. 227/14–18; *Ṣubḥ*, iv, p. 31/11–16; *Ḥusn*, ii, p. 94/27–ult.
202 In the *Sulūk* the phrase "the Great Chest" is found under the years 724/1324, 774/1372–3, and 777/1375–6 (ii, p. 256; iii, pp. 207, 255).
203 I.e. *naẓar al-buyūt*. Cf. *Khiṭaṭ*, ii, p. 224/27–30; *Ṣubḥ*, iv, p. 31/17–19; *Ḥusn*, ii, p. 94/ult.–95/1.
204 In Section 37.
205 I.e. *naẓar bait al-māl*. Cf. *Khiṭaṭ*, ii, p. 224/30–7; *Ṣubḥ*, iv, p. 31/20–2; *Ḥusn*, ii, p. 95/1–3. See Gaudefroy-Demombynes, p. lxxiii.
206 I.e. *naẓar al-isṭablāt*. Cf. *Khiṭaṭ*, ii, p. 224/37–9; *Ṣubḥ*, iv, p. 32/1–4; *Ḥusn*, ii, p. 95/3–4. See Gaudefroy-Demombynes, p. lxxiii.
207 See Quatremère, *Histoire*, ii, part 2, p. 65, note 26.
208 For the districts of Jerusalem, Hebron and Nablus, cf. *Ṣubḥ*, iv, pp. 100–3 (for which see Gaudefroy-Demombynes, pp. 59–63). Detailed descriptions of the Ḥaram al-Sharīf at Jerusalem (based on the *Silsilat al-Asjad* by Aḥmad ibn Amīn al-Mulk) will be found in *Masālik*, pp. 133–67, and of Hebron (or al-Khalīl), which al-ʿUmarī visited in 1345 A.D., in op. cit. pp. 168–76. See further Section 48.
209 According to the traditional dating the direction of prayer was changed from Jerusalem to Mecca in Shaʿbān 2/February 624.
210 *Koran*, 17, v. 1.
211 The author identifies the Mount of Olives (*Ṭūr Zaitā*) with the mountain on which Moses spoke with God and received the Law. Normally this is identified with Mount Sinai (*Ṭūr Sīnā* or *Jabal Mūsā*), situated in the south of the Sinai Peninsula. However, Yāqūt (iii, p. 220) locates the *al-Ṭūr* of Moses in Syria (*al-Shām*), whereas Ibn

Shaddād, *Liban*, pp. 243, 283, places *Ṭūr Sīnā* near Nablus and identifies Mount Tabor with the mountain on which God spoke to Moses.

212 Sharaf al-Dīn Aḥmad ibn Yūsuf al-Tīfāshī (died 651/1253) wrote a work whose title was *Faṣl al-khiṭāb fī madārik al-ḥawāṣṣ al-khams li-ūlī al-albāb* (cf. Brockelmann, *Supplément*, i, p. 904). This present title, *The Soul's Delight* etc. (*Surūr al-Nafs*), is that of a version by Ibn Manẓūr (died 711/1311), apparently a selection from what was an exceedingly large work. Ibn Manẓūr's book has been edited by Iḥsān ʿAbbās, Beirut (1400/1980) but does not contain the text quoted by al-ʿUmarī.

213 For the wider sense of the Aqsa Mosque, meaning the whole area of the Ḥaram, see van Berchem, pp. 426–7, and *EI*, 2nd ed., s.v. *al-Ḥaram al-Sharīf.*

214 Cf. the author's comments in *Masālik*, p. 169. There are two accounts of the discovery of the burial place of Abraham and his sons in a cave in 513/1119–20, given by Ibn Shaddād, *Liban*, pp. 239–40, 289–90 (one of the accounts is from Ibn Qalānisī, p. 202).

215 For fuller descriptions of the Meccan and Medinan sanctuaries refer to *Masālik*, pp. 92–111 and pp. 123–7 respectively, and *EI*, 2nd ed., iii, s.v. *al-Madīna*; iv, s.v. *al-Kaʿba*. For the Ḥasanid ruler of Mecca, see *Ṣubḥ*, iv, pp. 272–5 (the Banū Qatāda), and de Zambaur, pp. 21–2; for the Ḥusainids of Medina, see *Ṣubḥ*, iv, pp. 298–301, and the sketchy list in de Zambaur, p. 114.

216 The proverbial saying may be found in al-Zamakhsharī, ii, pp. 412–13: "that is, he pretends to tend the cream while sipping the milk; said of someone who pretends one thing, but intends another".

217 No doubt the Ilkhānids tried to establish their suzerainty over the Hijaz both because of the great prestige involved in that and because it was an expression of their rivalry with the Mameluke state. However, the actual recognition of the Ilkhānids came about rather because of disputes within the ruling family of Sharifs. After an abortive attempt in 1315 A.D. Ḥumaida ousted his brother Rumaitha with Mongol help in 1317 A.D. (*Sulūk*, ii, pp. 147–8, 175–6). By the beginning of 1322 A.D. al-Nāṣir Muḥammad's name had been restored to its place in the khutbah before Abū Saʿīd's (*Sulūk*, ii, p. 215). See Melville, "Year of the Elephant".

218 Abū Saʿīd succeeded at the age of thirteen in 1316 A.D. and died in late 1335. His father, otherwise known as Öljeitü, was the brother of the great Ilkhānid, Ghazān Khān.

219 Examples of diplomas given to the rulers of Mecca and Medina will be found in *Ṣubḥ*, xii, pp. 233–58.

220 Manuscripts A and P read *quwwatihi*, "his power".

221 I.e. the *Kaʿba.*

222 See Section 75 below and cf. the section on Hama and its dependencies in *Ṣubḥ*, iv, pp. 236–9 (including two passages quoted, or rather expanded, from the *Masālik*). See also *EI*, 2nd ed., s.v. *ḥamāt.*

223 Al-Muẓaffar III died Thursday 20 August 1299 (Abū'l-Fidā, iv, p. 41; *Sulūk*, i, p. 881; Ibn al-Dawādārī, ix, pp. 7, 14). All the sources agree that his name was Maḥmūd, not Shādī as in the text.

224 None other than the historian Abū'l-Fidā himself. By his own account he was invested with the sultanate of Hama in Cairo by al-Nāṣir Muḥammad on the morning of Thursday 28 February 1320 (Abū'l-Fidā, *Mukhtaṣar*, iv, p. 87). He died 30 October 1331 (*Sulūk*, ii, p. 354; Ibn al-Dawādārī, ix, p. 364). For an authoritative account of the restored Ayyubid branch, see Abū'l-Fidā, *Memoirs*.

225 Al-Afḍal succeeded through the intercession of the Emir Tankiz on Thursday 2 January 1332 (Ibn al-Dawādārī, ix, pp. 365–6). He was eventually deposed in early September 1341, and died soon afterwards (*Sulūk*, ii, pp. 573, 615). As our author refers to al-Afḍal as "the present ruler", that places the composition of this work within the period of a little under nine years, but see the next section.

226 For Cilicia or Lesser Armenia, see *Ṣubḥ*, iv, pp. 130–7, and for a summary of Muslim relations with its rulers, see *Ṣubḥ*, viii, pp. 29–33. A resumé of military contacts etc.

will be found in *EI*, ii, s.v. Cilicia. This section has been translated in Gaudefroy-Demombynes, p. 100, note 1. See also Amitai.

227 The author seems to have in mind Leo II, King of Armenia (1269–89), five of whose sons ruled after him, not to speak of other relatives. He was, however, son of Hethum I (1226–69), not of Mleh, who was a Rupenid, son of Leo I, and Lord of the Mountains in 1170–5.

228 The ruler at the time of the composition of the *Masālik* was Leo IV (1320–41), a grandson of Leo II (see Rödt-Collenburg, especially Table III (H2). Note that by others these Leos are numbered III and V.

229 The expedition set out in Sha'bān 737/March 1337, and returned in early 738/August 1337 (*Sulūk*, ii, p. 428; Zetterstéen, pp. 193–4).

230 See Sections 2 and 3.

231 Under the year 704/1304–5 Maqrīzī mentions a large emerald (175 *mithqāl*s in weight) taken from the mine, which the *ḍāmin* (normally "tax farmer", here perhaps something like "concession holder") attempted to sell to the rule of Yemen (*Sulūk*, ii, p. 12 and references there cited).

232 The medical theory derived from the Greeks taught that health depended on a balance of the four qualities (hot, cold, dry and moist) in the four humours of the body (blood, phlegm, yellow and black bile). See Ullmann, pp. 57–8.

233 The manuscripts read <s.b.s.b.>, which is unidentified. Perhaps read *saisbān*; Dozy, ii, p. 703, has "arbrisseau d'Égypte, dont les feuilles y sont employées comme purgatives".

234 This section has been translated in Quatremère, *Histoire*, ii, part 2, pp. 70–3; Gaudefroy-Demombynes, pp. xc–xcii; Mayer, pp. 58–60 (on the basis of *Khiṭaṭ*, ii, pp. 227–8). Cf. also *Ṣubḥ*, iv, pp. 52–3.

My translation differs from Mayer's in that I have assumed a constant distinction between *taḥt*, "below" in the sense of "worn beneath" and *dūna*, "below" in the sense of "lower in a hierarchical classification".

235 This was the typical headdress of the military élite, see Mayer, p. 28 and references there cited.

236 For an example of an Ayyubid belt, see Mayer, plate ix.

237 This translation is deliberately vague, because of the uncertainty over the Arabic. The Beirut edition reads *yumraj* which is backed by the manuscripts. A meaning of the verb *m.r.j.* is "to mix", and one might well have made a simple emendation to *yumzaj* (with the same meaning), especially as the form *mumtazij*, "mixed", appears a few lines below. *Khiṭaṭ*, ii, p. 227, in a parallel passage, plays safe with *yunsaj*, "woven". The Cairo edition of our text reads *yumawwaj*, which is effectively the reading found in *Ṣubḥ*, iv, p. 53 (*mumawwaj*). Dozy, ii, p. 631, gives this the sense of "*ondé*, fait, façonné en onde, *moiré*, ondé comme la moire".

238 There are textual and translation problems with this term too. The manuscripts A and T clearly support this present reading, which is that of the Beirut edition. The Paris manuscript has no diacritical points and based on that reading alone Quatremère, *Histoire*, ii, part 2, p. 77 (note), proposed *mutammar*, which he interpreted as meaning a stuff embroidered with representations of dates (followed in this by Dozy, i, p. 152). Could one suggest that *muthammar* might mean "fruit-patterned"? *Mutammar* is also found in *Ṣubḥ*, iv, p. 53, and that reading was adopted by the Cairo edition, although it fits badly with the reading from *mawwaja* (see previous note), suggesting wavy patterns. A *mutammar* robe of honour is mentioned in Ibn Ijās, iv, p. 199. Mayer (see p. 14, note 4) queried this form of the word and made a further suggestion of *munammar* (cf. Dozy, ii, 733, "*tavelé, tacheté, marqueté*").

239 Serjeant, p. 142: "*Ṭardwaḥsh* seems to be a Persian compound name and is thought to be a cloth embroidered with animals and scenes from the chase, of which there are numerous examples extant today". See Marzouk, *History*, plates xv, xvi.

240 An unidentified type of fabric.

241 See Dozy, s.v. *kanjī* and *quṭnī*: cotton and silk material, made originally in Ganja in Arran. The parallel passages in *Khiṭaṭ* have *kamkhā* instead of *kanjī*.
242 See Dozy, s.v. *maḥram*: "sorte d'étoffe . . . mais la leçon est incertaine". Cf. Mayer, pp. 59–60.
243 See Quatremère, *Histoire*, ii, part 2, pp. 73–4; Gaudefroy-Demombynes, p. xcv.
244 Dozy, s.v.; Mayer, p. 50 and references there given.
245 Dozy, s.v. *ṭarrāḥa*. Mayer, p. 13, translates as "head shawl", and on p. 51: an item of dress of "high ecclesiastic functionaries . . . a scarf worn over the turban and the neck, so as to fall on the shoulders".
246 Cf. Section 35.
247 See *EI*, 2nd ed., s.v. *khaṭīb* and *masjid*.
248 I.e. the *minbar*.
249 In Arabic *muballigh*. See *EI*, 2nd ed., s. v. *dikka*; Lane, *Manners and Customs*, pp. 86–7, 127.
250 For this *ḥadīth* or tradition of the Prophet, see Wensinck, vi, p. 130, for references; al-Bukhārī (*bāb al-jumʿa*, 36), pp. 304–5.
251 Cf. *Khiṭaṭ*, ii, p. 229/8–12; *Ṣubḥ*, iv, pp. 52–3.
252 See the broad picture drawn by Levanoni; and also Ayalon, "Expansion and Decline".
253 I.e. *al-jūkāndār*.
254 These departments of the household are respectively the *ṭisht-khāne*, the *sharāb-khāne* and the *firāsh-khāne*.
255 The meaning of *ghāyāt* in this context is not clear.
256 For the encouragement and inducements offered to slave merchants, see *Sulūk*, ii, pp. 524–5.
257 *Sulūk*, ii, pp. 525–30. speaks of al-Nāṣir Muḥammad's passion for horse, and the high prices he paid to the Arab Bedouin.
258 Cf. *Ṣubḥ*, iv, p. 73; and see Section 39.
259 In the Arabic *al-Qumāma*, see above p. 84, note 469.
260 This centre of Greek Orthodox Christianity is situated on the Kalamun plateau north of Damascus and was, according to Yāqūt, iii, p. 441, "famous for the number of its vines and its outstanding wine". See Dussaud, p. 283. Al-ʿUmarī earlier in this work mentioned the monastery of Ṣaydanāyā: "It is known as the Monastery of Our Lady. . . . It benefits from many religious trusts, receives ample resources and abundant votive gifts. Frankish Christians seek it out and pay visits. I have seen them asking the Sultan [al-Nāṣir Muḥammad] to allow them to do so. When written permission is given to visit the Sepulchre but not Saydanāyā as well, they press their requests for it to be granted. They have a particular belief about it . . . . Once letters from the Kings of France and Aragon were brought by their envoys. They asked that their envoys should be allowed to go there on a blessed pilgrimage. The Sultan granted their request and sent them there on post horses" (*Masālik*, pp. 356–7).
261 This refers to the titular kings of Jerusalem after the loss of that city.
262 The author is incorrect here. One should understand the Church of St Mark.
263 See *Ṣubḥ*, viii, p. 39; and cf. *Masālik* (facsimile), iv, p. 29. In 673/1274–5 a letter came to Cairo (via Yemen) requesting the appointment of a metropolitan by the Patriarch (see Ibn Shaddād, *Taʾrīkh*, pp. 430–1). Ibn ʿAbd al-Ẓāhir's reply is quoted in *Ṣubḥ*, viii, p. 41.
264 In the chapter on Abyssinia al-ʿUmarī names several informants, Muslim lawyers from the area, merchants and also the Coptic Patriarch in Egypt, Benjamin. See *Masālik* (facsimile), iv, pp. 17, 22, 27, 28.
265 For the spiritual authority of the Alexandrian Patriarch and the elaborate ceremonial here described, see also *Ṣubḥ*, v, pp. 308–9.
266 They are Masyaf, Khawabi, Qadmus, Rusafa, Kahf, Ullaiqa and Mainaqa. See *Ṣubḥ*, iv, p. 147.
267 Sinān, the "Old Man of the Mountain", ruled the Syrian Assassins from 558/1163 till his death in 589/1193. See Hodgson, pp. 185–209; Thorau, *Die Burgen*, pp. 132–58.

268 These agents were referred to as *fidāʿīs* (cf. the modern Fedayeen). "He [al-Nāṣir] could kill anyone he wanted through these agents, because he bestowed large sums of money on them" [!] *Sulūk*, ii, p. 537. In 720/1320 the Sultan al-Nāṣir sent assassins from Masyaf against the rebel Qarā Sunqur, but all were unsuccessful (*Sulūk*, ii, p. 207). See further Melville, "Sometimes by the Sword".

Al-ʿUmarī is somewhat neutral about the use of such agents, but Ibn Taimiyya in a fatwa states that it is a cardinal sin to employ members of the sect in castles, in the army or on the frontier. The authorities should dispense with them as soon as possible (quoted in *Sulūk*, ii, appendix 1, pp. 935–41).

269 Cf. *Khiṭaṭ*, ii, pp. 204–5; *Ṣubḥ*, iii, pp. 372–9. See Creswell, ii, pp. 1–40 (this passage translated p. 260); Rabbat.

270 Bahāʾ al-Dīn Qarāqūsh al-Asadī, a leading emir of the early Ayyubid period, died 1 Rajab 597/7 April 1201 (see ʿAbd al-Laṭīf al-Baghdādī, p. 109; Ibn Khallikān, iv, pp. 91–2).

271 Al-ʿĀdil displaced his brother's direct line and became sultan of Egypt in 596/1200 (see *EI*, 2nd. ed., i, pp. 197–8).

272 Building began on 13 Rabīʿ I 713/8 July 1313, and was completed 10 Jumādā I 714/22 August 1314. See Creswell, ii, pp. 260–4.

273 For the aqueduct that brought the water from the Nile and the water supply in general, see *Khiṭaṭ*, ii, pp. 210, 229–30; *Ṣubḥ*, iii, p. 377/2–6.

274 This refers to the fashion of building in alternate coloured courses, which was called *ablaq* ("piebald").

275 The Arabic term is *al-maʿjūn*. By "paste" the author may possibly mean the bitumen mixture, red or black, that made inlaid designs on marble. Later examples survive, e.g. the mihrab of Qijmās al-Isḥāqī's mosque in Cairo (Meinecke, plate 114 (b)). The two terms that follow are translated speculatively.

276 This area for polo and military exercises, normally called the Great Hippodrome (*al-maidān al-kabīr*) but referred to a little below as the Green Hippodrome, was restored and replanted by Sultan al-Nāṣir Muḥammad in 712/1312–3 (see *Khiṭaṭ*, ii, pp. 228–9).

277 The text has simply "at the times of the feeding of the birds (*al-ṭair*)". *Ṣubḥ*, iii, p. 377/14–15, is clearer: "at times the royal birds of prey (*al-jawāriḥ*) are fed there".

278 For Sultan al-Nāṣir Muḥammad's building works in general, see *Sulūk*, ii, pp. 537–8, 544.

279 This appears to mean that he does not worry about money, nor fear that death will expunge his achievements, in the spirit of Horace's *monumentum aere perennius*.

280 Cf. *Ṣubḥ*, iii, pp. 370–1.

281 I.e. the island of Roda.

282 I.e. *al-miqyās*, which is the well-like structure with a calibrated pillar that measures the height of the Nile (see Popper).

283 The Beirut edition (p. 146) reads *al-ṭarāʾif*, which has been emended to *al-ṭawāʾif*.

284 Ismāʿīl ibn Muḥammad ibn Yāqūt al-Sallāmī (born 671/1272–3, died Jumādā II 743/ November 1342) was an influential importer of mamluks and carried out diplomatic missions, notably in connection with the peace made with the Ilkhānid Abū Saʿīd in 723/1323. See Ibn Ḥajar al-Asqalānī, i, p. 407; al-Ṣafadī, ix, pp. 220–1.

285 In Arabic *sajʿa*, lit. "a phrase in balanced rhyming prose".

286 Cf. *Khiṭaṭ*, i, pp. 202–3, 236; *Ṣubḥ*, iii, pp. 400–1. See Garçin.

287 Arabic: *funduq*, inn, storehouse, entrepôt.

288 This is not the well-known author of the biographical dictionary, who was Khalīl ibn Aibak.

289 Widely believed to be poisonous and to cause skin diseases.

290 See the entry for this person, who died in 745/1344–5, in Ibn Ḥajar al-Asqalānī, ii, pp. 326–7.

291 The same anecdote is found in *Khiṭaṭ*, i, pp. 189–90; *Ṣubḥ*, iii, p. 397.

292 Cf. *Ṣubḥ*, iii, pp. 407–8; also cf. Yāqūt, i, pp. 254ff (p. 260/4ff: its fabulous whiteness, p. 260: the grid pattern), and *Khiṭaṭ*, i, p. 162/20–1.

293 This description, in Arabic *Dhū'l-Qarnain*, derives from the *Koran*, 18, vv. 83–94, where it is generally understood to refer to Alexander the Great, perhaps on account of representations on coins. *Khiṭaṭ*, i, pp. 153–4 summarises other views.
294 Al-Qalqashandī claims (*Ṣubḥ*, iv, pp. 24, 27) that Alexandria was first raised to the rank of a vicegerency (*niyāba*) in 767/1365–6, previously being a *wilāya* (governorship). However, a *nā'ib* of Alexandria is mentioned as early as 740/1339–40 in *Sulūk*, ii, p. 493.
295 Lit. "buried", meaning perhaps "with a hint of patterning". See Dozy, i, 450, s.v.
296 Sic *Masālik* (Beirut), unexplained. *Masālik* (Cairo) reads *al-muftariḥ*; see Dozy, ii, 249, s.v.: sorte d'étoffe d'Alexandrie.
297 See also for textiles and materials Sections 22, 35, 44 and 45. Many sorts mentioned here are not identifiable. In general, consult Lombard.
298 See Section 5.
299 This sentence is translated with some modifications of the printed text.
300 Cf. *Khiṭaṭ*, i, pp. 71/7ff, pp. 169–72.
301 For its representation as a three-tiered city, see *Khiṭaṭ*, i, p. 126/15.
302 See Section 39, p. 39.
303 In Arabic *Kitāb al-Tartīb*. The work is unrecorded and the identity of the author is uncertain. Possible candidates are mentioned in Yāqūt, ii, pp. 115–16; and al-Ṣafadī, viii, p. 181.
304 For this anecdote see Ibn ʿAbd al-Ḥakam, pp. 12, 37–44 (the queen is there called Kharūyā, daughter of Ṭūṭīs); al-Masʿūdī, *Murūj*, pp. 99–109 (al-Masʿūdī, *Prairies*, ii, pp. 313–19).
305 For the sea-monsters, see al-Masʿūdī, *Murūj,* ii, pp. 101–2 (al-Masʿūdī, *Prairies,* ii, pp. 314–15). In some versions it was something like primitive "bathoscopes" that were lowered so that the monsters could be drawn prior to making accurate copies to put on columns as talismanic figures.
306 Cf. *Khiṭaṭ*, i, pp. 155–8; *Ṣubḥ*, iii, p. 321; *Ḥusn*, i, pp. 43–5. See also al-Masʿūdī, *Murūj*, ii, pp. 104–8 (al-Masʿūdī, *Prairies*, ii, pp. 316–19); Yāqūt, i, pp. 291–3.
307 Cf. end of Section 66.
308 See Hinz, p. 29: = 312 dirhems = 967 g. Note an official called al-Jarawī, *Khiṭaṭ*, i, pp. 178–9.
309 See *Khiṭaṭ*, i, pp. 213–26.
310 This refers to the periods in which the Fifth and Sixth Crusades were directed against Damietta, i.e. 1217–21 and 1248–50.
311 See *Khiṭaṭ*, i, pp. 176ff. For its popular name and the visit of Jesus, see Yāqūt, i, p. 883.
312 See *Khiṭaṭ*, i, p. 189/2–10
313 The verb used is *jafara*.
314 At this point I read *fa-mā*, not *mimmā*, although the difference is not crucial.
315 Reading *al-istabraq* as an apposition, without the preposition (*li-*) that precedes it in both the Beirut and the Cairo editions.
316 Cf. *Taʿrīf*, pp. 219–24; *Ṣubḥ*, iii, pp. 396–410.
317 For this paragraph, cf. *Khiṭaṭ*, i, p. 74/5–8.
318 *Masālik* (Beirut), p. 111, reads *gharb*, but *Masālik* (Cairo) p. 97, has *ʿArab.*
319 The Cairo edition follows the manuscripts A, P and T in reading *ʿalā al-*[*ʿ.r.y.*] with the sense of "region, vicinity" (see Lane, *Lexicon*, s.v. ʿ.r.w.). The reading of the Beirut edition (as also of the *Khiṭaṭ*) is "to the west" (*ʿalā al-gharbī*).
320 Cf. *Khiṭaṭ*, i, p. 74/8–12.
321 In the margin of manuscript A, corrections in the hand of Maqrīzī: "This is an error. Manūf [i.e. Memphis] which was the old capital of the land of Egypt, is an area on the Giza side, known as Badarshīn. I have a considerable amount of information about it in *An Account of the Sites and Relics* etc. [i.e. *al-Khiṭaṭ*]". In *Ṣubḥ*, iii, pp. 402, 409, there is a correction of al-ʿUmarī's statement. There is a confusion between Manf and Manūf (Memphis), for which see Maspero & Wiet, s.v.

322 From the margin of manuscript A: "The correct form should be the Island of the Banū Naṣr, for it is named after the Banū Naṣr ibn Muʿāwiya ibn Bakr ibn Hawāzin. The Banū Hammās ibn Ẓālim ibn Juʿail ibn ʿAmr ibn Dahmān ibn Naṣr ibn Muʿāwiya ibn Baḥr ibn Hawāzin were very powerful in Egypt. They multiplied and eventually took control of and dominated the Delta, until they were challenged by the Liwāta, one of the Berber tribes. The Banū Naṣr were humbled, adopted a settled existence and became village people in a place that came to bear their name, in the middle of the Nile, that is to say, this Island of the Banū Naṣr. Take note accordingly".
323 Also known as Ashmūn al-Rummān.
324 Cf. *Taʿrīf*, p. 224; *Khiṭaṭ*, i, p. 74/12–13, p. 234, p. 236/14–16.
325 Al-Bakrī, an author from Andalus, died in 487/1094. This passage is in *Kitāb al-Masālik wa'l-Mamālik d'Abu Ubayd al-Bakrī*, i, p. 330, para. 541. The text differs, most importantly in reading "This area is fertile and prosperous (*khaṣiba rākhiya*)" instead of "In this area are found alum and vitriol (*shabbiyya wa-zājiyya*)".
326 See *Ṣubḥ*, iii, pp. 395–6.
327 The North African author Alī ibn Mūsā ibn Saʿīd died in Tunis in 1286; see Meisami & Starkey, i, p. 368.
328 For this ʿAqaba (near modern Salloum) as the limit of Egyptian territory, see *Ṣubḥ*, vii, p. 376 (called ʿAqaba of Barqa) and *Masālik (Qabāʾil)*, p. 180 (called *al-ʿAqaba al-Kabīra*, the Great Pass).
329 Ibn Ḥajar al-Asqalānī, iv, p. 31: Nāṣir al-Dīn Muḥammad ibn Bilik al-Muḥsinī. No mention of connection with Barqa. One manuscript of *Durar* gives his year of death as 754/1353. Another Muḥammad al-Muḥsinī's career, which included being Prefect of Manūfiyya and Cairo, some time in Syria and eventual promotion to emir of a hundred in 762/1360–1, may be followed in *Sulūk*, iii, see index.
330 I.e. the *ʿadād*, a tax on sheep, camels etc. extracted from the bedouin (see Quatremère, *Histoire*, i, part 1, p. 189, note 69).
331 A bedouin Emir called Fāʾid accompanied a military expedition led by the Emir Aitamish al-Muḥammadī in 719/1319 to extract allegiance and dues from the Emir Jaʿfar ibn ʿUmar of Cyrenaica (*Sulūk*, ii, pp. 190–2).
332 He was born at Zawāwa in North Africa in 664/1265–6, had a career as a Mālikī judge, scholar and prolific author in Egypt and Syria, and died in Rajab 743/December 1342 (Ibn Ḥajar al-Asqalānī, iii, pp. 289–91).
333 See the study of Munajjid.
334 For al-Idrīsī, the famous geographer who wrote for Roger II of Sicily and who was born in 493/1100 and died in 560/1165 (although the dates are uncertain), see *EI*, 2nd ed., iii, pp. 1032–5.
335 *Koran*, 30, vv. 2–3.
336 In Arabic: *al-Mīzāb*. This refers to the water-spout for the clearing of rain-water, which juts out from the north-west wall of the Kaaba.
337 Born in Damascus in 449/1105, Ibn ʿAsākir was an eminent Shāfiʿī scholar. His work referred to here is in fact entitled *History of the City of Damascus*, a biographical encyclopaedia on a vast scale. He died in 571/1176 (see *EI*, 2nd ed., iii, pp. 736–7).
338 For this and the following two paragraphs, cf. Ibn ʿAsākir, i, pp. 12/15–13/8.
339 See al-Ṭabarī, i, pp. 220–1; Yāqūt, iii, pp. 6–7: "mountain in Upper Mesopotamia".
340 These are the stars Beta and Gamma of Ursa Minor.
341 The Arabic verb used here is *ijtaḥafa*.
342 Hadith scholar and philologian (885–940), see Meisami & Starkey, i, pp. 89–90.
343 *Koran*, 56, v. 9, and 90, v. 19.
344 Cf. Ibn ʿAsākir, i, pp. 13/15–14/5
345 The various elements in Section 64 will be found in Ibn ʿAsākir, pp. 14–16. See the selected passages translated in Gaudefroy-Demombynes, pp. 40–8.
346 A Yemeni Jew who was an early convert to Islam and a source of much Jewish lore. He died, probably in Homs, in the 30s/650s (see *EI*, 2nd ed., iv, pp. 316–17).

347 The modern Turkish Colap.
348 I.e *Iram Dhāt al-ʿImād*, which is mentioned in *Koran*, 89, v. 6. It was interpreted either as a tribal name or as a toponym, the latter often identified with Damascus, although other more fabulous explanations are given. See *EI*, 2nd ed., iii, p. 1270.
349 A Yemeni of Persian descent (born 34/654–5), he was an important source of biblical stories and exegesis for later Muslim writers. He died in 110/728–9 or 114/732–3.
350 For the author see Brockelmann, i, p. 103;, and *Supplément*, i, p. 162, but no work of this title is mentioned. However, the work is quoted in *Ṣubḥ*, iv, p. 92/8.
351 See Yāqūt, vii, p. 448.
352 For similar testing of soil, see Virgil, *Georgics*, ii, vv. 226–37.
353 Cf. Ibn Shaddād, *Damas*, pp. 17/20–18/7.
354 Ibn Shaddād, see above, has al-Riyya. Yāqūt, ii, p. 752 reads al-Rubba.
355 Abū Bakr al-Khwārizmī (323–83/934–93), prose stylist and poet, known especially for his literary duel with Badīʿ al-Zamān al-Hamadhānī, the author of the *Maqāmāt*. See *EI*, 2nd ed., iv, p. 1069.
356 Reading *jannāt*, instead of the Beirut edition's *al-jawānib*, "sides, directions", which is also in all the manuscripts. Ibn Shaddād, *Damas*, p. 309, quotes al-Khwārizmī in a different form: "The earthly paradises (*jinān*) are four . . . I have seen all [including the Ghuta] and none is more beautiful than the Ghuta". When the quotation is referred to again (see Section 68 below, p. 69) in yet a different form, "paradises" (*jinān*) is the undoubted reading.
357 For these three extracts from Ibn ʿUnain (Damascus poet, 549–630/1154–1233; see *EI*, 2nd ed., iii, p. 962), see his *Diwān*, pp. 4–5, 69, 84.
358 He was Abūʾl-Nadā Ḥassān ibn Numair al-Kalbī (born 486/1093, died 567/1171–2). His *Diwān* has been published by Aḥmad al-Jundī, Damascus (1390/1970). For a brief biographical note and then a selection from his *Diwān* (not including this piece), see ʿImād al-Dīn, *Kharīda*, i, pp. 178–229.
359 Both editions, following the manuscripts, read ʿUkbarā, which is in Iraq. The *Dīwān* has ʿAshtarā, which is a village in the Hauran (see also this poem quoted in Ibn Shaddād, *Damas*, pp. 357–8). ʿĀliqain is a village of Damascus.
360 ʿĀlij is a sandy area on the Iraqi pilgrimage route; Kāḥima is on the coast between Basra and Bahrain; Wadi al-Qurā (the Valley of the Villages) is between Damascus and Medina.
361 He was Abū ʿUbāda al-Walīd ibn ʿUbaid (206–284/821–897), poet of the Caliphal court and anthologist (*EI*, 2nd ed., i, pp. 1289–90). See his *Diwān*, Dār Ṣādir edition, Beirut (1962), i, pp. 25–6.
362 Reading *namzujuhā*, as quoted in Ibn Shaddād, *Damas*, p. 335.
363 Reading *yumsī* instead of *yamshī*.
364 Reading *al-suqāt*, rather than *al-shifāh* (lips).
365 See towards the end of Section 55.
366 For a similar comment on Damascus, see Bahaʾ al-Dīn, p. 239: "a year of copious rains and the water was running in the streets like rivers".
367 Cf. *Ṣubḥ*, iv, p. 183/5–14.
368 Cf. *Ṣubḥ*, iv, p. 93/3–7, 16–18. See also Gaudefroy-Demombynes, pp. 35, 44–5.
369 Sauvaget, "La Citadelle".
370 See p. 65.
371 Reading *sharafai-hā* as in *Masālik* (Cairo), p. 114.
372 For this and preceding paragraphs see *Ṣubḥ*, iv, pp. 94–5.
373 See *Masālik*, pp. 353–6.
374 Built for the Ḥanafīs by the Ayyubid sultan of Damascus, al-Muʿaẓẓam ʿĪsā (died 624/1227), son of al-ʿĀdil. It was built in 621/1224 (see Ibn Shaddād, *Damas,* p. 220).
375 Yāqūt says: "The Pass of Dummar overlooks the Ghūṭa of Damascus . . . to the north on the Baalbek road".

376 Cf. *Ṣubḥ*, iv, pp. 93/14–94/ult. See also Gaudefroy-Demombynes, pp. 45/24–46/11.
377 Baibars I built it in 665/1266–7 (see Meinecke, ii, pp. 24–5). It was a royal residence until its destruction by Tamerlane in 803/1400 (see *Sulūk*, i, p. 561). The Sultan al-Nāṣir Muḥammad built the Striped Palace (*al-Qaṣr al-Ablaq*) in the Cairo Citadel to rival that of Baibars outside Damascus, according to *Sulūk*, ii, p. 129.
378 Baibars, the great Mamluk sultan, ruled from 658/1260 until his death in 676/1277. See Thorau, *Lion of Egypt*.
379 See Ibn Ḥajar al-Asqalānī, i, pp. 424–6. Āqqūsh, a Circassian mamluk of al-Nāṣir Muḥammad, held this position from Jumādā I 698/February 1299 until the sultan's third return to power in 709/1309–10. He died in Hamadhan in the service of the Ilkhanids after 720/1320.
380 This polo and exercise ground was situated west of the town between the Baradā and the Qanawat. In 690/1291 some buildings were demolished to enlarge the area (see Meinecke, ii, p. 72). For the Hippodrome in Cairo (also called "the Green" in this text), see Section 50, p. 5.
381 Contrary to the Beirut and the Cairo editions, no paragraph break is made here. "The river valley" is understood to be linked by the conjunction to "the Ghuta", and the following *kāmil* ("perfect . . .") refers back to "the palace" (*al-qaṣr*), i.e. the description of the palace continues, not that of the valley.
382 Cf. *Ṣubḥ*, iv, pp. 95/9–96/6. See also Gaudefroy-Demombynes, pp. 46–8.
383 Fīja is situated between Zabadani and Damascus. For ʿAzzatā, see Ibn ʿUnain, p. 69 & note 5; *Masālik*, p. 81.
384 The Sultan of the Zangid dynasty and great champion of Islam against the Crusaders, born 511/1118 and died 569/1174. A full study of his career will be found in Elisséeff, *Nūr al-Dīn*.
385 *Koran*, 23, v. 50. See Ibn Shaddād, *Damas,* p. 181, where this identification is denied. Al-ʿUmarī himself (*Masālik*, i, pp. 206–8) notes that Koranic exegetes have variously located Rabwa at Damascus, Ramla, Jerusalem and even Alexandria and Kufa, although he clearly considers all opinions unfounded; consult further Ibn ʿAsākir, ii/1, pp. 96–8; Yāqūt, s.v. *Rabwa*; Gibb, *Travels of Ibn Baṭṭūṭa*, i, pp. 146–8.
386 The Beirut edition reads *afrāsh* and just before *aḥlāl*. I have taken both as IVth form *maṣdar*s. Note that the Cairo edition has *iftirāsh* and *iḥlāl.*
387 For more on the watercourses of Damascus, see Ibn Shaddād, *Liban,* pp. 12–18; Thoumin.
388 A long list of the sub-divided streams and channels (sing. *qanāh*, pl. *qanan* or *qanawāt*) is in Ibn Shaddād, *Liban*, pp. 19–32.
389 Cf. *Ṣubḥ*, iv, p. 96/7–97/5. See also Gaudefroy-Demombynes, p. 48.
390 They were Companions of the Prophet and generals during the early conquests of Islam.
391 The author gives a detailed description of the Umayyad Mosque towards the beginning of his whole work and refers to the serious fire that occurred in 740/1341, quoting a *maqāma* by al-Ṣafadī on the subject (*Masālik*, pp. 178–203). None of the early sources (al-Ṭabarī or al-Balādhurī) speak of any sharing (*munāṣafa*) of space, although a Muslim place of prayer certainly stood adjacent to the Church of St John the Baptist before the latter was demolished by al-Walīd. See *EI*, I, 2nd ed., ii, pp. 280–1, s.v. Dimashḳ; and also the collection of traditions in Ibn Shaddād, *Damas*, pp. 50–8.
392 Cf. *Ṣubḥ*, iv, pp. 97–114, where the divisions are different.
393 Thus in the three manuscripts and also in *Sulūk*, i, p. 811, where it is described as a village (*qarya*) of Damascus. The Beirut edition reads ʿUsail, following Yāqūt, ii, p. 31, where it is said to be "a district (*nāḥiya*) between Damascus and Baalbek, consisting of several villages". It is in fact both the name of a village and of the immediate area, see Dussaud, p. 279.
394 See al-Balādhurī, *Futūḥ*, p. 126.

395 That is, the mountains of Edom, east of Wadi ʿAraba and west of Maʿān (see Le Strange, index).
396 According to *Ṣubḥ*, iv, p. 105/ult., the castle was built in 580/1184–5. Ibn Shaddād, *Liban*, pp. 86–91, gives no date. ʿIzz al-Dīn Usāma, lord of Kawkab (Belvoir) and ʿAjlūn, originally an emir of Saladin (and hence frequently called al-Ṣalāḥī), played a significant role in politics after Saladin's death. He was arrested in 608/1211–2, and imprisoned in Kerak, where he subsequently died (see Ibn Wāṣil, iii, pp. 209–10).
397 This paragraph should be compared with Ibn Shaddād, *Liban*, pp. 86–7.
398 For this paragraph, cf. Ibn Shaddād, *Liban*, pp. 83–4.
399 It was the residence of members of the ʿAbbāsid family while the *daʿwa*, the movement that brought them to power, was in progress in the eastern Islamic lands.
400 This quotation does not exactly reproduce any passage in the *Futūḥ*.
401 This son of al-ʿĀdil Abū Bakr (and nephew of Saladin) ruled after his father as Ayyubid sultan of Damascus till his death in 624/1227.
402 Cf. Ibn Shaddād, *Liban*, pp. 83–4. The translation "insulted" assumes *fa-sabbūhunna*. The Beirut edition reads *fa-sabawhunna*, "they made them captive". The Cairo edition is non-committal, and the parallel text in Ibn Shaddād, op. cit., p. 84, also vocalises only the first consonant.
403 This was a brother of al-Nāṣir Yūsuf, the last Ayyubid ruler of Aleppo and Damascus. They were born in the same year, 627/1229–30 (see Ibn Wāṣil, iv, p. 283). This ʿAlī is not to be confused with al-Ẓāhir Ghāzī ibn al-ʿAzīz, a younger full-brother of al-Nāṣir Yūsuf. The editor of Ibn Shaddād, *Liban*, has erroneously replaced the ʿAlī found in two manuscripts with Yūsuf (p. 63, where incidentally the name of the deputy at Sarkhad is given as Saʿd al-Dīn ʿUmar Qilij).
404 The Mongol Ilkhanid who conquered Baghdad and ended the Abbasid caliphate in 1258 A.D.
405 The wealthy widow who became the Prophet Muḥammad's first wife and an early convert to Islam.
406 Al-Balādhurī, *Futūḥ*, p. 112. Baḥīrā met the youthful Muhammad and recognised his future as a prophet.
407 Op. cit., p. 126.
408 Ṣarkhad is not found in the index of de Goeje's edition of al-Ṭabarī's chronicle.
409 No case comes to mind concerning Sarkhad or Bosra. Sallār, the Vicegerent and associate of Baibars II, after the return to power of al-Nāṣir Muḥammad, retired for a short while to Shawbak in 709/1310.
410 Cf. Ibn Shaddād, *Liban*, pp. 42–54; *Ṣubḥ*, iv, p. 109/2–110/8. See also Gaudefroy-Demombynes, pp. 70–1 (this section is translated into French p. 72).
411 He was al-Malik al-Amjad Majd al-Dīn Bahrāmshāh ibn Farrukhshāh ibn Shāhinshāh, who ruled Baalbek for 49 years until his death in 627/1229–30 (Ibn Wāṣil, iv, pp. 284–93).
412 Ibn Baṭṭūṭa, p. 102, comments on Baalbek's production and export to Damascus of "many preparations of milk" (Gibb, *Travels of Ibn Baṭṭūṭa*, i, p. 117).
413 Probably built in the reign of al-Nāṣir Muḥammad, see Meinecke, ii, p. 189.
414 Manuscript P has the corresponding word without diacritical points; manuscripts A and T read the outline as *n.f.ṭ*, i.e. oil, or in the historical context "Greek fire". The present translation emends the outline to *n.q.ṭ*, forming part of a typically elaborate image. The crennelations on towers are seen as basic letter shapes, that are waiting for a shower of missiles, the diacritical "dots".
415 The last phrase echoes *Koran*, 12, v. 18; 21, v. 112. Al-Qāḍī al-Fāḍil probably refers either to the conquest of Baalbek (by Saladin) in 570/1174–5 or to the siege in 574/1178–9.
416 Cf. *Ṣubḥ*, iv, p. 112/9–113/11. See also Gaudefroy-Demombynes, pp. 75–7.
417 This is based on reading *al-bazz*, which is found in manuscript T, and see also the reference below to Homs as a textile centre. The Beirut edition reads *al-birr* (charitable gifts?!). The Cairo edition gives no vowelling. Could *al-burr*, "wheat", be intended?

418 Cf. *Ṣubḥ*, iv, p. 73/12–ult.; Gaudefroy-Demombynes, pp. 2–3.
419 A rather different text of al-Qāḍī al-Fāḍil is quoted in Abū Shāma, *Rawdatain*, i, p. 618/8–9. For the special sense of "mangonel scorpions", see Gaudefroy-Demombynes, p. 3, note 1. For a variety of translated extracts on Homs, see Le Strange, pp. 353–7.
420 This difficult description is literally "the littleness of its water and the 'male quality' (*fuḥūla*) of its body". The verb *tafaḥḥala* is given (in the *Qāmūs al-muḥīṭ*) as meaning "to affect *fuḥūla* in one's clothing and food, thus to make them rough, coarse".
421 See Section 41 above. Cf. *Ṣubḥ*, iv, pp. 139–40; Gaudefroy-Demombynes, pp. 106–8.
422 Following the text of *Masālik* (Cairo), p 127. *Masālik (*Beirut), p. 197 reads *kull mā li-maḥall min-hā* (?).
423 For the two districts, see *Ṣubḥ*, iv, pp. 141–2.
424 Cf. *Ṣubḥ*, iv, pp. 116–139; Gaudefroy-Demombynes, pp. 81–5.
425 This is contradicted by Ibn al-Shiḥna, p. 157: "This is not so. Its earth is grey (*shahbāʾ*) like its name".
426 The Banū Ḥamdān were a family of Arab descent, several members of which ruled in Mesopotamia and in Syria (centred on Aleppo) in the fourth/tenth century (see *EI*, 2nd ed., iii, pp. 126–31).
427 The River Sājūr rises near ʿAintāb (modern Gaziantep), passes north of Manbij and flows into the Euphrates. What is referred to here is the works carried out under Arghūn, Sultan al-Nāṣir Muḥammad's vicegerent in Aleppo, who constructed a canal from the Sājūr to the upper Fuwaiq to supplement the flow of the latter which dried up in summer (see Ibn al-Shiḥna, pp. 132, 170).
428 Abū Naṣr Aḥmad ibn Yūsuf al-Manāzī (died 437/1045), see Ibn Khallikān, i, pp. 143–5; al-Ṣafadī, viii, p. 285. According to ʿImād al-Dīn al-Isfahānī (*Kharīda,* ii, p. 348) he belonged to a family of viziers who served the Marwanids in Diyar Bakr. The Andalusians attributed these verses to Ḥamda bint Ziyād, according to Jawdat Rikabi, *Fīʾl-adab al-Andalusī*, Dar al-Maʿārif (1960), pp. 99–100.
429 The dependencies of Aleppo are listed in *Taʿrīf*, pp. 232–5, and *Ṣubḥ*, iv, pp. 118–30 (summary translation of *Ṣubḥ* text in Gaudefroy-Demombynes, pp. 85–97). Al-Qalqashandī (*Ṣubḥ*, iv, p. 119/10–13) points out that the present list and that in the *Taʿrīf* do not correspond.
430 *Ṣubḥ*, iv, p. 123/8–15: "names of two castles a bow shot distance one from the other".
431 Formerly called Qalʿat al-Rūm (Castle of the Greeks), until the name was changed by Sultan al-Ashraf Khalīl after his capture of it in Rajab 691/June 1292 (see *Sulūk*, i, p. 778; also Stewart.
432 In Section 76.
433 See *Taʿrīf*, pp. 235–6. Cf. *Ṣubḥ*, iv, pp. 142/13–143/ult.; Gaudefroy-Demombynes, pp. 110–7.
434 This dynasty (mostly recognising Fatimid suzerainty) ruled 462–502/1070–1109 (*EI*, 2nd ed., i, p. 448, s.v. ʿAmmār)
435 He was Vicegerent of Tripoli from 701/1301–2 until 709/1310. He moved to Hama and then to Aleppo, but was arrested in 710/1311 and died probably the following year, see Ibn Ḥajar al-Asqalānī, i, pp. 414–15; Zettersteen, pp. 110, 144, 151–4; al-Ṣafadī, pp. 248–9.
436 Sulaimān ibn Dāʾūd ibn Sulaimān al-Dimashqī, Chief Physician (*raʾīs al-aṭibbāʾ*), died in Shaʿbān 732/May 1332. He gained fame from this cure, but is said to have known no "theory" (*ḥikma*) but "only knew medicine through practical experience" (see Ibn Ḥajar al-Asqalānī, ii, p. 246).
437 In the Arabic text there are rather unusual singular verbs after *kathīran* ("many"), which necessitates the bracketed insertion. *Ṣubḥ* in the parallel passage says "but they gave me no answer about it", with a plural verb. Among the manuscripts, T clearly has *kathīran*, A has no diacritical point on the second consonant, while P reads *kabīr* with no *tanwīn*. However, the phrase *kabīr min al-aṭibbāʾ* ("an eminent doctor") would itself be slightly odd.

438 Al-Qalqashandī (*Ṣubḥ*, iv, p. 143/9–12) refers the "curative property" of the proximity of camels to a Prophetic tradition, for which see al-Bukhārī, book 77 (*Ṭibb*), pp. 29/1. For tribesmen cured by camel milk and urine, see Ibn Saʿd, ii (1), p. 67.
439 He was *kātib al-sirr* (privy secretary) in Tripoli and died in 735/1334–5, see al-Ṣafadī, x, pp. 253–8. Ibn Baṭṭūṭa, p. 85, described his learning and generosity and presumably met him on his visit to Tripoli.
440 "Water flows into the city from all sides, and there is an aqueduct on arches which brings the water from a valley in the mountains. This aqueduct carries the water at a height of near 70 ells, and is about 200 ells long". This is from al-Dimashqī, quoted in Le Strange, p. 351.
441 According to D. Latham, in a personal communication, *khawāriq* are "arrows that pass through the target and drop to the ground behind it". It does not appear as a technical term in Latham & Paterson.
442 For the Ismāʿīlīs see also Section 49. For Ismāʿīlī castles, cf. *Ṣubḥ*, iv, pp. 146/10–147/18; Gaudefroy-Demombynes, pp. 114–16.
443 This paragraph is the acknowledged source of *Ṣubḥ*, iv, p. 74/12–14.
444 Cf. *Ṣubḥ*, iv, p. 74/15–18, where this "place" is called a *ṣadʿ*, "crevice".
445 For this paragraph and the preceding, cf. *Ṣubḥ*, iv, p. 74/12–18; Gaudefroy-Demombynes, p. 3.
446 Cf. *Ṣubḥ*, iv, p. 74/4–11; Gaudefroy-Demombynes, pp. 3–4. This is the so-called "Sabbatical River", see Le Strange, p. 57 (and references there cited); Josephus, iii, p. 535.
447 Cf. *Ṣubḥ*, iv, p. 74/1–3; Gaudefroy-Demombynes, p. 3, where "Bordj al Jaṣṣāṣ" is given. The second element in the name is devoid of diacritical points in all the manuscripts, and is so printed in the Beirut edition. Ibn al-Shiḥna, p. 255, also reads al-Jaṣṣāṣ (along with an unacceptable alternative, Burj al-Raṣṣāṣ, "the Tower of Lead", which is situated near Dulūk, north of ʿAintāb) and then adds, "nowadays they call it al-Baḥṣāṣ (?)".
448 Cf. *Ṣubḥ*, iv, pp. 149/9–155/9; Gaudefroy-Demombynes, pp. 118–24. Elements from this section were used (with differences in the text) by al-ʿUthmānī in his *Taʾrīkh Ṣafad* (see Lewis).
449 The text (literally "the kidneys [!] of weeping etc.") apparently means that the water supply was not copious. Read *malaʾat* as in *Masālik* (Cairo), p. 134, and cf. the simpler version in Lewis, p. 480: *wa-lā malaʾat al-aḥdāq* ("nor fill the pupils").
450 Reading (with some trepidation) *al-jalaba*, which is given in Lane's Arabic lexicon as a variant of *al-jalab*, "imported goods or slaves", for which compare the more normal *julbān* or *ajlāb*. Manuscripts A and T have *al-ḥilya* (adopted by the Beirut edition) but without any obvious meaning in the context. Manuscript P gives "j" as the first consonant and leaves the third without diacritical points. The Cairo edition reads the perhaps too obvious *al-ḥalqa*, which is also tautologous with *al-jund*.
451 The translation of this paragraph is very tentative.
452 Baibars I took Safed on Friday, 18 Shawwāl 664/23 July 1266, according to Ibn ʿAbd al-Ẓāhir, pp. 260–1. According to Ibn Shaddād, *Liban*, pp. 149–50, Safed fell between 2 Shawwāl 664/7 July 1266 and the date Baibars left the place, 17 Shawwāl/22 July 1266.
453 See the list in *Taʿrīf*, pp. 236–7, where only six of them are mentioned.
454 For the lake (the Sea of Galilee), see also *Ṣubḥ*, iv, p. 83.
455 A town overlooking the lake of the same name, otherwise known as Lake Huleh.
456 Saladin took Tibnīn in Jumādā I 583/July 1187 (Bundārī, p. 304) and Ḥunain soon after. See Ibn Shaddād, *Liban*, pp. 152–3. Al-Muʿaẓẓam ʿĪsā dismantled the castles after 617/1220, and they returned to Frankish control in 638/1240–1, until Baibars I took them back in 664/1266.
457 The northern part of Galilee, see *EI*, 2nd ed., i, p. 436.
458 ʿAthlīth is the Crusader Chateau Pèlerin on the coast below Haifa.
459 Haifa was taken by al-Ashraf Khalīl in 690/1291.

460 Known to the Crusaders as Belvoir, it was surrendered to Saladin in the middle of Dhū'l-Qa'da 584/5 January 1189.
461 Historian and secretary of Saladin (born 1125, died 1201); for a sketch of his life, see Richards, "'Imād al-Dīn".
462 This refers to the castle on Mount Tabor, west of Tiberias. A fort built there by the Franks had been destroyed by Saladin, and rebuilt by al-'Ādil in either 608/1211–12 or 609/1212–13 (Ibn Wāṣil, iii, p. 215). According to Yāqūt (iii, p. 557) it was built by al-Mu'aẓẓam 'Īsā, the son of al-'Ādil, and was demolished in 615/1218. Ibn Shaddād names al-'Ādil as the builder, but agrees that his son dismantled it (and also Kawkab); see Ibn Shaddād, *Liban*, pp. 161–2.
463 For a fuller description of Jerusalem, see *Masālik*, pp. 133–67; cf. *Ṣubḥ*, iv, pp. 100–2 (Gaudefroy-Demombynes, pp. 59–62); Ibn Shaddād, *Liban,* pp. 185–238.
464 The external walls of the former Temple, Herodian in construction, are now the base of the walls enclosing what came to be called the Noble Sanctuary (*al-Ḥaram al-Sharīf*). The Aqsa came to refer exclusively to the mosque on the south side of the Ḥaram.
465 In Arabic: Ṣilwān. The reference is to a tunnel used to divert the waters of the Spring of Gihon to Siloam, cut in the reign of Hezekiah of Judah before 701 B.C. See *II Kings* 20:20 and *II Chronicles* 32:30, and *Encyclopaedia Judaica*, s.v. Siloam.
466 One would not expect "black". Cf. al-'Ulaimī, ii, p. 55: "it is all constructed of white dressed stone".
467 "Roads" (*masālik*) could refer to access roads, leading up to Jerusalem. Cf. al-'Ulaimī, ii, p. 50: "The city's streets (*shawāri'*) are partly level and partly steep".
468 The use of this title shows that Baktimur's time as Vicegerent in Egypt is meant (see Section 36). He was appointed in Shawwāl 709/March 1310, arrested in Jumādā I 711/October 1311, and executed probably in 716/1316–17 (see *Sulūk*, ii, p. 102; Ibn Ḥajar al-Asqalānī, ii, pp. 18–19). However, according to *Ṣubḥ*, iv, p. 101/4, the Citadel was restored in 716/1316–17.
469 See Section 39, last paragraph. Note this dismissive way of referring to the Holy Sepulchre.
470 This refers to the building works of the powerful Emir Tankiz, appointed Vicegerent of Damascus in Rabī' II 712/August–September 1312, arrested in Dhū'l-Ḥijja 740/June 1340 and executed soon afterwards (al-Ṣafadī, x, 420–35).
471 This is the Tankiziyya, adjoining the Ḥaram's Chain Gate. It was built in 729/1328–9, see Burgoyne & Richards, pp. 223–39. The Hospice of Qalāwūn (see Burgoyne & Richards, pp. 129–40) is in fact some way to the north in the street that leads to the Ḥaram's Bāb al-Nāẓir (Overseer's Gate).
472 For a school founded by an emir at Jerusalem in the fourteenth century, see Richards, "Primary Education under the Mamlūks".
473 For the secular constructions of the Emir Tankiz, see Burgoyne & Richards, pp. 273–98.
474 Cf. Ibn Shaddād, *Liban*, pp. 239–42; *Ṣubḥ*, iv, p. 102/12–ult.; Gaudefroy-Demombynes, p. 62.
475 For Baktimur, see Section 80. He made an endowment for the maintenance of this water supply and for sick relief in the town, which was being administered by his descendants late in the sixteenth century (see Burgoyne & Richards, p. 65).
476 Cf. *Ṣubḥ*, iv, pp. 155–6; Gaudefroy-Demombynes, pp. 125–9. This passage is translated in Quatremère, *Histoire*, ii, part 1, pp. 242ff; Gaudefroy-Demombynes, pp. 131–3.
477 It was taken by al-'Ādil Abū Bakr in Ramaḍān 584/October–November 1188 ('Imād al-Dīn, *Fatḥ*, pp. 161–2; Ibn Wāṣil, ii, pp. 271–2).
478 As Beirut edition *li'l-ruqā*, which preserves the rhymed prose, but note Cairo edition *li'l-ruqiyy* "to climbing".
479 As the Cairo edition, reading *thiql*, while the Beirut edition has *na'l* (shoe, sandal). The word is devoid of diacritical points in manuscripts A, T and P.

480 Undoubtedly refers to the experience of al-Nāṣir Muḥammad, son of Sultan Qalawūn, who in 708/1309 gave up his throne and retired to Kerak and made it his base for his final return to power.
481 This piece by al-Qāḍī al-Fāḍil was written on the fall of Kerak, expressing here the wish that Shawbak would soon follow, which it did.
482 This translates *al-ghazāh*. The Beirut edition reads *al-ghuzāh*, "the warriors for the Faith", but the following feminine singular pronoun is then awkward.
483 Situated near the Gulf of Aqaba, it was raided by the Prophet in 9/630 (see Ibn Hishām, ii, pp. 515–27).
484 The final phrase is literally "whose *ḥubwa* the mountain has tied", and *ḥubwa* is explained as "a piece of cloth used as a support when sitting".
485 The three manuscripts and both editions read *silla*, for which I can provide no obvious meaning. I have preferred to emend to *sikka*, and then *al-dūr* can be taken as thought it were *dūr al-ḍarb*, "mints".
486 A probable reference to the threat posed by Reynaud de Chatillon, as in his expedition to the Hijaz in Shawwāl 578/February 1183 (see Abū Shāma, *Rawḍatain*, ii, pp. 35–7).
487 There are echoes of *Koran*, 7, v. 54 in this sentence.
488 *Koran*, 4, v. 94; 57, v. 10.
489 Cf. Ibn Shaddād, *Liban.*, pp. 80–1; *Ṣubḥ*, iv, pp. 156/18–157/10; Gaudefroy-Demombynes, p. 133.
490 A reference to *Koran*, 56, v. 33.
491 See Section 82.
492 Cf. Ibn Shaddād, *Liban*, pp. 67–8.
493 There is no such text in al-Balādhurī's *Futūḥ*. For ʿArandal, see Ibn Shaddād, *Liban*, p. 67; Yāqūt, iii, p. 657: "a village in the Sharāt district".
494 For the battle between the force sent by the Prophet and Byzantine troops in 8/629, see Ibn Hishām, ii, pp. 373–89. Jaʿfar ibn Abī Ṭālib, who was the elder brother of ʿAlī and a cousin of the Prophet, was killed during the battle. His tomb there, of obvious antiquity, is still extant according to *EI*, 2nd ed., ii, p. 372.
495 Cf. Ibn Shaddād, *Liban* etc., pp. 264–6; *Ṣubḥ*, iv, pp. 98/11–99/6; Gaudefroy-Demombynes, pp. 50–2.
496 Al-Shāfiʿī, i.e. Abū ʿAbd Allāh Muḥammad ibn Idrīs, the eponymous founder of the school of law, was born in 150/767. After many travels he died in Egypt in Rajab 204/ January 820. His mausoleum, built by the Ayyubid al-Kāmil in 608/1211, is still a place of pilgrimage.
497 The Vicegerent of Gazza, the Emir ʿAlam al-Dīn Sanjar al-Jāwulī, during his period of office, 712–20/1313–20, is credited with much building activity (*Khiṭaṭ*, ii, p. 398). The hospital too is normally attributed to him (see Meinecke, ii, p. 117) but Maqrīzī adds: "He made considerable charitable donations (*waqfs*) in its favour on behalf of al-Malik al-Nāṣir" (*Khiṭaṭ*, loc. cit./34).
498 The expedition against Lesser Armenia set out in Shaʿbān 737/March 1337 and returned to Aleppo in Dhūʾl-Ḥijja 737/July 1337.
499 For the various centres that were annexed, see *Ṣubḥ*, iv, pp. 133–8; Gaudefroy-Demombynes, pp. 98–103.
500 That is *Koran*, 106, vv. 1–2.
501 No information has been traced on this poet. His ode was presumably in imitation of the ode on the same subject, known as *al-Mudhahhaba* (also said to have been of some 300 lines), by Kumait ibn Zaid al-Asadī (died 126/743, or in 127). See Sezgin, ii, pp. 347–9.
502 This was the name of a hill to the north outside Maʿlā Gate and also of a cemetery on its lower slopes (see Yāqūt, ii, p. 215; Gibb, *Travels of Ibn Baṭṭūṭa*, i, pp. 206–8). al-Nuwairī, xvi, p. 37, says that ʿAbd Shams was buried in Ajyād, an area south-west of the city.
503 Most sources mention only four sons, omitting Abu ʿAmr.

504 I.e *al-badrān*. There is a reference to the use of this soubriquet in al-Balādhurī, *Ansāb*, i, p. 61.

505 This expression presents difficulties. The two editions read *quddāḥ al-nuḍār* (or *al-naḍār*), presumably as a plural of *qādiḥ*, but with what meaning intended? Manuscripts P and A have the *shadda* on the "d" but no manuscript gives any vowel. The *Lisān al-Arab* (Ibn Manẓūr), s.v. *n.ḍ.r.*, makes a strong connection between *nuḍār* ("best wood", variously identified but most often as "tamarisk") and *qadaḥ* ("drinking bowl"). It says, for example, "it is the most excellent wood for a vessel (*āniya*) because from it is made both bowls (*aqdāḥ*) that are delicate and broad and those that are thick". One could read *qidāḥ* as the plural of *qadaḥ*, and translate as "the arrow shafts of finest wood". However, because of the explanations in the *Lisān al-Arab*, I have preferred to emend the manuscripts to *aqdāḥ* (adding an initial *hamza*). It may be noted that this phrase applied to the sons of ʿAbd Manāf has been traced nowhere else.

506 In al-Balādhurī, *Ansāb*, i, p. 58, the story is told how Hāshim fed the people of Mecca in a time of drought etc., and that ʿAbd Allāh ibn al-Zibaʿrā then spoke these verses.

507 This narrative (cf. Muḥammad ibn Ḥabīb, *Kitāb al-munammaq fī akhbār Quraish*, Hyderabad (1384/1964), pp. 31–6; Ibn Hishām, i, pp. 144–7; al-Ṭabarī, i, pp. 1091ff) reproduces the traditional account of Meccan trading initiatives before Islam and provides the standard exegesis of the obscure text and vocabulary of *Koran*, 106, vv. 1–3. See *EI*, 2nd ed., iii, p. 1093; Crone, esp. pp. 109–14.

508 This is ʿAbd Allāh ibn al-Zibaʿrā al-Suhmī, see Sezgin, ii, pp. 275–6.

509 The prosody fault is a change in the vowel (*al-majrā*) after the rhyming letter (*al-rawī*) in the "loose rhyme" (*al-qāfiya al-muṭlaqa*), see Wright, ii, p. 357. The poem itself is quoted in various forms and attributed to various poets. A version quoted by Ibn Hishām, i, p. 178, lacks the crucial last *bait* (the last two lines in the translation), which removes the "fault" in the prosody. The author of the last *bait*, referred to in Section 87 as "their local poet at Mecca" is alternatively said to be Maṭrūd ibn Kaʿb al-Khuzāʿī (al-Ṭabarī, i, pp. 1088–9).

510 Cf. *Ṣubḥ*, iv, p. 99; Ibn Shaddād, *Liban*, pp. 181–4.

511 Umayyad caliph, ruled 96–9/715–17

512 *Masālik* (Beirut), p. 221, reads *li-mithli-hā* (for such as them), probably a printing error.

513 Manuscript P ends with the following:

> Here ends the third part, thanks to God and His help. Blessings and peace be upon our Lord, Muhammad.
>
> Written by Muḥammad al-Saʿūdī, may God pardon him, his father, his patron, and all Muslims.

References

Arabic texts

ʿAbd al-Laṭīf al-Baghdādī. *The Eastern Key: Kitāb al-ifāda waʾl-iʿtibār*, trans. K.H. Zand, J.A. Videan and I.E. Videan, London (1965).

Abūʾl-Fidā. *Al-Mukhtaṣar fī akhbār al-bashar*, al-Maṭbaʿa al-Ḥusainiyya, Cairo (n.d.).

——. *The Memoirs of a Syrian Prince*, trans. P.M. Holt, Wiesbaden (1983).

Abū Shāma. *Kitāb al-rawḍatain fī akhbār al-dawlatain*, Bulaq edition, Cairo (1287–8/1870–2).

——. *al-Dhail ʿalā kitāb al-rawḍatain* or *Tarājim rijāl al-qarnain al-sādis waʾl-sābiʾ*, ed. M. al-Kawtharī, Cairo (1366/1947).

Alī ibn Hudhail. *Ḥilyat al-fursān wa-shiʿ*ār al-shujʿān, ed. L. Mercier, Paris (1922).

Bahāʾ al-Dīn ibn Shaddād. *The Rare and Excellent History of Saladin*, trans. D.S. Richards, Farnham (2001).

al-Bakrī. *Kitāb al-Masālik waʾl-Mamālik d'Abu Ubayd al-Bakrī*, ed. A.P. Van Leeuwen & A. Ferre, Tunis (1992).

al-Balādhurī. *Ansāb al-ashrāf*, Cairo (1959).

——. *Kitāb futūḥ al-buldān*, ed. M.J. de Geoje, Leiden (1866).

al-Bukhārī. *Les traditions islamiques traduits de l'arabe avec notes et index*, trans. O.V. Houdas, Paris (1903–14),

al-Bundārī. *Sanāʾ al-Barq al-Shāmī*, Cairo (1979).

Ḥusn = al-Suyūṭī. *Ḥusn al-muḥāḍara fī akhbār Miṣr waʾl-Qāhira,* Cairo (1321/1903).

Ibn ʿAbd al-Ḥakam, *Futūḥ Miṣr*, ed. C. Torrey, Leiden (1920).

Ibn ʿAbd al-Ẓāhir. *Al-Rawḍ al-zāhir fī sīrat al-Malik al-Ẓāhir*, ed. ʿAbd al-ʿAzīz al-Khuwaiṭir, Riyāḍ (1396/1976).

Ibn ʿAsākir. *Taʾrīkh madīnat Dimashq*, Damascus (1986).

Ibn al-Athīr. *Al-Kāmil fīʾl-taʾrīkh*, Dār Ṣādir edition, Beirut (1965–7).

Ibn Ḥajar al-Asqalānī. *Durar al-kāmina fī aʿyān al-miʾa al-thāmina*, ed. M. Jād al-Haqq, Cairo (1385/1966).

Ibn Baṭṭūṭa. *Riḥla Ibn Baṭṭūṭa*, ed. Ṭalāl Ḥarb, Beirut (1407/1987).

Ibn al-Dawādārī. *Kanz al-durar wa-jāmiʿ al-ghurar*, vol. viii, ed. U. Haarmann, Cairo (1971); vol. ix, ed. Hans Roemer, Cairo (1960).

Ibn al-Furāt. *Taʾrīkh*, eds. Costi K. Zurayk & Nejla Izzedin, ix, Beirut (1938).

Ibn Ḥabīb. *Tadhkirat al-nabīh fī ayyām al-Manṣūr.wa-banīh*, Cairo (1976).

Ibn Hishām. *Al-Sīra al-nabawiyya*, ed. M. al-Saqā et al., Cairo (1955).

Ibn Ijās. *Die Chronik des Ibn Ijās*, ed. M. Mostafa, Cairo (1960).

Ibn Kathīr. *Al-Bidāya waʾl-nihāya*, Beirut (1977).

Ibn Khallikān. *Wafāyāt al-aʿyān wa-anbāʾ abnāʾ al-zamān*, ed. Iḥsan ʿAbbās, Beirut (1977).

Ibn Manẓūr. *Lisān al-Arab al-muḥīṭ*, Beirut (1389/1970).

Ibn Qāḍī Shuhba. *Ta'rīkh Ibn Qāḍī Shuhba*, ed. 'Adnān Darwīsh, Damascus (1977).

Ibn Qalānisī, *Dhail*, ed. H.F. Amedroz, Leiden (1908).

Ibn Sa'd. *al-Ṭabaqāt*, ed. E. Sachau, Leiden (1904–40).

Ibn Shaddād, 'Izz al-Dīn. [*Damas*] *al-A'lāq al-khaṭīra fī dhikr umarā' al-Shām wa'l-Jazīra (ta'rīkh madīnat Dimashq)*, ed. Sāmī al-Dahhān, Damascus (1956).

——. [*Liban*] *al-A'lāq al-khaṭīra fī dhikr umarā' al-Shām wa'l-Jazīra (ta'rīkh Lubnān wa'l-Urdunn wa-Filastīn),* ed. Sāmī al-Dahhān, Damascus (1963).

——. *Ta'rīkh al-Malik al-Ẓāhir*, ed. Aḥmad Ḥutait, Wiesbaden (1983).

Ibn al-Shiḥna. *The History of Aleppo known as ad-Durr al-Muntakhab by Ibn ash-Shiḥna*, ed. K. Ohta, Tokyo (1990).

Ibn al-Suqā'ī. *Tālī kitāb Wafayāt al-A'yān*, ed. J. Sublet, Damas (1974).

Ibn 'Unain. *Diwān*, ed. Khalil Mardum Bey, Beirut (1974).

Ibn Wāṣil. *Mufarrij al-kurūb fī akhbār Banī Ayyūb*, ed. al-Shayyal, Cairo (1953–77).

Ibn Ẓahīra. *Al-Faḍā'il al-bāhira fī maḥāsin Miṣr wa'l-Qāhira*, Cairo (1969).

al-Idrīsī. *Opus Geographicum*, eds. A. Bombaci et al., fasc. 4, Naples (1974).

'Imād al-Dīn al-Isfahānī. *Al-Fatḥ al-quṣṣī fī'l-fatḥ al-qudsī*, ed. C. de Landberg, Leiden (1888).

——. *Kharīdat al-qaṣr wa-jarīdat al-'aṣr (qism shu'arā' al-Shām)*, ed. Shukrī Faiṣal, Damascus (1955).

Khiṭaṭ = al-Maqrīzī. *Kitāb al-mawā'iẓ wa'l-i'tibār fī dhikr al-khiṭaṭ wa'l-āthār*, Bulāq, Cairo (1853–4).*Masālik* = Ibn Faḍl Allāh al-'Umarī. *Masālik al-abṣār fī mamālik al-amṣār*, i, ed. Aḥmad Zakī, Cairo (1924).

Masālik (Beirut) = Ibn Faḍl Allāh al-'Umarī. *Masālik al-abṣār fī mamālik al-amṣār, dawlat al-mamālīk al-ūlā*, ed. Dorothea Krawulsky, Beirut (1986).

Masālik (Cairo) = Ibn Faḍl Allāh al-'Umarī. *Masālik al-abṣār fī mamālik al-amṣār, mamālik Miṣr wa'l-Shām*, ed. Ayman Fuad Sayyid, Cairo (1985).

Masālik (facsimile) = Ibn Faḍl Allāh al-'Umarī. *Routes towards Insight into the Capital Empires: Masālik al-abṣār fī mamālik al-amṣār*, ed. F. Sezgin with A. Jokhosha & E. Neubauer, Frankfurt am Main (1988–9).

Masālik (*Qabā'il*) = Ibn Faḍl Allāh al-'Umarī. *Masālik al-abṣār mamālik al-amṣār*, Book 15, *Qabā'il al-Arab*, ed. Dorothea Krawulsky, Beirut (1985).

al-Mas'ūdī. *Murūj al-dhahab wa-ma'ādin al-jawhar*, ed. C. Pellat, Beirut (1965–79).

——. *Les Prairies d'Or*, trans. C. Pellat, Paris (1962–77).

Munajjid, S.D. *Waṣf Dimashq fī Masālik al-Abṣār lil-'Umarī, Revue de l'Institut des Manuscrits arabes*, iii/1 (1957), pp. 113–26.

al-Nuwairī. *Nihāyat al-arab fī funūn al-adab*, Cairo (1923–76).

al-Yūsufī. *Nuzhat al-nāẓir fī sīrat al-Malik al-Nāṣir*, ed. A. Ḥuṭaiṭ, Beirut (1986).

al-Ṭabarī. *Kitāb akhbār al-rusul wa'l-mulūk*, ed. M.J. de Goeje et al., Leiden (1879–1901).

Ta'rīf = Ibn Faḍl Allāh al-'Umarī. *Al-Ta'rīf bi'l-muṣṭalāḥ al-sharīf*, ed. M.Ḥ. Shams al-Dīn, Beirut (1408/1988).

al-Ṣafadī. *Kitāb al-wāfī bi'l-wafāyāt*, ed. Hans Ritter et al., Wiesbaden (1931–in progress).

al-Sam'ānī. *Kitāb al-ansāb*, Hyderabad (1401/1981).

Ṣubḥ = al-Qalqashandī. *Ṣubḥ al-a'shā fī kitābat* [or *ṣinā'at*] *al-inshā,* Cairo (1913–18).

Sulūk = al-Maqrīzī. *Kitāb al-sulūk ilā ma'rifat al-duwal wa'l-mulūk*, ed. M. Mostafa Ziyada et al., Cairo (1956–73).

al-'Ulaimī, Mujīr al-Dīn. *Al-Uns al-jalīl bi-ta'rīkh al-Quds wa'l-Khalīl*, Amman, Jordan (1973).

Waṣf Ifrīqiyya = Ibn Faḍl Allāh al-'Umarī. *Waṣf Ifrīqiyya wa-Andalus*, ed. Ḥasan Ḥusnī 'Abd al-Wahhāb, Tunis (1341).

Yāqūt al-Ḥamawī. *Mu'jam al-buldān*, ed. F. Wüstenfeld, Leipzig (1866–70).
al-Ẓāhirī, Khalīl. *Zubdat kashf al-mamālik*, ed. P. Ravaisse, Paris (1894).
al-Zamakhsharī. *Al-Mustaqṣā fī amthāl al-arab*, Beirut (1977).
Zetterstéen, K.V. *Beiträge zur Geschichte der Mamlūkensultane*, Leiden (1919).

Secondary sources

Adler, E.N., ed., *Jewish Travellers*, London (1930).
Amitai, R. "Dangerous Liaisons: Armenian–Mongol–Mamluk Relations (1260–1292)", in G. Dédéyan and C. Mutafian eds., *La Méditerranée des Arméniens, xiie-xve siècle*, Paris (2014), pp. 191–206.
Ayalon, D. "The Expansion and Decline of Cairo under the Mamluks and its Background", in *Itineraires d'Orient: Hommages à Claude Cahen*, in *Res Orientates*, iv, Bures-sur-Yvette (1994).
——. "Studies in the Structure of the Mamluk Army", *Bulletin of the School of Oriental and African Studies*, xv (1953), pp. 203–28, 448–76; xvi (1954), pp. 57–90.
——. "The System of Payment in the Mamluk Military Society", *Journal of the Economic and Social History of the Orient*, i (1958), pp. 257–71.
Balog, P. "History of the Dirhem in Egypt from the Fātimid Conquest until the Collapse of the Mamlūk Empire.", *Revue Numismatique*, 6th series, iii (1961), pp. 109–46.
van Berchem, M. *Matériaux pour un Corpus Inscriptionum Arabicarum,* Deuzième Partie: Syrie du Sud, Tome Deuzième – Jérusalem "Ḥaram", Mémoires de l'Institut Français d'Archéologie Orientale, Cairo (1927).
Blachère, R. "Quelques réflexions sur les formes de l'encyclopédisme en Égypte et en Syrie du VIIIe/XIVe siècle à la fin du IXe/XVe siècle", *Bulletin des Études Orientales*, xxiii (1970), pp. 1–19.
Brockelmann, C. *Geschichte der Arabischen Litteratur*, Leiden (1937–43).
Burgoyne, M.H., & D.S. Richards, *Mamluk Jerusalem: An Architectural Study*, London (1987).
Cahen, C. "Un texte inédit relatif au Ṭirāz égyptien", *Arts Asiatiques*, xi (1964).
Clauson, G. *An Etymological Dictionary of Pre-thirteenth Century Turkish*, Oxford (1972).
Cooper, R.S. "A Note on the *dinar jayshi*", *Journal of the Economic and Social History of the Orient*, xvi (1973), pp. 317–18.
Creswell, K.A.C. *The Muslim Architecture of Egypt*, Oxford (1952–9).
Crone, P. *Meccan Trade and the Rise of Islam*, Princeton (1987).
Dozy, R. *Supplément aux dictionnaires arabes*, Leiden (1881).
Dussaud, R. Topographie historique de la Syrie antique et médiévale, Paris (1927).
EI = The Encyclopaedia of Islam.
Elisséeff, N. *La Description de Damas d'Ibn 'Asakir*, Damascus (1959).
——. *Nūr al-Dīn, un grand prince musulman de Syrie au temps des Croisades*, 3 vols, Damascus (1967).
Ernst, H. *Die mamlukischen Sultansurkunden des Sinai-Klosters*, Wiesbaden (1960).
Floyer, E.A. "Mines of Northern Etbai", *Journal of the Royal Asiatic Society*, xxiv (1892), pp. 811–33.
Fulcher of Chartres, *History of the Expedition to Jerusalem, 1095–1127*, trans. F.R. Ryan, Knoxville (1969).
Garçin, J.-C. *Un Centre Musulman de la Haute-Égypte Médiévale: Qus,* Cairo (1976)
Gaudefroy-Demombynes, M. *La Syrie à l'Époque des Mamelouks*, Paris (1923).

Gibb, H.A.R. "The Armies of Saladin", in Stanford J. Shaw and William R. Polk eds., *Studies on the Civilization of Islam*, London (1962).Gibb, H.A.R. *The Travels of Ibn Baṭṭūṭa*, Cambridge (1985, 1962, 1971).

Gil, M. "Building Operations and Repairs in the House of the Qodesh in Fustat", *Journal of the Economic and Social History of the Orient*, xiv (1971), pp. 136–95.

de Goeje, M.J. *Catalogus Codicum Orientalium Bibliothecae Academiae Lugduno-Batavae*, Leiden (1873).

Hartmann, R. "Politische Geographie des Mamlukenreiches", *Zeitschrift der Deutschen Morgenlandischen Gesellschaft*, lxx (1916).

Hinz, W. *Islamische Masse und Gewichte*, Brill (1970).

Hodgson, M. *The Order of the Assassins*, The Hague (1955).

Joinville. *The Life of Saint Louis*, trans. M.R.B. Shaw, in *Chronicles of the Crusades*, London (1963).

Josephus, *De bello judaico (The Jewish War)*, Loeb ed.

Kister, M.J. "You Shall Only Set Out for Three Mosques", *Museon*, lxxxii (1969), pp. 173–96.

Lane, E.W. *Manners and Customs of the Modern Egyptians*, London (reprinted 1954).

——. *An Arabic–English Lexicon* etc., London and Edinburgh (1863–77).

Latham, J.D., & W.F. Paterson, *Saracen Archery*, London (1970).

Le Strange, G. *Palestine under the Moslems*, London (1890). Reprinted Beirut (1965).

Levanoni, A. *A Turning Point in Mamluk History: the Third Reign of al-Nāṣir Muḥammad ibn Qalāwūn, 1310–1341*, Leiden (1995).

Lewis, B. "An Arabic Account of the Province of Safed-I", *Bulletin of the School of Oriental and African Studies*, vol. 15 (1953), pp. 477–88.

Little, D.P. "The Nature of Khanqahs, Ribats, and Zawiyas under the Mamluks", in *Islamic Studies Presented to Charles J. Adams*, ed. W.B. Hallaq and D.P. Little, Leiden (1991).

Lombard, M. *Les textiles dans le monde musulman VIIe–XIIe siècle*, Paris (1978).

Lucas, A. *Ancient Egyptian Materials and Industries*, revised J.R. Harris, 4th ed., London (1962).

MacAlister, D.S. "The Emerald Mines of Northern Etbai", *Geographical Journal*, xvi (1900), pp. 537–49.

Marzouk, M.A. *History of the Textile Industry in Alexandria*, 331 B.C.–1517 A.D., Alexandria (1955).

——. "The Tiraz Institutions in Medieval Egypt", *Studies in Islamic Art and Architecture in Honour of A. Creswell*, Cairo (1965), pp. 157–62.

Maspero, J., & G. Wiet, *Matériaux pour servir à la geographie de l'Égypte*, Cairo (1919).

Mayer, L.A. *Mamluk Costume*, Geneva (1952).

Meinecke, M. *Die Mamlukische Architektur in Agypten und Syrien*, 2 vols., Glückstadt (1992).

Meisami, J.S., & P. Starkey, eds. *Encyclopedia of Arabic Literature*, 2 vols., London (1998).

Melville, C. "'Sometimes by the Sword, Sometimes by the Dagger': the Role of the Ismāʿīlīs in Mamluk–Mongol Relations in the 8th/14th Century", in F. Daftary ed., *Mediaeval Ismaʿili History and Thought*, Cambridge (1996), pp. 247–63.

——. " 'The Year of the Elephant': Mamluk–Mongol Rivalry in the Hejaz in the Reign of Abū Saʿid (1317–1335)", *Studia Iranica*, xxi (1992), pp. 197–214.

Northrup, L.J. "Al-Bīmāristān al-Manṣūrī – Explorations: The Interface between Medicine, Politics and Culture in Early Mamluk Egypt", in Stephan Conermann ed., *History and Society during the Mamluk Period*, i, Bonn (2014), pp. 107–42.

Paul, A. *A History of the Beja Tribes of the Sudan*, Cambridge (1954).
Popper, W. *The Cairo Nilometer*, Berkeley (1951).
Quatremère, E. *Histoire des Sultans Mamlouks de l'Égypte*, Paris (1837–45).
——. "Memoire sur la Mine d'emeraudes", *Memoires geographiques et historiques sur l'Egypte et sur quelques contrées voisines*, Paris (1811), ii, pp. 173–80.
Rabbat, N.O. *The Citadel of Cairo: A New Interpretation of Royal Mamluk Architecture*, Leiden (1995).
Rabie, H. *The Financial System of Egypt*, Oxford (1972).
Richards, D.S. "Arabic Documents from the Karaite Community in Cairo", *Journal of the Economic and Social History of the Orient*, xv (1972).
——. "Documents from Sinai Concerning Mainly Cairene Property", *Journal of the Economic and Social History of the Orient*, xxvii (1985).
——. "ʿImād al-Dīn al-ʿIsfahānī: Administrator, Littérateur and Historian", in Maya Shatzmiller ed., *Crusaders and Muslims in Twelfth-Century Syria*, London (1993), pp. 133–46.
——. "A Mamlūk Emir's 'Square' Decree", *Bulletin of the School of Oriental and African Studies*, liv (1991), pp 63–7.
——. "A Mamluk Petition and a Report from the Dīwān al-Jaysh", *Bulletin of the School of Oriental and African Studies*, xl (1977), pp. 1–14.
——. "Primary Education under the Mamlūks: Two Documents from the Haram in Jerusalem", *Proceedings of the 20th Congress of the Union Européenne des Arabisants et Islamisants*, part one, ed. K. Dévény, Budapest (2002), pp. 223–32.
Risciani, N. *Documenti e Firmani*, Jerusalem (1931).
Rödt-Collenburg, W.H. *The Rupenides, Hethumides and Lusignans: the Structure of the Armeno-Cilician Dynasties*, Paris (1963).
Sadi. *Gulistan* [*Flower-garden of Shaikh Sadi of Shiraz*], trans. James Ross, London (1823).
Sauvaget, J. "La Citadelle de Damas", *Syrie*, xi (1930), pp. 59–90, 216–41.
——. *La Poste aux Chevaux dans l'Empire des Mamelouks*, Paris (1941).
Serjeant, R.B. "Material for the History of Islamic Textiles up to the Mongol Conquest", *Ars Islamica*, ix (1942), pp. 54–92; x (1943), pp. 71–104.
Seton-Kerr, H.W. "The Egyptian Emerald Mines", *Geographical Journal*, xviii (1901).
Sezgin, F. *Geschichte des Arabischen Schrifttums*, Leiden (1967).
Stern, S.M. *Fatimid Decrees*, London (1964).
——. "Petitions from the Ayyūbid Period", *Bulletin of the School of Oriental and African Studies*, xvii (1964), pp. 15–16.
——. "Petitions from the Mamluk Period", *Bulletin of the School of Oriental and African Studies*, xxix (1966), pp. 251–2.
Stewart, A.D. "Qalʿat al-Rūm/Hromgla/Rumkale and the Mamluk Siege of 691 AH/1292 CE", in Hugh Kennedy ed., *Muslim Military Architecture in Greater Syria: From the Coming of Islam to the Ottoman Period*, Leiden (2006), pp. 269–80.Thorau, P. "Die Burgen der Assassinen in Syrien und ihre Einnahme durch Sultan Baibars", *Die Welt des Orients*, xviii (1987), pp. 132–58.
——. *The Lion of Egypt Sultan: Baybars I and the Near East in the Thirteenth Century*, London and New York (1987).
Thoumin, R. "Note sur l'amenagement et la distribution des eaux à Damas et dans la Ghouta", *Bulletin des Études Orientales*, iv (1934), pp. 1–16.
Trimingham, J.S. *The Sufi Orders in Islam*, Oxford (1971).

Ullmann, M. *Islamic Medicine*, Edinburgh (1978).

Vermeulen, U. "Une note sur les insignes royaux des Mamelouks", in U. Vermeulen & D. De Smet eds., *Egypt and Syria in the Fatimid, Ayyubid and Mamluk Eras*, Orientalia Lovaniensia Analecta 73, Leuven (1995), pp. 355–61.

Webster, R. *Gems: Their Sources, Descriptions and Identification*, 3rd ed., London (1975).Wensinck, A.J., J.P. Mensing et al., *Concordance de la Tradition musulmane*, Leiden (1943–88).

Wright, W. *A Grammar of the Arabic Language*, 3rd ed., Cambridge (1896–8).

de Zambaur, E. *Manuel de généalogie et de chronologie pour l'histoire de l'Islam*, Hanover (1927).

Index

When a name is given in full, "b." stands for "ibn" (son of) and should be ignored for alphabetical ordering. However, "Ibn" is maintained when given as the initial element of a name. The Arabic direct article "al-" should also be ignored.

dress of men of the sword 24, 32, 35
dress of preachers 42

Egypt: beautiful at springtime 97; infested with snakes 97
emerald mine 13–14, 40
emir jandar 27, 33
emirs: grants and allowances 21–2; pay 21
exordium, various levels of 28, 50

farajiyya-gown 31
fauna 16
Fayyum 15, 57
al-Fīja 68
flora: of Egypt 16, 20; of Syria 20, 34–5
Friday prayers, sultan's attendance at 26–7
Fustat 17

Gaza 85–7
Ghuta 67
Great Hall 43, 47, 48

Haifa 81
ḥalqa 21–2, 24, 29
Hama: nominally ruled by Ayyubids 39; 75–6
Harem 47
Hāshim b. ʿAbd Manāf 86–7
Hebron 82–3
Hippodrome 67
Homs 74
Horse Market 47–8, 67
household departments 34
Hūlegū 69

Ibn ʿUnain 64–5
Ibn al-Zibaʿra 88
īlāf (Quraish trade compact) 86–8
ʿImād al-Dīn al-Isfahānī 81
inspector of the chest 36
inspector of the stables 36
intelligence gathering 27
*iqṭā*ʿ 22, 29, 40; form of appointment document 50–1

janā'ib (reserve mounts) 23, 25

kalauta-cap 24
kanji 24, 42
khāṣṣikīya 24
kunbūsh-caparison 31

Ismailis: their castles and doctrines 45–6, 79

Jerusalem 37–8, 81–2
Jordan river 69–70, 80–1

Kerak 83–5
al-Khalīl 37, 70
al-Khawābī 79
Krak des Chevaliers 79

Lebanon, mount 73
Lydda 70, 88–9

major-domo 34
Manha canal 15
Manṣūrī Hospital 18, 82
marshal of the army 34, 43
Masyāf, centre of Ismāʿīlī *daʿwa* 79
meals provided by sultan 26
Mecca 37–9
medical support 26
Medina 37–39
men of the learned class 37
men of the pen 30, 35
men of the sword 24, 32, 35
mīthara 31
monuments, ancient Egyptian 18
al-Muʿaẓẓam ʿĪsā b. al-ʿĀdil Abī Bakr 71, 84
Muʿaẓẓamiyya madrasa 67, 73
Muḥammad b. Qalāwūn, al-Malik al-Nāṣir 18
Muḥyī al-Dīn b. al-Zakī 18
Muqattam Hills 46

Nablus 38
Nāṣir al-Dīn Muḥammad b. al-Muḥsinī 58
Nilometer 48
Nūr al-Dīn Maḥmūd b. Zankī 68–9

oases: administered by local *iqṭā*ʿ holder 57
Orontes river 39, 75

Palace of Justice 24, 35, 47
Pharos, its measurements, its destruction 18, 54
peasants, sympathy for 49
pensions, inheritability of 18
petitions 33
pigeon post 27
produce of Egypt 15–17

products of the realm 20
privy purse, inspector of 35
privy secretary 27, 35
province: northern 57; southern 57

Qadi al-Fāḍil 18, 65, 73–4, 83
Qadmūs 79
Qalāwūn, al-Malik al-Manṣūr 18
Qarāfa cemetery 18
Qarāqūsh 17, 46
Qasyun, mount 67
Qulla gate 46–7
Qūs, trade routes to India, Yemen and Abyssinia 13, 49–50

Rajā'b. Ḥayāt 88–9
Ramla, foundation of 88–90
robes of honour 41–2

Safed 80–1
Ṣāliḥiyya 67
Sarkhad district 71–2
Saydanāyā, church of 44
sepulchre 38, 44,
sessions to hear complaints 24–5
shaqqa 26
sharb 24
Shawbak 84
Sidon district 72
signature, in form of motto 28
Sīs 39
sorcery with scorpions 50
Striped Palace 46
Sulaimān b. ʿAbd al-Malik b. Marwān 88
sultan's bounty, recipients of 22

ṭabl-khānah 21–2
Tadmor district [Palmyra] 72
ṭailasān-hood 42
takalāwāt 44
ṭamankiyyāt 31
ṭardwaḥsh 41
ṭarḥa-shawl 41
textiles, varieties of 16–17, 31, 51
Tinnis, lake of 55
travelling routine of sultan 25
Tripoli 78
ṭughrā 29
Tuqṣubā, governor of Qūs 50

Umayyad Mosque 70
ʿUqaiba, suburb of Damascus 20
ūshāqiya (corps of pages) 23

vicegerent 32–3
vizier 24, 30, 35

weights and measures 15, 55

Zabadānī 68
al-Ẓāhir Baibars 67, 71, 81
zunnārī 31